Life Within Limits

Michael Jackson

Life Within Limits

Well-being in a World of Want

DUKE UNIVERSITY PRESS

DURHAM AND LONDON

2011

© 2011 Duke University Press

All rights reserved

Printed in the United States of

America on acid-free paper ∞

Designed by C. H. Westmoreland

Typeset in Whitman by

Tseng Information Systems, Inc.

Library of Congress Cataloging-in-

Publication Data appear on the

last printed page of this book.

Ships at a distance have every man's wish on board. For some they come in with the tide. For others they sail forever on the horizon, never out of sight, never landing until the waiter turns his eyes away in resignation, his dreams mocked to death by Time. That is the life of men.

—ZORA NEALE HURSTON,
Their Eyes Were Watching God

The gospel of detachment is as well suited to a culture of excess as it is to a society of radical poverty. It thrives in circumstances in which one's wants are dangerous because they are surely going to be deprived—or because they are pulled in so many directions that they pose a threat to the integrity, the unity of one's self. Of course, wanting too much, wanting the wrong thing, wanting what you can't have is one definition of the human condition; we all have to learn how to make some liveable compromise between the always insatiable self and the always insufficient reality principle.

—EVA HOFFMAN,
Lost in Translation: A Life in a New Language

Contents

Imagining Firawa

THIS BOOK IS AN ESSAY in understanding human well-being, not as a settled state but as a field of struggle. As with goodness and reasonableness, our difficulty of achieving wellness does not diminish its hold over our imaginations, for it signifies a hope without which existence would be untenable — that life, for ourselves and those we care about, holds more in store for us than less. Though it is rare to meet people who are completely and permanently satisfied with their lot, it is rarer to meet people who expect nothing of life, abjectly accepting the status quo, never imagining that their situations could or should be socially, spiritually, or materially improved. This sense that well-being remains elusive, transitory, and unevenly distributed is felt by the rich as well as the poor, and in all societies. To explore this condition of existential dissatisfaction, I traveled to a West African country described in a recent UN report as the "least liveable" in the world.[1] In going to Sierra Leone, I wanted to see if current Western preoccupations with socioeconomic development and human rights prevent us from adequately understanding the priorities and values of ordinary Africans and whether, on balance, Sierra Leoneans have a harder time of it than Europeans and Americans in dealing with scarcity and insufficiency. African people have always faced forces from without that imperil lives and livelihoods. Though these minatory forces assume different forms at different times — slave raiding, warfare, epidemic illness, colonial domination, state interference, religious zealotry, economic exploitation, and corrupt government — they are subject to the same mix of magical and practical reactions that we in the affluent West deploy against terrorist threats, illegal immigration, market collapse, and economic recession. But well-being is always contingent on more than one's particular historical or cultural situation. It reflects a sense of discontinuity between who we are and what we might become[2] — questions of *existential well-being* and personal fate that

Paul Gauguin depicted in his 1897 masterpiece from Punaauia (Marquesas Islands): *Where do we come from? What are we? Where are we going?*[3]

I also went back to Sierra Leone to keep a promise I had made to myself many years ago. For reasons that remain obscure to me, even now, the remote village where I did my first fieldwork in 1969–70, and where I lived with my first wife and daughter during the dry season of 1979, had become a lodestone, compelling my return. Although I had revisited Sierra Leone often over the years, I had never managed to get back to the place that had figured most imperatively in my thoughts. I would find myself remembering the laterite path that skirted the hill before Firawa, distressed grasses in the late afternoon light, stands of contorted lophira trees, the sandy shallows of the Konkoron stream, and be overwhelmed by an emotion that resembled nostalgia but which I could not exactly name.

While it is true to say that my initiation into ethnography took place in Firawa,[4] beginnings are different from origins. One can date or determine a beginning, but origins are like the succession of low hills that blur into the bluish haze of the Loma Mountains beyond Firawa. Origins are like echoes—antecedent events that continue to make their presence felt in the here and now, or recollections sparked by a piece of music only to fade when the music stops.[5]

Methodologically, this difference between beginning and origin resembles Gabriel Marcel's distinction between a "problem" that admits of a solution, and a "mystery" that can never be entirely solved. "A problem is something met with which bars my passage. It is before me in its entirety. A mystery, on the other hand, is something in which I find myself caught up, and whose essence is therefore not to be before me in its entirety. It is as though in this province the distinction between in me and before me loses its meaning."[6]

When Paul Ricoeur speaks of "the enigma of anteriority," this sense of something "always-already-there," he is alluding to the gap between what we can define or decide and all that foreshadows us, having the force of fact or fate, yet remaining as fugitive as memory.[7] I also like to think that the origin suggests our common humanity, whose presence is never entirely obliterated by our singular identities or the particular situations in which we find ourselves. But can we posit an original sense of well-being, grounded in our social nature, that underlies all modes of seeking or securing a good life? Just as Ricoeur claims that "the political is almost without origin" since "before Caesar there is another Caesar,"[8] I will suggest that both the problem of well-being and the question as to what makes life worthwhile are grounded in the mystery of existential discontent—the question as to why human beings, regardless of their external circumstances, are haunted by a sense of insufficiency and loss.

My approach to the study of human well-being reflects a long-held assumption that while philosophers have often asked the most searching questions regarding the human condition, ethnographic method offers one of the most edifying ways of actually exploring these questions. The radical empiricism of William James insists that "the world is a pluralism," not a unity, despite the consoling myths, cognitive maps, and interpretive models with which we camouflage the world's complexity, contradictoriness, and contingency.[9] Well-being is, therefore, one thing for the young, another for the old, and varies from place to place, person to person. Moreover, what holds true today will seldom hold true tomorrow, particularly if the day in question disappoints.

This brings me to the question of hope—that sense that one may become other or more than one presently is or was fated to be. For

Gabriel Marcel, hope is the feeling that time is not closed to us,[10] a sentiment echoed by Pierre Bourdieu, for whom hope is the belief that our social investment in the world will pay off, if not immediately, then at some time in the future.[11] For Hannah Arendt, hope is synonymous with the appearance of the new which has the character of "startling unexpectedness"—something that is "inherent in all beginnings and all origins" and occurs despite "the overwhelming odds of statistical laws and their probability, which for all practical, everyday purposes amounts to certainty."[12] This sense of promise and potential transformation that Marcel refers to as "enthusiasm for living" (l'entrain de la vie),[13] Bourdieu as "the forthcoming,"[14] Arendt as "natality," and Ernst Bloch as "the spirit of utopia" finds expression in millennial dreams and revolutionary ardor as much as in the banal pleasure of an excursion to somewhere new, the anticipation of a lottery draw, a sporting contest, the denouement of a mystery novel, a child's Christmas, or the impatient excitement with which one counts the days before a vacation, prepares for a new departure, or awaits the return of an absent lover or friend. Like Hannah Arendt, Ernst Bloch makes pregnancy a metaphor for this yearning for the new, this heightened anticipation of what will surprise us, take us out of ourselves, or give us a new lease on life. Yet, he argues, all such aspirations have their origin in a sense that something is missing in our lives, and that there is more to life than what exists for us in the here and now.[15] Because it is notoriously difficult to pin down exactly what it is we lack or what will complete us, our imaginations wander from one thing to another as though searching for a mislaid article. At times we imagine that the lost object was once in our possession—a loving family, an organic community, an Edenic homeland, a perfect relationship. It was there before we realized what we had; it slipped from our grasp or was stolen, leaving us to hope that it might be restored to us, as well as to dread that it is irrecoverable. At times we imagine that what we need lies ahead, promised or owed but as yet undelivered, unrevealed, or unpaid, not yet born. In this yearning for what is missing, but that we regard as rightfully ours, lies our sense of natural justice. But as Ernst Bloch observes as he discusses these questions with Theodor Adorno, our sense of what is possible is always tempered by a sense of impossibility and danger. Accordingly, hope is never the same as confidence, since one who hopes is haunted by the sense that he is hoping for the impossible, that his hope is, deep down, a hope for life everlasting or absolute security, and that he knows, equally deep down, that he is bound to die. Because hope always arises with fear and anxiety, we tell ourselves to be careful what we wish for, since experience teaches us that the fulfillment of a dream often leads to disappointment. Hopes are dashed as often as they are realized, just as romantic love often flourishes when it is unrequited.

My fieldwork would touch on many of these issues and lead me to conclude that the anxieties of hope—in both the affluent societies of the north and the poor societies of the south—spring from the fundamentally unstable and ambiguous nature of our relationships with others and with the world.

Herein lies another assumption I make as an anthropologist—the assumption of intersubjectivity. Just as human existence is never simply an unfolding from within but rather an outcome of a situation, of a relationship with others, so human understanding is never born of contemplating the world from afar; it is an emergent and perpetually renegotiated outcome of social interaction, dialogue, and engagement. And though something of one's own experience—of hope or despair, affinity or estrangement, well-being or illness—is always one's point of departure, this experience continually undergoes a sea change in the course of one's encounters and conversations with others. Life transpires in the subjective in-between, in a space that remains indeterminate despite our attempts to fix our position within it—a borderlands, as it were, a third world.

For these reasons, intersubjectivity is not only what an ethnographer studies; it is the matrix, method, and means whereby an understanding is reached, albeit provisionally, of the other and of oneself. So it was not without significance that I learned about Ricoeur's "enigma": and Bloch's "utopian function" in the course of conversations with Harvard friends (Davíd Carrasco and Patrick Provost-Smith), and that the books themselves were conversational in form (Bloch is in conversation with his friend Theodor Adorno; Ricoeur with François Azouvi and Marc de Launay). Nor was I surprised that these conversations came to resonate with the conversations I had in Firawa—an oblique proof that the empirical and the philosophical—so often separated in the academic tradition of the West—are as necessarily and inevitably entwined as biography and history.

Fathers and Sons

OUR FLIGHT WAS DELAYED. Instead of leaving Gatwick at midnight we were confined to the Departure Concourse in the North Terminal and obliged to wait. The airport was deserted, the duty free shops locked down. Aluminum grilles sealed us off from Harrods Tax Free, World of Whiskies, Seafood Bar, Next, and Sunglass Hut, though W H Smith reopened briefly so we could exchange our £10 vouchers for snacks, magazines, and cold drinks. Most of those waiting were Sierra Leoneans going home for the holidays, and though everyone was dog tired the delay was taken in good heart. Some fell asleep in the Instant Massage Chairs; others sat in circles, chatting in Krio, sharing crisps and candies as kids chased each other around an illuminated Christmas tree. Two men strolled up and down the concourse, deep in conversation. And my seventeen-year-old son Joshua played his Game Boy.

My other traveling companion was a young man I had gotten to know in Freetown in 2002 while researching my biography of S. B. Marah.[1] Sewa had been working as a chauffeur for his uncle S.B. at the time, and his ambition was to get to England. This he achieved eighteen months later, and over the next few years I visited London several times, chronicling Sewa's adjustment to metropolitan life. When I asked Sewa if he would accompany me to Sierra Leone, he jumped at the chance. He had found it difficult to keep in touch with his natal village and was eager to impress friends and family with what he had made of himself. Dressed to the nines, with silver rings, a diamond ear-stud, and a silver chain around his neck, Sewa projected a complacent image of migrant success. But his outward cheerfulness belied doubts that he would be able to meet the demands kinsmen might make on his limited resources. Though he had done his best to keep his baggage under the maximum weight allowance (Joshua and I had transferred some of his surplus to our own bags), Sewa had been obliged to leave several intended gifts behind and this bothered him.

I found it ironic that the duty-free stores were closed to us, for many young Sierra Leoneans feel they have been locked out of a world where one's worth depends on purchasing power and the conspicuous consumption of foreign goods. In the Sierra Leone hinterland, access to imported commodities like salt, sugar, cement, cloth, cows, and medicines has long been as vital to well-being as the traditional staples of rice and kola. Nowadays, one can add a multitude of manufactured articles, digital devices, and various forms of symbolic capital, such as education and geopolitical mobility, to this ever-enlarging repertoire, so that even in the remotest village a person's destiny will be determined as much by doing his or her duty as by being duty-free. For my friend Sewa, it had not been easy striking a balance between his desire to make his mark in the world and his determination to keep faith with a traditional ethos that encouraged one to accept one's lot, honor one's elders and ancestors, and live within the limits set by one's birthright, one's circumstances, and the powers that be.

It wasn't until three thirty in the morning that we got an update on our flight. We were now free to move to Gate 48, though we would not be able to board for some time; the aircraft had developed a "technical fault." Some of the passengers moved quickly toward the gate as if their haste might speed our departure. Sewa, Joshua, and I saw no point in hurrying and when we finally reached the cold dingy gate area, with its mottled gray carpet, gray walls, gray ceiling panels, and dim fluorescent lights, the crowd was already expressing anger and irritation at not being able to proceed any further. Minutes later, things began to get out of hand. A middle-aged man began berating a female airline official, demanding an explanation for the long delay and cursing the airline for treating us like cattle. A second man stood nearby, preparing his own tirade. I was too far away to hear what the airline official was saying, but her calm and impersonal manner seemed to enrage the two protesters even more, and with several women now stridently pitching in, the beleaguered official turned her back and summoned security on her walkie-talkie.

"We've reached the end of our tethers," a woman next to me explained. "Why don't they tell us what's going on? It's common courtesy."

With the arrival of security police, the confrontation became a stand-off, and though it was announced that our aircraft's technical problems could not be fixed, we were quickly assured that there was no need for panic, and that baggage, catering, and crew were being transferred to another aircraft and boarding would soon begin. Though this was enough to placate the crowd, it wasn't until six o'clock that we found ourselves in a long line, hunched against an icy wind, inching our way across the tarmac and up the gangway into an unmarked aircraft that had obviously seen better days.

WE LANDED IN FREETOWN just after midday. Many of the passengers clapped as we touched down, either in relief that we had made it or in joy at being back home.

Rugie was at the airport to meet us. I found it hard to reconcile the overweight and affluently attired woman I now embraced with the slip of a girl I had known in 1970. Her mother and Sewa's mother were twins, though Rugie had been raised by her maternal grandmother, Aisetta Sanfan. For many years she had been called Musukura (lit. "new girl"), a name parents often assign a baby girl until they can think of a personal name for her.

I climbed into the backseat of the 4Runner with Joshua and Sewa; Rugie sat in front beside her driver—a wiry, affable man in his midforties who answered to the name of American. As we sped along the road from Lungi toward the ferry crossing, a warm breeze blew against my face, and the smells of salt water, charcoal, and orange peel carried me back to another time.

Joshua plied me with questions—the very questions to which I sought answers when I first arrived in Sierra Leone almost thirty-eight years ago. What kind of palms are those? What are they selling at those roadside stalls? How should I greet people? Where will we stay? What is Rugie saying?

I was explaining my research to her. How I intended to explore the Kuranko notion of well-being (kendeye). How I would begin by asking people about the sweetest and hardest experiences of their lives.

Rugie said that the hardest experiences would be the war. She had lost her daughter during the war years, unable to get the medicines she needed when she fell desperately ill. Now Rugie herself was unwell, with diabetes and heart problems. She hoped to avoid costly bypass surgery in Ghana by cutting down on carbohydrates.

Shouting to make myself heard above the noise of the engine and the buffeting wind, I asked Rugie if she was still in politics.

She had stood as the Sierra Leone People's Party candidate for

Sengbe-Mongo in the recent national elections but lost to her All People's Congress opponent. People had become disenchanted with the SLPP government and wanted a change. No hard feelings. That's the way things go. And with her health bad, she was happy to take it easy for a while.

At the ferry crossing, Rugie summoned a young man to buy our ferry tickets, another to secure our place on the ferry, another to bring oranges for Joshua. Immediately I saw her uncle S.B. in her, the same compelling physical presence, the same assumption of authority, and again I found it hard to believe that this charismatic and confident woman was once a reticent ten-year-old with bare feet and tattered dress who used to bring messages and food to my wife and me from her grandmother's house and sit in our parlor without speaking, shyly sipping the cup of lemon tea Pauline made for her and declining our invitation to eat.

As the ferry pounded its way across the Sierra Leone River, I pointed out to Joshua the site of Fourah Bay College on Mt. Aureol, and the great silk cotton trees around Kissy Cemetery where my friends S.B. and Noah were both buried. I told him how much the city had grown during the war years, the refugee shanties now covering even the most inaccessible slopes. But Joshua was already feeling overwhelmed, and I was reminded of when I first came to West Africa, my disorientation compounded by jetlag, the brouhaha of a strange language, the press of bodies, the unfamiliarity of almost everything I saw or heard or smelled.

As Joshua refocused on his Game Boy, I observed a scratch-card lottery seller working his way through the crowd on the ferry deck. Unlike the orange sellers, he was doing a brisk trade.

"You going to buy a card?" I teased Sewa.

"They don't have the right numbers," Sewa said.

"How do you know unless you buy one?"

"I checked before. They've got to have the right pattern. Not jumbled."

I was reminded of a Kuranko adage Sewa had invoked the previous summer, talking with me about the stress he had experienced during his first two years in London. "There is a lot of water in this world, but the water you drink is meant for you alone." When I had asked Sewa to elaborate, he told me that you take what God puts in front of you. You can't take what's not meant for you, or what is meant for someone else. You can't force things to happen. You can't use underhand tactics to bring good fortune your way. You must be patient and keep faith. Certain things are in your future, but only God decides when and how they will come to you. It might mean a long wait, years of hard work, but eventually the day will arrive when what has been destined for you will find its way into your hands.

One thing that had steadied and sustained Sewa during his years of struggle in London was the "belief" he had inherited from his father—by which he meant both Islam and a sense of what in Kuranko is known as *bimba che*—ancestral legacy or birthright. "*Ni le wola*," he said. "My life is from them." Not a day passed that he did not offer prayers to his late father, asking him to beg God to open a path for him, to give him what he needed to make his way in the world. He would make this plea every morning over a bowl of cool water, then drink some of the water with Ade, his wife, and sprinkle water on the threshold of his room, so bringing coolness to his heart and peace to the house before he headed off on his bicycle to work on the other side of the city. If woken by bad dreams in the middle of the night, Sewa found that speaking the name of God and praising Allah would dismiss dread and anxiety from his mind. Just as he had a rough idea of his lucky number, and would recognize it when it came up, so he had a strong sense of his destiny.

As a scion of a ruling house, Sewa had always been aware that a political career, either at the local or national level, was in his stars, and that, God and the ancestors willing, it was only a matter of time before these things unfolded for him. But for the time being, it was important that he remain in England, earning money, encouraging his kinsmen back home to do everything in their power to retain the staff of chieftaincy in Diang. "That is my destiny," he said. "One day, when the moment is right, I will go home. You see, you have to do what you have to do, and be patient that things will work out. Like with my cinema job, I could see that the supervisor was not hard working. He would phone me in the morning, say 'Oh Sewa, I can't make it, can you go and cover my shift?' I would say 'Yeah, no problem.' Then, come to the summer, he went to Kent and saw his girlfriend, and Kent is far from Wandsworth, so he phoned me and asked if I would do his shift as well as my own. So I knew that one day this fellow would be sacked. It was just a matter of time. And I was waiting, waiting. Even if it had taken two or three years I would still have waited, because I knew definitely that if he went I would be the next supervisor, you see. You have to know what you're doing in life, you have to get focus."

Inevitably, Sewa became a supervisor. But his philosophy was neither fatalistic nor thoughtless. "When people do things or say things, you have to think twice, think why, why they're doing this, is it because of this? I'm young. I've got to think that even if the [Diang] chief lived a long life or I die, I have kids coming up, and if I have access to the chieftaincy they might be interested, you know. People don't write history, they don't write things down. You have to remember everything. We say, '*i tole kina i bimba ko*' [your ear is as wise as your grandfather's words]. When my father was young he was listening to the elders talk about things that happened long before his time. Then he told me those stories, and I will tell them to my son. They're not written down, but if you listen you will know them. Those are the things you have to think about, that you have to know deep down. Ade says, 'You think too much,' but I tell her there are things you have to think about, things beyond normal, so that you'll know."

Sewa's father, the late Paramount Chief Sheku Magba II, was his role model. As a small boy, Sewa had been nicknamed "walking-stick" because of the way he followed his father everywhere, dogging his heels, head down, concentrating on placing his feet exactly where his father placed his, literally walking in his father's footsteps. This was the "kingly way of walking" that his uncle S.B. had often upbraided him for, thinking it impertinent that a small boy should comport himself as a chief. But Sewa had inherited more than his father's way of walking; he wanted to emulate the political even-handedness and incorruptibility for which his father was known during forty years as paramount chief of Diang. By contrast, the present incumbent, Sewa's brother Sheku, was at odds with the older section and town chiefs and increasingly embattled and unpopular. "If Sheku gave up the chieftaincy," Sewa told me, "and I was called upon to go home tomorrow and contest, I would do so, even though I am only twenty-nine."

From the ferry landing it was only a short drive to Sewa's mother's house in Kissy. We sat on the front porch for a while, paying our respects, before Rugie drove Joshua and me to our hotel.

I was assailed by a familiar odor of varnished wood and mildew, and for a moment I was back in the apartment at Fourah Bay College where Pauline and I lived before heading north to Kabala in 1969. Outside, I heard the murmur of voices, the cheep of a bird, the bleat of car horns, and the thrum of traffic along Kissy Road.

I asked Joshua how he was feeling.

"I'm fine," he said. "I just need to pace myself."

I knew what he was experiencing and was deeply moved by his courage and common sense. Months ago, when I began planning my trip, Joshua insisted on accompanying me. I had tried to dissuade him, with daunting descriptions of local food and living conditions, but he had not been put off. Even now, using his old Game Boy as a parallel universe into which he could escape and recover some sense of being in command of things, he had the presence of mind to say that no matter how difficult the day had been he had no misgivings about the journey ahead.

I WOKE IN DARKNESS to the muezzin's call from a nearby mosque and a crowing rooster. When the hotel generator started up and a light came on in our room, I wrote in my journal. But since neither Josh nor I had eaten a full meal since London, I soon left off writing and went out in search of some bottled water, bread, and bananas.

When I got back Joshua was awake. He wanted to know my plans for the day. I explained that Sewa would need to drop off gifts at the houses of friends and family. I would try to conclude arrangements for hiring Rugie's Land Cruiser for our trip north, buy some supplies downtown, and visit Kaimah. "You don't have to come if you don't want to," I said. "If you prefer to stay here and rest . . ."

But Josh was eager to come, and when Sewa turned up with American and D.Y., the two drivers Rugie had assigned to us, we piled into the 4Runner and headed into the city.

We were immediately stalled in traffic along Kissy Road. Peddlers offered up trays of biscuits, key rings, electrical cords, ballpoint pens, razors, trinkets, and chewing gum at the open windows of our vehicle as the crowd surged past. Women sat at roadside stalls, selling limes, peppers, magi cubes, onions. Sewa complained of "this postman business" and rummaged yet again in the back of the vehicle for another plastic bag of clothing marked with a kinsman's name.

"Did you ever think of going to America instead of England?" Joshua asked Sewa.

"America was my first dream," Sewa said. "Everyone wants to go to America. If you got out of the vehicle right now and stood in the street and said you were going to take one person to America, you'd be mobbed. I'd have to come and rescue you!"

I bought the supplies I needed from a Lebanese trader—bottled water, cooking oil, tomato paste, onions, toilet paper, dried milk, salt—then found an Internet cafe where I could e-mail my wife Francine that we had arrived safely in Freetown.

While waiting for a computer, I watched the sites that the cafe clients were surfing. One young man was on Arsenal's website, looking at scores and stats. Another was working his way down a page called Education Destination; another was studying the criteria for undergraduate admissions to the Australian National University. Joshua had recently remarked that sports, like religion, are alternative names for hope. But when was hope wishful thinking, and therefore in vain; when was it realistic and reasonable? Or did the existential necessity of hopefulness render these distinctions between abstract and concrete utopias irrelevant?[2] And I thought of Kaimah, whom I had been helping through university for several years. Though he saw education as a way out of Sierra Leone, a way of securing a future abroad, I was beginning to wonder if this would ever happen.

At Rugie's I discovered that the Land Cruiser was undergoing major engine repairs and might not be ready that day. Since Sewa still had many calls to make, I asked American to drive Joshua and me back to our hotel. We would wait there until Sewa phoned us.

At two thirty Sewa called. There had been an accident in the city. Some gas cylinders had exploded. Several people had been killed. It was impossible to get through to the East End.

Realizing that our chances of leaving Freetown that day were fast diminishing, even if the Land Cruiser was repaired, I tried to book another hotel room for the night. But the hotel was already full.

Sewa and American picked us up a couple of hours later. Sewa was even more impatient than I was to get out of Freetown. A day of delays, demands, and deliveries had exhausted him.

Night had fallen by the time we reached Rugie's compound near Congo Cross, and it was hard to make ourselves heard over the hubbub of voices in the eroded laterite lane, the noise of a diesel generator, the reggae beat in a nearby bar. The smell of ganja was ubiquitous.

Rugie introduced me to the children crowded into the main room of the house, watching a video. Some were her offspring, some were staying with her so they could attend school in Freetown. Among these children was the late chief Tala Sewa's daughter from Firawa. "This is home," Rugie said, smiling at the crowded room, "and there is no place like home, surrounded by people who love you, who care. Unlike England, where no one cares who you are, everyone in a rush."

The Land Cruiser was in a backyard workshop not far away. I went there with Sewa and American to see how the work was progressing. The mechanics were reassembling the engine. We waited as they bolted it back in place. Checked the wiring. Tried the ignition. Nothing. They tried to jump start it by having some local kids push it down the potholed lane. Still no sign of life.

I decided to give ourselves a couple of hours before deciding what to do, and I asked Sewa and American if they would drive me to Kaimah's place, which was only a short way along Main Motor Road at Congo Cross.

I HAD KNOWN KAIMAH from the year of his birth. During my first stint of fieldwork in Sierra Leone, his father, Noah, worked as my research assistant. When Noah died in 2003, I took Kaimah under my wing until he graduated from Njala University in June 2006. When I found myself unable to meet the costs of his further education in the UK or South Africa, Kaimah enrolled for an MSci degree in rural development at Njala. But even these fees proved beyond my means, and like many other young West Africans who had allowed themselves to believe that education would guarantee them a bright future, Kaimah had come to the realization that without local benefactors, inside connections, and the means to pay bribes he would probably never find employment in Sierra Leone, no matter how qualified he was. In the darkness of his single room, his clothes hanging from the ceiling above his bed, and surrounded by the books I had sent him over the years, Kaimah seemed close to despair.

I felt desperately sorry for him, and guilty that I could not help. But as he shared his story with me in that candlelit and claustrophobic room, it became clear that he regarded me as his *yigi* (hope or mentor), his *sabu* (enabler), and that he felt both frustrated and humiliated to find himself, at age thirty-eight, still unable to earn a living, marry, or support a wife and family.

"What of your girlfriend who worked in the hospital?" I asked. "Are you still together?"

Aisetta had left him. Kaimah knew from the very start of the relationship that it would end this way, because she had a beau before him. This man had gone to London with his family during the war years. When he came back to Sierra Leone he was able to offer Aisetta security, income, prospects—so she went back to him. "You can't expect love when you have nothing to give but love," Kaimah said. "Love without money counts for nothing here. You have to have money. Only with children is this any different."

Kaimah then shared with me a story he had never confided to his own father.

In 1992, when Noah was working as a trade inspector in Koidu and Kaimah was a student at the local high school, Kaimah had fallen in love with another student who was known as Lango. Lango, whose given name was Fatmata Massaquoi, lived with her aunt and uncle in the same compound as Kaimah's family. Not long before the Revolutionary United Front invaded Kono and only a few months after Lango gave birth to their love child, the Massaquoi family left Koidu, possibly because of the shame that Lango had brought upon them, possibly because they had heard rumors of the impending invasion. For the next ten years, as war destroyed the country, with villages burned to the ground, thousands killed or maimed, and every scrap of moveable property plundered, Kaimah's family moved, with thousands like them, from one district to another seeking refuge from the fighting and the atrocities. Despite continual disruptions to his education, Kaimah passed his O levels in 1994 and sought admission to Fourah Bay College. Unable to find anyone to help him pay his fees, he gained his A levels and tried again, to no avail. Kaimah struggled to accept, as his father once had, that he might never gain a higher education, but when I returned to Sierra Leone in January 2002, just as the war was ending, Kaimah found the mentor he had been seeking, and went to university.

During the war years, Kaimah had done everything in his power to locate Lango. But it wasn't until after his graduation in June 2006 that a breakthrough came. "I began having dreams, the same dream over and over again," Kaimah said, "and in these dreams Lango was telling me about our child. In the same dreams, an old man appeared, someone I knew in Koidu town when Lango and I were living there. I was sure these dreams meant that I was soon going to see her again. So one day I went to Koidu with my younger brother, and we found the old man who had appeared in my dreams. I asked him if he remembered Lango, if he knew where she was, and how I could find her. He told me that Lango was dead. She had died in Bo ten years ago. He said she had been seriously ill for some time. So I traveled to Bo next day and found the family. They were where the old man told me they were. I greeted them, and explained who I was, and how much I wanted to see my child. It was very difficult. No one remembered me, no one could identify me. But thanks to God, Lango's aunty Sarah, who Lango lived with when she was in Koidu, happened to be visiting Bo from Moyamba and she identified me and told the rest of the Massaquoi family about my friendship with Lango and about our love child."

Kaimah's son was in the St. Mary's Children's Home in Bo, and after visiting the boy several times, Kaimah petitioned the coordinator of the home to grant him custody, promising that he would dedicate himself to his son's education, and showing evidence that he had already secured a place for him at the St. Edward's Secondary School in Freetown.

As Kaimah concluded his story, and as if what now happened had been carefully stage-managed for dramatic effect, Kaimah's fourteen-year-old son appeared at the door and I was introduced to Michael Bangura—named for me and for Kaimah's late mother, Yebu Bangura. As Michael sat on the bed beside his father, Kaimah proudly showed me his son's school reports. I had a sudden sense of history unfolding before me and tears welled up in my eyes as I recalled how Kaimah's grandfather, Tina Kome, taught himself to read and write while serving with the British in the Cameroons during the First World War (the first Kuranko man to become literate in English), of how Kaimah's father, Noah, had struggled to complete his education after his elder brother S.B. took him out of high school to help in his political campaigns, of how Noah's mother argued against Noah pursuing studies in New Zealand, fearful that he, like Tina Kome, would throw his life to the winds and "become a child of the white men," and of how, despite Kaimah's years in the wilderness, he was now on the threshold of realizing a dream whose origins lay in his grandfather's conviction that the future lay in a world very different from the world into which he was born.

I asked Michael about his favorite subjects at school. As shy as his father, he spoke little and in whispers. Turning to Kaimah, I assured him I would visit him again when I returned from Firawa. We would discuss the possibility of his going to the UK, just as Sewa had done, and enrolling for a course of study there. He was ready to give up his MSci studies at Njala, and if I could help pay for his airfare to the UK, he would find a college course there and stay with his cousins until he found his feet in England.

"But I am concerned about Michael," I said. "What will become of him if you go to England to live?

"I have thought about that already," Kaimah said. "My sister Zainab lives close to here, close to Michael's school. She will care for Michael if I go abroad."

Forty Days

WE DROVE THROUGH THE NIGHT, American at the wheel and
D.Y. dozing beside him. The journey was less comfortable than it
would have been in the Land Cruiser but after consulting American, who had firsthand knowledge of the roads we would have to
negotiate in the far north, I decided to take the 4Runner and avoid
further delays in Freetown. And so we sped along a pitch black and
abandoned road, blind to the landscape around us, our headlights
picking out potholes in the asphalt or momentarily pinning a group
of startled villagers against a backdrop of elephant grass. We were
all relieved to have put the city's thronged and polluted streets behind us.

At Paygay's Guest House in Kabala, the bleary-eyed Limba pro-
prietor unlocked the gate and showed us to our rooms. Joshua and I
threw our rucksacks into the corner, collapsed on the bed, and fell
fast asleep. But Sewa had other matters on his mind. As we slept, he
visited the grave of his best friend, cousin, and namesake (*togema*),
who died a year ago, not long after graduating from Milton Margai
Teacher's College. Sewa Balansama had been in a motorcycle accident the previous year and had died of complications from internal
injuries.

That afternoon, Sewa told me what this friendship had meant to
him. "We were the same age. We bore the same name. We went to
the same school, and were in the same class. We came from ruling
houses and had the same code of conduct. When we came to Kabala
for high school we were always together. Every evening, strolling
up and down the street in Yogomaia. Even our girlfriends were sisters . . ."

Sewa hesitated, as if struggling to find the right word. "He was the
quiet one," Sewa said at last. "Intelligent. Perfect in every way."

Sewa was suffering from a swollen throat. His eyes were sore. Perhaps from the Harmattan. Did I have any medicine that might help?

"There is no medicine for grief," I said.

"I have not been so tearful since my son died," Sewa said, alluding to last summer in London when Ade gave birth prematurely. The baby survived only a few hours before his lungs failed.

It was not only these tragedies that oppressed Sewa. That morning he had learned that a Canadian NGO was planning to build its headquarters on the site where his friend was buried. No one had told the Canadians that the place was a graveyard, and they had not bothered to find out.

Later I would visit Sewa Balansama's grave with Sewa, hard under the great granite wall of Albitaiya, and we would stroll past the house where Sewa's namesake used to live and see his name still painted on the closed wooden shutter of his room.

How long can we expect our lives, or the lives of those we love, to be memorialized in objects and in places? How hard, I wondered, would it be for me to go back to the house at One-Mile where my first wife and I lived thirty-eight years ago, and find it gone?

In his 2006 Nobel Lecture, Orhan Pamuk argues that a writer must assume that the experiences that seem so unique to himself or herself are shared by people everywhere; indeed, it is on one's ability to transcend the boundary between oneself and others that one's writing stands or falls. "When a writer uses his secret wounds as his starting point, he is, whether he is aware of it or not, putting great faith in humanity. My confidence comes from the belief that all human beings resemble one another, that others carry wounds like mine—and that they will therefore understand. All true literature rises from this childish, hopeful certainty that we resemble one another."[1]

LATER THAT MORNING, as our vehicle lurched through the scrub, I breathed a sigh of relief. In Kabala, I had been besieged by memories, as well as jostling crowds, incessant demands, relentless commerce, car horns, and palaver. The bush would be a space of silences, broken only by the piping of a bird or an imagined footfall.

But it was slow going, the road eroded by rains, and on the steep hills our tires scrabbling to gain purchase on the loose laterite. Several times we had to climb down and walk behind the vehicle, leaving American to wrestle with the wheel and the reluctant gearshift as he inched the 4Runner over an outcropping boulder or across a deep rut.

As we neared Firawa, I asked American to stop and let me down. I wanted to see if the landscape — the familiar hill, the long grass, the lophira trees, the path — was as I remembered it.

It was. It had remained constant. Despite all the changes in my life, and the changes I would undoubtedly confront when I walked the last hundred yards into the village, this had remained the same.

After a long minute alone with my thoughts, I turned to Joshua, telling him that Abdul Marah was the section chief, the brother of my old friends Noah and S.B., and that in all likelihood we would be lodged in his house. And I warned Joshua that there would be a lot of speechmaking, praise-singing, and gift-giving. He should be patient. It was protocol. He did not have to participate. If anything perplexed him, I would explain it to him later.

ABDUL'S PORCH WAS CROWDED with older men, gathered for prayers. It was, Abdul quickly explained, the last day of a *labinane* and, even as we embraced, he apologized for the inconvenience.[2]

I begged him not to; we had given him no definite date for our arrival; if anything, we were putting him out.

Abdul was seventy-three years old, and as solidly built as when I first knew him. Not for nothing was he nicknamed *kin gbilime* (heavy-foot), for as a young wrestler he was unbeatable. Once he had taken his stance, he could not be moved. Not even ten adversaries could throw him off balance. And long after his wrestling days had ended, he showed the same strength of mind in settling disputes or laying down the law. "Heavy-foot has stepped into the ring," people would say, for whatever Abdul determined would be done.

We clasped each other, allowing the reality of the moment to sink in. It had been a long time, I told Abdul. I had dreamed of returning, dreamed of this moment. So many years passing. So many losses and sorrows. S.B. and Noah no longer with us. The war . . .

"I am sorry," Abdul said, using the conventional phrase of sympathy for the bereaved.

"I too am sorry," I said, "for all *you* have lost," for I had already glimpsed, a few yards from Abdul's modest, mud brick dwelling, the mound of earth and rank weeds that was all that remained of his former house, burned to the ground by rebels in their second and most devastating assault on Firawa ten years before.

Several of the elders recognized me. As we shook hands, they expressed astonishment that I had returned. Some had assumed I was dead. Others were baffled as to who I was. But Abdul explained patiently that Noah and I had been best friends. Many years ago, I came to Firawa from London where I was pursuing my studies. I had written books about Barawa history, Kuranko life and customs. I had helped people, done good things, had been close to S.B. and written his life story. I had returned to Barawa often over the years and stayed in Abdul's house. Once, I came with my wife and daughter, who was born in Sierra Leone. After my wife died, I remarried and had two more children. Now I had returned, bringing my son with me . . .

Abdul broke off and ordered the chief's drum beaten, summoning the praise-singers to his house.

Within minutes a *jelimusu* and her son, lugging a heavy xylophone, hurried into the compound and began singing my praises and the praises of the lineage to which, by adoption, I belonged—the ruling lineage of the Marah.

"Give me money, sir!" The Kuranko plaudits were all followed by this English refrain. "Give me money, Oh give me money, sir!" The peremptory demands sounded vulgar in English, though every Kuranko celebration of ancestral power, heroic deeds, and chiefly wisdom is followed by the same extortions. I shelled out thirty leones, relieved that now we were in Firawa a little money went a long way. Grinning in satisfaction at my gift, the *jelimusu* now turned her attentions to Sewa, extolling his lineage, which had been allied with the Barawa rulers for many generations (Sewa's mother, Tina, was Abdul's sister, and her marriage to Sewa's father—paramount chief of Diang—had been arranged in order to cement this old alliance). The praise song was one of Sewa's father's favorites, and it brought tears to Sewa's eyes. He was in his mother's place (*na ware*), in the chiefdom of his maternal uncles, the Marah. He felt at home here; indeed, more at home in some ways than he felt in Diang, where his brother was chief, though making a poor fist of it, and where he was subject to all manner of demands, as well as envious gossip.

When the welcome was over, Abdul signaled that our baths were ready. Buckets of hot water, one for Joshua and one for me, had been left by one of his junior wives in the latrine. This was Josh's first experience of a pit latrine, and he quailed at the thought of it and of the room in which we were to sleep—the dirt floor, the grimy mosquito net, the eviscerated mattress, the boxes stacked oppressively against the mud brick wall, the piece of flattened roofing iron that served as a shutter, the large spider hanging from the rafters . . .

THAT NIGHT, JOSHUA AND I were kept awake by the widows and other women singing in an adjacent room. Poignant and unflagging, the singing went on until dawn. At times a dirge in Arabic, led by the local imam; at other times a succession of improvised praise songs in which the widows took turns to celebrate the late Yira Marah's virtues—what a fine man he was, how many children he had brought into the world, the clothes and jewelry freely bestowed, the consideration and respect, the untroubled life.

Where does it spring from, this universal disinclination to speak ill of the dead? Why, when a friend or family member dies, do we slip so immediately and naturally into panegyric, overlooking all faults, transforming flaws into mere foibles, the loved one unparalleled in virtue? The greater our distance from the real person, the purer he or she becomes until, in passing into the great beyond, he or she embodies perfection itself. Is it for the same reason that we see victims as virtuous? Do we sympathetically respond to absolute loss by overcompensatory gestures—bringing the dead back to life in language, indulging in commemorative rites, creating shrines around their photographs, fetishizing memorabilia, making them exemplars of everything that is true and good? Certainly I found myself doing all of this, in some measure or another, when Pauline died. Just as, in time, I experienced her metamorphosis into pure spirit, present and diffuse in, of all places, the grasslands of Barawa.

A DEATH THROWS THE WORLD into momentary chaos, a chaos that is at once social and emotional. Unassuageable grief—like love, fury, anger, and deep resentment—signals both a loss of self-control and a disruption of social relationships. As Mary Douglas remarked, human beings everywhere tend to construe such disorderliness as a dangerous state of impurity.[3] Such is the case among the Kuranko.

Not only are the bereaved tainted by death; anyone intimately related to the deceased, or anyone who comes into close contact with the corpse or the grave, is tainted by association and must be ritually cleansed.

After a death, the extended family observes a relatively brief mourning period of seven days. By contrast, widows are obliged to remain in their late husband's house, isolated from the ongoing life of the village, for forty days. As Kuranko see it, the women's physical, social, and emotional closeness to their late husband places them in a dangerous situation that requires quarantine. Moreover, anyone who has not experienced bereavement should avoid such women, lest they become contaminated, as it were, by the death. It is as though past experience of loss gives one a degree of immunity to its devastating effects.

During *labinane* widows may let their hair go unbraided, neglect their appearance, and appear indifferent to life — manifestations of their inner distress, perhaps, but more significantly for Kuranko, signs that they are momentarily outside the pale of quotidian life. At the same time, it is said that placing them in isolation protects them from their late husband's shade, which lingers, loathe to depart this world, still attached to his wives, his children, his property, and his home, and sometimes angry and vengeful at having been abandoned and ostracized by the living. This is also why wives and daughters of the deceased are enjoined to avoid all contact with the corpse. They are also placed in the care and custody of a sister's son of their late husband throughout their forty-day confinement to ensure they remain separated both from the dead and from the living. Any communication with the widows must go through the sister's son.

As for why a sister's son has this power to protect the widows, the Kuranko reasoning follows from the fact that he is "acting in the place of the dead man's sister." As one informant explained, "We permit the sister's son [*berinné*, lit. 'little maternal uncle'] to watch over the widows because if the dead man's shade [*yiyei*] approaches it will see the sister's son there on the porch of his house [where he keeps vigil, day and night]. It will not go past him and frighten the women; it will immediately think of the sister's son as the sister [i.e., recall the taboo against a man showing undue familiarity with his sister]. And the sister will also be inside the house to console the widows and prevent them from being frightened by their late husband's shade."

The *intersubjective* separation of the widows from others who are less deeply or directly touched by bereavement is paralleled on the *intrapsychic* plane by forgetting—which is, in essence, an *inward* strategy for detaching the living from the dead. But whether separation is accomplished physically or psychologically,[4] the goal is to ensure that a death does not pollute, overshadow, or destroy the lives of the living, and that life itself goes on.

Just as the confinement of widows is temporary—a prelude to a new phase of life—so forgetting is never simply a matter of putting something or someone from one's mind; it is a process of *transmutation* in which the idiosyncratic or living image of the person who has passed away gives ground to a new, generalized image of him or her as abstract presence or moral ideal. As anyone who has suffered bereavement will attest, this transmutation occurs naturally but may be resisted and lamented, since it is also natural to want to retain a vivid image of a loved one, to keep it alive, to not allow it to fade. Perhaps this is why, in mortuary rituals throughout the world, the transmutation of a loved one into an abstraction has to be ritually encouraged. As in many other human societies, Kuranko are simultaneously concerned with the passage of the shade to its extraworldly destination, the transformation of the deceased *person* into an ancestral *figure*, the transition of the widows to a new life, and the passing of the property of the dead into new hands. Each element entails the others. Thus, excessive weeping and lamentation at a funeral will make it difficult for the spirit of the deceased to pass into the place of the dead. The ancestors already there will allegedly say, "The spirit is not with us until those on earth have kept quiet." Clearly, reactions to loss—particularly protest, searching, and despair—are attributed to *both* the bereaved *and* the deceased. But as long as one clings to the life one shared with the other, neither will achieve the detachment that makes possible a new life—the widow remarried, the deceased become an ancestor.

AS DAWN BROKE the widows left the house, escorted by the sister's son of their late husband. The sister's son held a small drum, which he beat dolefully, warning away those who had not yet lost a loved one. I did not follow the small procession but knew that it was headed for the streamside for the final rite of purification. This would be the last chance for the widows to confess any grievances they bore their late husband, any infidelity or ill-will. In the past, a two-cotyledon kola nut would be split, and the two halves cast on the ground. If these fell facing each other, no confession was required; if they fell the other way, then some undeclared issue required absolution. Not to confess would invite retribution from the husband's vengeful ghost.

The sun, rising through the mist, resembled a cake of soap. The air was cold, and Abdul and I huddled on a bench in the yard with several of his grandchildren, our hands extended toward the fire at our feet. Abdul's youngest wife had placed a pot of water on the fire, and it was now coming to the boil. Abdul ordered his wife to fetch a thermos flask from his room — the room he had vacated for Joshua and me. He did not want to wake Joshua, though. Perhaps we should wait. "No," I said, "Josh will sleep through anything." And so, after pouring a coffee for Abdul and another for myself, I helped Abdul navigate the photo album I had given him the previous evening, showing Firawa as it had been twenty-five to thirty years ago. His eyesight was not good, Abdul explained. I would have to help him identify some of the people in the photos. "Is that Yeli Maliki?" "Yes," I said, and recalled how he recounted the history of Barawa to me. "And this? Is this Saran Salia Sanoh?" "Yes. I took the photo of him outside his house — the house he gave me and Pauline to stay in when we were here in 1979."

"His house was also burned by the rebels,"[5] Abdul said. "There is nothing there now."

THAT MORNING, WHILE THE WIDOWS were at the streamside, the men of the lineage gathered in Abdul's compound to sacrifice a red goat to the ancestors. We stood around the goat, our arms outstretched, as the imam named the ancestors, beginning with the recently dead and working back toward the dimly remembered ones. And as the names were called we murmured *amina* in unison, beseeching the ancestors to accept our sacrifice, and begging Allah to receive Yira's spirit into *lakira*. This was *our* moment of purification, our last opportunity to declare any grudges we might have borne the dead man, for these would "spoil" the sacrifice.

The sacrifice was quickly over and from Abdul's porch I watched the young men butchering the goat. Each portion of the meat was carefully placed on banana leaves before being distributed according to custom—the upper foreleg to Abdul, the section chief, the rump to the lineage sisters, the neck to the sisters' sons, the heart and liver to a respected person (on this occasion I was the honored recipient), and the remaining meat to the household and lineage. Because the body of the consecrated animal stands for the body of the lineage itself, the distribution of the meat was a kind of social reconstitution of the animal, now symbolically reborn as a living community of kin and neighbors.

Traditionally, a few days would be allowed to elapse after the ending of *labinane* before the legacy was distributed and widows remarried. But things change. Some rituals become curtailed. Old rules no longer apply. Economies of time come into play.

It was late in the day, the sun already sinking in the western sky, when the senior sister's son of the late Yira Marah appeared in Abdul's compound with his uncle's box of clothes. Yira Marah's surviving brothers were there, too, together with his eldest son and a small crowd of elders and other relatives.

The protocol was familiar. The clothes piled on a mat in the compound; Abdul, as senior member of the Marah clan, ensuring that everything conformed to custom; the widows confined within the house behind us; the need to distribute the clothes as widely as possible, and so avoid the appearance of favoritism or bias.

According to the rule of primogeniture, the eldest son succeeds his father as family head. So he receives his late father's cap and gown, though never his trousers because his father's identity as progenitor and his identity as offspring preclude any action that might blur this boundary. As one man once put it to me, "He cannot wear his father's trousers because it is from his father's loins that he sprang." As the clothes were spread out on the mat and sorted, conversation turned to the question as to who would inherit Yira Marah's widows. According to the levirate, they would go to their late husband's brothers. But Abdul took pains to point out that he would reserve the final decision in this matter, and that the women would be asked if they had any preferences.

Abdul's remark precipitated a heated argument among the brothers. The elder pointed out that, according to custom, he had the primary claim. In any event, he argued, the women should be given before any clothing was distributed lest one brother end up with more than the others. The mother's brother, asserting his authority, demanded calm. The widows had expressed no preferences, and the *chefare* could not be postponed. Therefore, he would supervise the distribution of the clothes, and the widow business would be resolved another day. "After all, what do I get out of this?" he bantered. "The neck from the sacrifice? Nothing more!" And he snatched some shoes from the mat and stuffed them under his gown. This was part of the performance. A man enjoys a joking relationship with his maternal uncle and may freely snatch small articles of his maternal uncle's clothing or take food from his plate. It is a reminder, first that his father's lineage gave bridewealth to his mother's lineage, and second that his mother's brother is obligated to the sister whose marriage provided the bridewealth with which he could marry. In stealing from his mother's brothers he therefore asserts his mother's bridewealth-linked claim over her brothers, and the right he retains to the bridewealth his father gave his mother's lineage. As one man put it, explaining why the neck is given to the sister's son at a sacrifice, "When [the sister's son's] father married, he said he wanted that woman as his wife. These words came from

his throat/neck. So whenever the mother's brother sacrifices an animal, the sister's child takes the neck in recollection of the time his father married his mother's brother's sister."

The *chefare* wound up with more badinage and mock fighting. One brother hurried away with his haul of shirts, trousers, and shoes, only to be pursued by another who snatched a shirt back, smirking at me as he quickly hid it under his tunic. Another brother continued his tug of war with the sister's son. And the elder brother renewed his attempt to persuade Abdul to order the widows to decide their new husbands immediately.

IT HAD BEEN A LONG DAY, yet that evening, lying in the hammock outside Abdul's house, I found myself pondering the strange ways in which the past returns to life in the present, whether it be the wandering and vengeful ghost of a dead person, determined to remain in the land of the living, or the living themselves, unable to forget what has been taken from them or forgive those they hold responsible for their loss. Of the rebels who had destroyed Firawa in 1998, Abdul declared, *A ma heketu*—"It is not forgiven"—adding that the war still lay heavy on his hands. But the resolution of such matters depended on one's power to see that justice was done. Ordinary people were powerless to avenge the wrongs that had been done to them and their families; for them, acceptance was the only option. But for those who had the means to pursue justice, grievances were often nursed and opportunities sought for getting even. Abdul was in an unenviable position. As a chief whose house had been burned, possessions looted, and livelihood destroyed, he was bound to seek indemnification and revenge. But without powerful allies, he could do nothing.

That afternoon I had spoken with the late Yira Marah's eldest son, whose mother died during the war. Kulifa said she died of stress, forced to flee the village and subsist in the bush for three months, scavenging for food, living in a makeshift house, cooking without salt, bathing without soap. "Life is still hard for us here," Kulifa told me. "We live in a house with three rooms. Not enough space for all of us. We have no way of earning money, no way of getting our rice to the markets in Kabala and Makeni. If we sell our rice to the traders that come in their lorries from Kabala, we get a pittance and they make a huge profit. Without money we cannot buy even secondhand roofing iron. We certainly cannot buy cement."

It was difficult to know whether these complaints were pitched at me—a white man with money—or to what extent people dwelt in despair or accepted hardship, not wanting to appear weak or waste their breath bemoaning their lot.

Kuranko are skeptical about our ability to read the minds of others or infer inner experience from outward appearances. *N'de ma konto lon*—"I don't know what is inside." *N'de sa bu'ro*—"I am not in his belly." This contrast between what is between people (the intersubjective) and what is within people (the intrapsychic) finds expression in the crucial contrast between private and public space. The sociospatial distinction that Kuranko make between *kenema* (open to the public gaze) and *duguro* (lit. "ground-in") or *duworon* (covert, hidden, underhand) echoes the Latin distinction between the *res publica* (whatever belongs to or concerns the people as a whole) and the *res privata* (the domain of the domus or house). At the same time it suggests the European distinction between the open space of the agora and the space of oblique meanings and of allegory (*allos*, other + *agoreuin*, speak openly, speak in the assembly or market—the agora) and thus implies a wide array of differences between activities that take place in the light of day—within the hearing and in sight of others, and are thus common knowledge—and activities that are clandestine, duplicitous, or veiled by secrecy and darkness. In a society where inordinate emphasis is placed on creating a *semblance* of personal equanimity and social amity, what matters most is not so much what one *really* thinks or feels but how adroitly one is able to cultivate relationships with others—greeting a neighbor, paying one's respects to an elder or chief, keeping one's own counsel, and curbing one's impulse to gossip and spread rumor. Intelligence (*hankili*) thus connotes *social* adroitness rather than purely intellectual ability. By extension, well-being (*kendeye*) emphasizes *social* over physical or psychological health—an emphasis that contrasts strikingly with the priority well-intentioned Europeans give to dealing with epidemic diseases like HIV-AIDS, illiteracy, and economic underdevelopment in Africa.

It is because emotionality may disrupt or destroy *social* relationships that marriages were traditionally made for political reasons and not for love. For the same reason, initiation drilled into neophytes the importance of controlling their emotions and not yielding to passion. And this is also why the bereaved are sequestered, and why the overwhelming emotions of grief are enacted by surrogate mourners—granddaughters of the deceased—who are best able to perform these feelings without succumbing to them. Emotionality creates a "hot" and volatile situation; sociality requires "coolness" and calm. In the final analysis, it does not matter how a girl feels about her prospective husband, how a young person feels about the hardship of life, or how a widow feels about her late husband; what matters is that a person follow customary procedures that ensure that social life, and the continuity of life, is not built on the unstable foundation of feeling or subject to the shifting winds of desire.

Does this mean that Kuranko are not in touch with their emotions, or set no store by the expression of individual thoughts and feelings? Are they slaves to social appearance, sacrificing the needs of the ego to the demands of the superego, playing down private feelings in order to conform to public imperatives? I think not. In the first place, the fulfillment of one's social duty—as a mother, a father, a wife, a husband, a chief, a praise-singer—does not necessarily preclude the exercise of will or the expression of emotion; it simply provides a framework or channel for the realization of one's human capacity to make something of oneself within the limits set by one's environment. Even when a person devotes his or her time and energy to educational, economic, or political success, this means little unless the attainment is recognized *socially* and is seen to bolster the life of that person's lineage. Even in the modern West, with its allegedly dominant ethos of possessive individualism, profit and power are seldom praised unless they bring benefit to others. In the second place, the control of emotions in everyday life does not betoken an absence of feeling. To be able to hold one's tongue, not speak out of turn, refrain from gossip, and heed the advice of elders are virtues. Yet these accomplishments do not imply that one lives on automatic pilot, slavishly conforming to social demands, bereft of any inner life of one's own, any more than the individualistic ethos of modernity implies that people lack all sense of collective identity and responsibility or give no thought to family and community commitments.

Consider, for example, these two Kuranko tales that I recorded many years ago, both of which are as poignant as they are absurd (indeed, the narrator's use of ridicule is a way of encouraging us to distance ourselves from the emotional reality that both stories address).

In the first story, a man is so distressed when his wife dies that he severs her breasts and hangs them in the rafters of his house. When villagers come to express their sympathy, he tells them not to cry; his wife has not left him empty-handed. Assuming that the man is referring to the six children his wife had borne him, the villagers are impressed by his equanimity in the face of his loss. However, when the man spoke of not being empty-handed he was referring to his wife's breasts and the comfort they afforded him

Forty days pass and the breasts begin to putrefy. Grief-stricken, the man calls out for his wife, whose name was Jeneba. His neighbors grow impatient with him, and tell him to be quiet, to place his hope in God. "All well and good you telling me to be quiet," the man mutters, "but you are lying down beside your wives. Who have I to comfort me?"

The man grows so unhappy that he begins to visit his wife's grave at night, imploring her to return to him. "My wife, my wife, think of the children you left, think of your poor husband, think of your water pot, so empty now, your fishing nets, your pans . . ."

His neighbors become irritated at being kept awake and having to listen to this man crying like a baby in the night, calling for his wife. "As if his wife is the first woman to ever die," they say. "As if no one else in the world has lost someone they love." That night two strong young men go to the woman's grave and hide inside it. When the widower comes and calls for his wife, the men reach out and start pulling him into the grave. Frightened out of his wits, the man begs his wife to leave him be. "I was only joking, Jeneba. Besides, who would look after the children if I followed you into your grave? Don't take me so seriously," he implores. "I beg you, Jeneba, think of how we worked together, how we loved each other, and leave me be." The young men release him and he falls backward, scrambles quickly to his feet, and flees to his house. Next morning he takes his hoe and seals the grave. He is quiet all that day and for many days to come.

In the second story three widows are consumed by grief. Surrounded by sympathetic neighbors, they yield to their pain. "How will we ever live without our husband?" the youngest asks. "We must place our hope in God," says the eldest. But as soon as she is alone, she takes a knife and severs the penis from the body of her late husband. She then places the penis in a smoking basket and dries it over the fire. This done, she summons her co-wives to mourn the death of their husband. Their cries of grief are heard throughout the village. But their tears are crocodile tears. Their cries of grief are cries of pleasure. For the eldest wife is using the dried penis of their late husband as a dildo. And as she pleasures her co-wives, she sings:

> Allah has given us comfort today
> Allah has heard our cries and given us comfort
> Allah has given us comfort in our grief . . .

THESE STORIES ARE anthropologically illuminating. Everything that occurs in the course of Kuranko mourning rites—from the day of the death to the end of *labinane*—suggests a pervasive cultural tendency to externalize and spatialize experiences that in the modern West we tend to locate within the mind. While we might admit that an afterimage or memory survives the death of a loved one, Kuranko tend to project this afterimage as a socially isolated, wandering soul. And where we might speak of the bereaved experiencing ambivalence toward the dead—pining and drawn to them at the same time as they feel angry at having been abandoned by them— Kuranko attribute these mixed emotions to the shade itself. This is why ghosts are said to haunt and sometimes hound the living, for they are incensed at having been abandoned and ostracized. And yet, as these two stories make clear, this prevailing view does not preclude a very different picture of grief—a grief so deep that it may drive a person to self-destructive, antisocial behavior, and even the edge of insanity.

WHAT FACTORS FAVOR AN interpretation of the bereavement reaction that places less emphasis on private experience than on the integrity of the public realm? As a general principle we might say that in small-scale, traditional societies, experiences that are conducive to the well-being of the community will be reinforced, rehearsed, and retained, while experiences that jeopardize social integrity will be suppressed. But it is important to note, as these Kuranko stories suggest, that what is suppressed in the public sphere will make its appearance outside that sphere, in cries and whispers, in private thoughts, in stories told at night when quotidian conventions are in abeyance, and in fantasy and dream.

What holds true for private thoughts and feelings, holds true for what we call memory and forgetting, which Kuranko regard as modes of thought (*miria*). Specifically, remembering and forgetting are not simply spontaneous and natural mental events over which one has little control; they are under the sway of one's social intelligence (*hankili*), which is why such phrases as *n'hankili bilara a ko* (I remembered) or *n'hankili bora a ko* (I forgot) suggest that remembering and forgetting, like any other process of thought and feeling, must be constrained by social judgment. That is to say that though a person may be preoccupied by some period in the past when life was easier or happier, or be haunted by guilt at some harm he or she did a kinsman years ago, or cannot forget a humiliation suffered at the hands of a neighbor, he or she can avoid publicly *expressing* this nostalgia, confessing this guilt, or pursuing this grievance. One must decide when a residue of the past has *social* value and when it has not. This emphasis on social judgment helps us explain why it is largely irrelevant for Kuranko to see memory as a kind of intrapsychic hiccupping, in which the past unexpectedly and sometimes problematically repeats itself in one's consciousness and demands to be expressed. For what is at issue is not the compelling vividness or private significance of one's memories but how one reacts to them, how effectively one decides which experiences might be socially damaging to share, and how best to censor one's speech in order to promote social harmony.

It was curious to be brought full circle here, for the two Kuranko stories I had called to mind brought me to a reconsideration of the limits one must place on the sharing of private thoughts and feelings, of the ethical value of confession as a measure of authenticity, honesty, and truth, and of social judgment as a matter of deciding what is conducive to Life rather than just one's own life. And I thought of Sewa, going abroad to satisfy his ambition to become a man of substance, yet struggling also to fulfill his destiny in his natal village. His attempts to reconcile and balance these opposing imperatives had often led to frustration and doubt, for the more he succeeded in London the more he became a target of scavengers and the subject of envy. Yet only days ago he had told me how he longed to get to Firawa, to get away from the impossible demands people were making on his time and resources, to go fishing with a hook and line as he and his age-mates did when they were boys. Even in this, however, there was unintended irony. For the float (*lue fonfone*) that bobs up and down when a fish bites, communicating what is going on beneath the surface of the water, is a Kuranko synonym for a gossip or backbiter (*nafigiye*) — a person who trawls the muddy depths, as it were, dredging up information that would be better left unspoken and unshared.

Two days later, Sewa went fishing with Abdul's son Bockarie, D.Y., and American. They returned to the village empty-handed. It was the dry season. The river was low. There were no deep pools. Their patience and persistence had not been rewarded.

I was amused by their glum looks. For though they had caught no fish, they had had a good time. They had bonded.

But I said nothing. I could not be sure that a remark along these lines would not smack of condescension. For I had the money to buy all the fish in Firawa and enjoyed a liberty that many in Firawa did not possess — of rating sociability ahead of a full stomach.

Scenes from a Marriage

MOST OF THE DAY, Abdul sat in his bush-carpentered chair at the end of his porch, observing people as they came and went along the path that skirted his compound, chatting and sharing kola with elders, hearing complaints and settling minor disputes, or tinkering with the electric torch that he was trying to rig as a nightlight for our room. From time to time he would summon me to his side, to assist him in sorting through and interpreting the official letters in his battered briefcase, all of which appeared to concern his installation as Barawa section chief. Or he would ask my help in identifying some of the people and places in the photo album I had given him. Having done his bidding I would ply him with questions of my own. I was particularly keen to know what had become of his wives, Tilkolo and Ferema, who used to give me invaluable glimpses into the workaday lives of Kuranko women.

"They are there," Abdul replied offhandedly.

When I pressed him to explain exactly where "there" was, Abdul named the villages where Tilkolo and Ferema now lived. Having become too old to pull their weight in Abdul's compound, they had returned to their natal families.

"And Gbongbon?" I asked, remembering the unhappy and homesick girl—Abdul's youngest wife—who he had sent to live with his mother in Kabala, and who found her voice again, telling trickster stories to the children of the house.

"She passed away," Abdul said. And I immediately regretted asking after her. Even taking the war years into account, during which so many lives were lost, people seldom survived into late adulthood.

Turning the pages of the album, I came to the photos of Abdul's daughter, Fina, that I had taken in the dry season of 1969–70. These photos captured beautifully the inward and outward transformations that occur during initiation. In the first photo, taken shortly before she left Firawa for her period of sequestration with other neophytes in a bush house, Fina is sitting in the shade of an orange

tree in front of Abdul's house. She is combing out her hair in preparation for having it braided.

Her mother, Ferema, will use large white snail-shell toggles to create a hairstyle unique to neophytes. Fina is about thirteen or fourteen years of age, and on the morning I took the photograph, Abdul was sitting behind me on the high porch of his house, working at his treadle Singer sewing machine to complete the gown of narrow white strips of country cloth that Fina would put on after her initiation.

The second photograph was taken six weeks later, after Fina's re-

turn to Firawa from the bush. She is now an initiated woman. And the transfiguration is startling. Brimming with confidence and filled with happiness, she will soon leave home to enter into an arranged marriage with an older man in another Barawa village.

"And Fina?" I asked Abdul, with some trepidation. "Is she . . . ?"

"She is there," he said.

Fina was living in Timbira, some three miles away. She was old now, but she was well.

"I would very much like to see her," I said.

"Let her come here," Abdul replied, as if there was no good reason why I should put myself out in order to see an old woman, even if she was his daughter.

It was a curious introduction to a day in which everything seemed to fall into place, like a series of acts in a drama, each one complementing the others, and all echoing the events of yesterday.

IT WAS LATE IN THE MORNING when Fina arrived from Timbira, accompanied by her firstborn son, Fina Konkuro. At first I did not recognize her, though she remembered me, or said she did. Yet when she spoke, I heard the same soft voice and discerned the same inner quietness that she possessed as a girl.

Abdul showed Fina the photos.

"Eh!" she exclaimed, as if she could not believe her eyes. "This is me?"

"Yes, that is you," I said. "Before and after your *biriye*."

Fina seemed puzzled. She looked at me, smiled, then fell silent.

Seizing the moment, her son recounted details of his own life, and his marriages. His wife had borne him thirteen children, only four of whom were still alive. "Now she will bear no more. She will rest."

I took this to mean that his wife had passed the menopause.

I suddenly felt old. Aged by seeing Fina, and by hearing the brief history of her son's marriage. It was as if several generations had passed in Barawa within the space of what, for me, had been less than a single lifetime. It was as if I had known Fina in a previous incarnation.

When Sewa joined us, I suggested we all stroll to the edge of the village where we might talk without interruption, for already we were surrounded by a score of small children, curious to know what the white man was saying and what was going on.

Abdul gruffly ordered the kids to disperse.

Stopping where the path from the village passed under the hill, we found a place to sit in the shade of a locust tree. Fina untied her headkerchief and used it to sit on. Sewa and I squatted on the ground while Fina Konkuro walked about, as if undecided as to whether or not he wanted to participate in the conversation.

Rather than ask Fina to talk solely about herself, I suggested she speak a little about the changes she had seen in Barawa since the year of her initiation.

"Even in the old days," she said, "marriages would be arranged. But the girls would often go on *sumburi* [running away, usually with a lover]. Even betrothal marriages would end in this way. If a girl changed her mind like this, the bridewealth that had been paid would have to be returned. Still, some girls respected their father's wishes and remained with their husband, even though it was hard."

I was struck immediately by Fina's focus. Whereas Abdul's preoccupations were typical of a man in authority — chiefdom politics and legal matters — Fina had immediately launched into an account of the changing expectations and attitudes of women.

"What of you?" I asked. "Was your marriage arranged by your father?"

"Yes. I didn't like it, but in those days you had to accept it. But my first husband turned out to be a good man. He treated me with respect. For this reason my sister was also given in marriage to him."

"*Sole bambane fure*," I said (lit. "back hamper marriage"). This was the Kuranko term for sororal polygyny, since it was assumed that sisters would naturally be disposed to help each other, literally sharing the load. Such marriages were seen as a way of fostering affection and cooperation between co-wives, and of making the prospect of marrying a man in a distant place less daunting.

"That is it," Fina said.

"What was the sweetest moment in your life?" I asked. Given the radiant face in the photograph, I half expected her to say it was the day she returned home after her initiation.

"The birth of Konkuro, my firstborn," she said.

"And the hardest?"

"My husband died shortly after I gave birth to my second child. I was forced to marry his brother. He used to beat me and abuse me for no reason. He didn't like me and I didn't like him. He would accuse me of meanness and rudeness. With no justification, no provocation. I bore him four children, two boys and two girls."

"Did you ever think of *sumburi*, of leaving him?"

"Of course. But where would I have run to? I was no longer a young woman. Had I come back here to Firawa, to my father's compound, I would have been sent back to my husband. That is how it was in those days.[1] And I had my children to think of. Without a husband, how could I have farmed, found food, or clothed myself? But my son there [she nodded in the direction of Konkuro, still walking up and down the path, as if impatient for his mother to finish her conversation]—he could not bring himself to stay with my second husband. So he went and lived with my brother. He and my brother became very close. My son is completely loyal to him."[2]

"Is it different nowadays? Is it easier for a woman to leave a man who mistreats her?"

"Yes. There is more *sumburi* now than in the past."[3]

"What of kinship marriages [*nakelinyorgoye fure*]?" I asked, referring to arranged marriages between cross-cousins.[4]

"There are as many now as there were in the past. But they do not last. The girls want to decide for themselves. Even my granddaughter; she refused to marry the man my husband chose for her. She ran away with a young man from another village. This young man has refused to pay bridewealth and recompense the husband, but no one has been able to do anything about it. These days, girls want to marry men of wealth, not poor farmers."

"But is bridewealth [*furufan*] still important?"

"Of course. If you don't give or receive bridewealth a marriage is not a marriage."

WALKING BACK TO ABDUL'S compound with Fina and Sewa, I was reflecting on Fina's comment about young women nowadays insisting on deciding for themselves, but how this desire to have some say in whom they married had always existed. What, then, had militated against such freedom?

From the standpoint of older Kuranko men, it was imperative that a marriage be based on judgment, not passion—a quality that men allegedly possessed in greater measure than children and women. If both husband and wife kept to their different domains and fulfilled their distinct duties, a marriage would be viable and durable. Certainly, I had seen how mutual affection and respect could grow out of an arranged marriage, just as, in the modern West, divorce could quickly follow the falling out of love. Kuranko men argued that if one became emotionally too involved with one's wife, one would favor her over one's other wives, and this would cause dissension both among one's wives and among one's children. A disinterested attitude toward women meant, moreover, that one would be less inclined to jealousy or vengefulness should a wife prove unfaithful. What mattered most were one's relationships with other men. Women's fickle and unfaithful natures made them a constant threat to the political order that men believed themselves to uphold.[5]

Not only was men's distrust of women the subject of countless stories; it was proverbial. *Musu kai i gbundu lon*, "Never let a woman know your secrets." *Kele da ma si ban, koni musu ko kele ti ban*, "All quarrels come to an end, except the quarrels caused by women." *Yanfe da ma si no, koni musu yanfe wo ti fo*, "All conspiracies can be overcome, except conspiracies hatched by women." Just as young Kuranko men are told to think before they speak or act, and to be wary of women and strangers, so they learn that others are often Janus-faced, their appearances not to be trusted, their words not to be taken at face value. Perhaps social life is universally a matter of necessary masks and expedient lies. As the Kuranko adage puts it, "A person had blood inside him but it is saliva he spits out"—meaning that what a person says often belies what is in his heart, what is really on his mind.

I used to see this preoccupation with transparency and trust as a consequence of scarcity—of the "hungry time" during the last couple of months of the growing season, when people tell white lies about how much rice they have in their granaries lest the little that is left for their own needs is claimed by hungry neighbors and distant kin. Or as a fear of in-marrying women and visiting strangers, whose loyalties and intentions can never be readily divined, even by the *Doé dannu* (the Doé children), who specialize in such matters. Or as a diffuse memory of Samori Turé's *sofas*, who laid waste to Kuranko country a hundred years ago. Other ethnographers, struck by this same preoccupation with trust and betrayal, this world of clandestine desire, greed, envy, and resentment that so readily finds expression in witchcraft suspicions and fantasies, have sought to explain it in terms of the historical fear of slavers, invaders, or traders seeking to profit from relatively powerless villagers.

But how do women see themselves?

As Fina's remarks made clear, many women wanted more out of life than the dutiful performance of their domestic duties as wives and mothers. They wanted love, and they wanted to choose their own destinies—though these wants, I suspect, were practically identical.

Ironically, neither love marriages nor arranged marriages necessarily bring fulfillment. Without emotional intimacy in marriage, a person will be inclined to find fulfillment elsewhere—in love affairs, or in the closed worlds of women and the equally closed worlds of men. But marriages based on deep affinity and sexual love may quickly run aground when passion dies and interests change.

"What do you think?" I asked Sewa, after sharing my thoughts with him.

"It is difficult, Mr. Michael," Sewa said. "My wife often says I do not show her enough affection. But I say, 'We are married now. It is different.' But she wants me to behave like I did when I was courting her. And when I don't she gets jealous and thinks I have found someone else."

Back in Abdul's compound, I asked Fina to tell me what were the greatest hardships in her life.

"Farming is hard," she said, "especially these days, because everyone wants money. We all need money. It's hard to get seed rice from the business people. They demand exorbitant returns on the advance — two bags of rice for one bag of seed. And if you get seed rice from kinsmen, they'll try to make a profit too."

I was reminded of the battered Nissan truck with the logo above the windscreen, *Fear Not the World but the People*, that only yesterday had lurched and ground its way up the narrow path, loaded down with sacks of peppers, rice, cocoa beans, bananas, beans, cowpeas, and palm oil, purchased for a derisory amount from farmers in a village like Timbira, and headed to Kabala or Freetown where the profit would be considerable.

"And another thing," Fina went on. "In the old days, if you were elderly, you would be given salt, rice, and peppers. But not now. You get nothing but lies."

"What lies?"

"People talk nicely, but they are duplicitous and exploitative. Like people that promise seed rice at a certain price. When the demand goes up they ask for more, overcharging you, telling you — even though it isn't true — that another farmer is prepared to pay the higher price. So they ask you for more, always more. Even the *kere* [the labor cooperative] — they now call it *compin* [a Krio term, meaning 'company'] — you will get fined 2,000 leones if you don't turn up, even though it's a family group, a group of neighbors and friends, working one day on one person's farm, working the next on another. And you will have to pay each member 20,000 leones a day, brushing a farm, building a house. You see, there is no amity or affection [*dienuye*] anymore."

I later told Sewa that Fina's words reminded me of what he had told me in London a year ago. How, as a boy, he would go about the village with his friends, calling at one person's house to eat, calling at another, going to the farm together, scaring birds with slingshots. And in the dry season (*telme ro*), how people used to come to Kondembaia from outlying villages to dance, calling the *jelibas* (praise-singers) beating the drums and xylophones, dancing all night, cooking food, eating together.

"Yes," Sewa said. "There was *dienaye*" — a word he was using in the

Kuranko sense to mean fellow-feeling, mutual regard, communitas, and solidarity. "When I went back to Kondembaia last year, everything had changed. That love is not there."

IT IS A UNIVERSAL HUMAN FAILING to think that the world was a happier place in the past, and that things have fallen apart since one was young. Memory is always fallible, and the original is irrecoverable except as a partial trace. Undoubtedly, this idealization of the past is born of present dissatisfactions and reminds us that well-being is less an attainable goal than a necessary fiction without which we might conclude that we have little to live for. Like the idea of utopia, the idea of well-being captures a universal yearning to be more than we presently are and to have more than we presently possess. In Firawa, I quickly found that this yearning variously found expression in a desire for education, prosperity, migration, marriage, or even a reversion to what was said to be a more caring society. But people's thoughts about what they imagined they lacked inevitably led to thoughts about the injustices, underhand practices, historical misfortunes or local jealousies that might account for their impoverishment. There was thus a direct relationship between scarcity, secrecy, and suspicion.

THAT EVENING, I TOOK THE PATH that led from the southern edge of the village, past palm frond fences and overgrown gardens, across a stream, into the grasslands. There, midway between town and bush, shaded by a mango tree, was the hunters' shrine, named for the first hunter, Mande Fa Bori.[6]

The buffalo-horned clay effigy, stained black from sacrificial blood, took me back to my first fieldwork in Firawa, and my brief encounter with Karifa Mansaré of Momoria, with whom I hoped to record the epic of Mande Fa Bori. Though Karifa was now dead, and I was aware that I would probably never sit down with any of his successors to fulfill my youthful ambition, I could hear the sound of Karifa's harp-lute as clearly as I heard it forty years ago,[7] the buzz and drone of the instrument reminding me of swarming bees as the praise-singer's thumbs and forefingers plucked at the two sets of four strings and his nasalized voice recounted the deeds of the ancestral

hunter, half-brother to Sundiata (1217–55), renowned ruler of mid-thirteenth century Mali, whose story stands with the Mwindo Epic and the myth of the Bagre as one of Africa's great epics.[8] Though I regretted that time and poor technology prevented me from taping this epic that Karifa boasted would take days to record in its entirety, I had collected numerous folktales over the years, in which Mande Fa Bori also figured, as well as Karifa's own summary of the epic in response to my questions, "Who was Mande Fa Bori?" and "Where and when did he live?" And these stories echoed many of the concerns that had surfaced in my conversations that day.

A certain chief had nine daughters. The ninth and last-born was small and light. One day a wind carried her away into the bush, setting her down under a locust tree. She remained under that tree for forty years. During this time she became pregnant. The djinn sent a message to the chief, telling him that his daughter was with child. On the same day this message reached the town, all the old women in the town became pregnant. When news came that the daughter in the bush had given birth to a son, all the old women in the town gave birth as well—not to children, but to guns, gunpowder, and cartridges. The people collected up the things that the old women had brought into the world and took them to the chief. The chief was mystified as to where these things had come from, but the people said that God may have sent them on account of the chief's ninth daughter giving birth in the bush. So the people were keen to see this woman's child. They went into the bush, found the baby and brought it back to the town. It was covered in dirt and leaves, so the women decided to wash it. But as soon as they splashed water on the baby, it died. They now tried to bury the newborn child, but the body refused every grave that was dug for it. Finally, they dug a grave under a *yalé* tree and laid the body in it. Immediately, a snake appeared. It picked a leaf from the *yalé* tree, chewed it, and smeared it on the dead child. The child came back to life. He declared he would not return to the town. He climbed to his feet, took the guns, gunpowder and cartridges that the old women had brought into the world, and went into the bush. There, he killed two buffalos and three deer. He then took the dead animals to his mother, inviting her to eat. He told her he would not go back to the town again.

Mande Fa Bori's mother now became pregnant for the second time, and in due course delivered another baby boy. When the new child asked after his older brother, the woman told him that Bori was in the bush. The child went in search of his older brother. When he found him, he asked: "Will you come with me to the town?" Bori said no, he would never return to the town. He then killed many, many animals and presented the meat to his younger brother. He said, "Take this meat with you to the town. Distribute it to everyone there. I will never go back to the town myself." The old women tried

to get Mande Fa Bori and to shave his head.[9] He refused, at least until he had initiated many other young men into the lore and skills of hunting. He then disappeared into the forest, never to be seen again. This is why he is represented in clay in the Mande Fa Bori house. He himself is in the bush.

LÉVI-STRAUSS WOULD no doubt have appreciated the structural indeterminacies and mediations of which Karifa's synopsis is replete: a hunter's shrine situated between town and bush; an ancestral hunter born of the union between a marginalized woman and a bush djinn; two brothers, one of whom will govern the wilderness, the other the town.[10] But the narrative, brief as it is, broaches existential issues that structural analysis alone cannot reveal. Of these the most compelling is the implicit comparison between the relationship of town-bush and the relationship of men-women. Just as the bush is at once a place of plenty and peril, so women fall, albeit in the imaginations of men, into two polar categories — the scheming seductress and the faithful wife or loving mother. The bush is symbolized by the bush cow (*Syncerus caffer nanus*) or buffalo (*Syncerus caffer*) which are, at the same time, the most difficult and dangerous animals to hunt,[11] the most prized meats, and the shapeshifting seductresses from whose wiles and entrapments the hunter must be constantly protected. In several tales that allude to the epic but play freely upon its key images, the dilemmas of balancing the logos of the town against the wild logos of the bush are imaginatively explored.

DO YOU KNOW, there was once a great hunter called Mande Fa Bori? He had killed so many animals that the surviving animals called a meeting to discuss how they could protect themselves from him. The youngest animal at the meeting was the bush cow.[12] It volunteered to kill Mande Fa Bori. It changed itself into a beautiful woman, though its fetlocks remained unchanged. The woman sought out the famous hunter and greeted him. She said she wanted to marry him. Her husband, also a famous hunter, had died recently, but before he passed away he told her to remarry. But she should go to no one other than Mande Fa Bori.

Mande Fa Bori was flattered and captivated by the woman. But his mother, even though she was old, could see what her son could not see. She saw the young woman's fetlocks. She said, "My son, even though you are blind with happiness, you should see what I have seen. Look down at this young woman's legs." But Mande Fa Bori did not heed his mother, and became impatient. So his mother went away.

Wherever the young woman now sat, Mande Fa Bori sat. Wherever she went, he went. And that night, when she went to her room to sleep, he followed her.

Mande Fa Bori had two hunting dogs. They were always with him. So when the young woman, under cover of darkness, began to change back into a bush cow, the dogs saw what was happening and began to growl. The young woman then decided to keep her human form. She woke Mande Fa Bori and told him that when she had got up to pee his dogs had begun to growl. She said, "How can I sleep with you or live with you if your dogs are going to be so unfriendly to me?" Mande Fa Bori told the first dog to leave the house. When the dog had gone, the young woman said to herself, "How can I change into a bush cow and steal the eyes of Mande Fa Bori while his second dog is still here?"[13] She told Mande Fa Bori to send the second dog away.

As soon as Mande Fa Bori had closed his eyes in sleep, she changed into a bush cow, seized Mande Fa Bori's eyes, and fled with them into the bush.

When Mande Fa Bori woke next morning he found that he was blind and called for his mother. She said, "Is this not what I warned you against? Now an animal has taken your eyes, the same animal I warned you about yesterday."

When the bush cow reached its home in the bush, the other animals crowded around. They sang, "These are the eyes of that infidel [kafiré], these are the eyes of that infidel . . ."

In the village, Mande Fa Bori's mother changed herself into a cat. She went into the bush and joined the other animals as they sang and rejoiced, passing Mande Fa Bori's eyes from hand to hand. The mother asked if she could hold the infidel's eyes, for she too was an animal who had lost close kin to the predatory hunter. The animals agreed and gave her the eyes to hold. The mother joined her voice to the voices of the other animals, singing, "Yes, yes, these are the eyes of the one who made us suffer; these are the eyes of that infidel."

But the mother took the eyes, ran back to town and gave the eyes to her son. "Let that be a lesson to you," she said, "always to heed my advice."

IN OTHER VERSIONS of this story it is Mande Fa Bori's wife who saves him from the alluring stranger, seeing through her disguise, reading her mind, avoiding her snares. But in every case, one encounters the same ironies: that the four-eyed hunter who can see in the dark is blind to the true identity of the bush cow or buffalo that has come to steal his sight and rob him of his power, and that it is a loyal wife or caring mother who outwits the Delilah-figure or foils her plan. While warning us to put our trust in the familiar and be on our guard against the strange, the stories nonetheless address

• our Oedipal fate — that we must leave the security of our natal world and assume responsibility for ourselves in a world that will be of our own making. On the most mundane level, this means that men must accept the hazards of entering the bush to hunt, tap palm wine, and farm, just as women must brave the wilderness to collect medicinal plants and marry a stranger in a village far from home. Without tapping the energy reserves of the bush, the village would die. On another level, however, journeys into the wilderness are ways in which one acquires extraordinary powers, for it is by suspending ordinary social ties that one opens oneself up to the possibility of alliances with djinn and the mastery of music, dancing, storytelling, healing, shape-shifting, and sorcery. The Mande Fa Bori stories suggest, therefore, that the modern imperative to migrate (or remain existentially impoverished) has its origins in an older imperative. For well-being has always been, in the Kuranko social imaginary, a matter of bringing the vital forces of the wild into the precinct of the village — which means transgressing the symbolic boundaries that separate the secure space of home from the unknown and the beyond.

Local attitudes to the outside world are always ambivalent. Mande Fa Bori's mother undoubtedly wants to see her son marry but fears he might marry a schemer who saps his powers or betrays his trust. The animals undoubtedly admire the great hunter and wish they possessed his powers of second sight, yet if they are to survive they must find a way of curbing his power. In conversations with Sierra Leoneans in London, I had observed the same ambivalence. To remain in the village was to doom oneself to a life of toil, limited horizons, and social stasis. But to go abroad meant estrangement from close kin, and the possibility of losing oneself in a world of strangers. Global space is thus a kind of bush in which one hopes • to trap or capture new forms of well-being without, however, becoming snared, captured, or lost. Kuranko descriptions of urban life bear an uncanny resemblance to the way that cities were depicted in the social imaginaries of rural England after the Industrial Revolution, when thousands of hopeful migrants left the countryside for the burgeoning new towns. Though the streets of these towns were allegedly paved with gold, they were actually littered with those who had fallen by the wayside, incapacitated, unemployed, rejected, and alone. Young men like Sewa and D.Y. would ruefully explain to me that city girls would not bother with a man without money, and that without contacts one could get nowhere. Though the city was a realm of fabulous opportunities, it was also a place of ambushes and pitfalls in which the vagrant hunter often became the hunted.

Smoke and Mirrors

I WAS UP BEFORE DAWN and joined Abdul by the fire in the compound, sharing a thermos of coffee and small talk, our morning routine now, as Joshua slept.

If I had wondered what the day would bring, I would not have had to wait long. Within minutes of finishing our coffee, Abdul and I were distracted by raised voices in the adjacent compound, a man shouting, a girl screaming.

Abdul knew exactly what was going on. The girl's name was Sayon Marah. She was sixteen, seventeen. Her husband, Ali Kamara, was about thirty. They were cross-cousins, and their arranged marriage has been fraught and fractious from the beginning. A few months ago, Sayon ran away to join her boyfriend in the diamond district of Tongo, leaving her five-month-old baby in the care of her parents. Not long afterward, her father happened to be Tongo, panning for diamonds, and heard of his daughter's presence there. The father found her and brought her back to Firawa.

Within days of his return home, the father fell ill and died. With no father around to force her to go back to her husband, Sayon remained in her parents' house at the opposite end of the village from her husband's compound. One evening, Ali went to visit her and found her with her lover, who had just arrived from Tongo. There was a fight, the lover fled, and Ali beat his wife unconscious. Her older sister helped get Sayon to the village dispensary where she recovered. But she would not break off her affair, so Ali had recourse to traditional law, binding her wrists with cord and bringing her before the section chief.

SHE WAS SITTING at one end of Abdul's porch. From the bruises and welts on her upper arms it was clear that she had been beaten. And the cord that bound her wrists behind her back had bitten so deeply into her flesh that blood had been drawn. As Abdul convened the moot, she sat with her head bowed, staring at her bare feet. Ali held one end of the cord, tugging it from time to time as though she were a disobedient dog that needed to be reminded who was its master.

Sayon would not respond to Abdul's questions, even though they were relayed to her through her elder sister, who was representing her. Abdul said he needed to hear from the girl, to hear why she had refused to return to her husband, what her intentions were, whether she would flee to Tongo again and continue to see her lover.

Despite repeating Abdul's questions and urging Sayon to speak, Sayon's elder sister could not get a word out of her. So she knelt, looking into her younger sister's impassive face, trying yet again to wring water from a stone.

Now smiling in exasperation, or in shame at the public debacle she had been drawn into, the elder sister glanced at Abdul as if admitting there was nothing she could do.

Abdul tried a different tack, describing the customary law that covered such a case. The girl was a Marah. She belonged to Abdul's own lineage. She was his grandchild. But Ali, the husband, was also a relative. This meant that Abdul had to be careful he did not favor one party over the other.

First, he upbraided the girl for her stupidity and obduracy and reminded her in no uncertain terms of her duty as a wife and mother. Again he implored her to speak. Again she sat stock still, staring at the ground in front of her, abject and immobile.

But Abdul's harsh words to Sayon had given him leave to reprimand Ali with equal severity. After telling Ali not to beat his wife again, lest her family take him to court on a charge of assault, he ordered Ali to untie her. As the cord was unwound from Sayon's wrists, the deep welts became apparent and I was amazed that only superficial damage seemed to have been done.

Having delivered his judgment against both parties, Abdul ordered Sayon to return to her husband. She had no other option.

Abdul then left his end of the porch and gently rubbed his open hand across Sayon's dusty head, assuring her that his affection for her had not been changed by the verdict against her.

Sayon's elder sister now led her down the steps from the porch and helped her sit on a folding chair a yard or two away from where

I was keeping notes. I found it heartwarming to watch another sister, perhaps no more than eleven years old, tending to Sayon's cuts, straightening her braids, bathing her bruises with warm water that Manti had had ready for some time. As the older and younger sisters continued to dab a moist cloth on Sayon's arms, head, and wrists, Ali's mother crossed the compound with a bowl of chicken broth. Sayon refused it. Nor would she speak. And as everyone dispersed, I could only wonder whether the peace would hold, the marriage survive, and whether the restoration of the appearance of amity was all that a court, or a ritual, could accomplish, and that deep down our grievances are never really addressed or our wounds healed.

"What would have happened," I asked Abdul later, "if Sayon and Ali had not agreed to make up? If she had refused to go back to him or he had refused to accept her back?"

"I would have fined the recalcitrant party, and they would have had to apologize to me," Abdul said.

I HAVE DESCRIBED the transformation that I observed in Abdul's daughter, Fina, in the space of a few weeks, from child to adult. But the transformation in Sayon Marah was just as remarkable. Within a day, the taciturn, bowed, and beaten young woman who had sat on Abdul's porch, listening to her fate being decided for her, would become a self-possessed, stylishly clothed coquette, publicly disdainful of her husband and determined to kick up her heels. The very evening after their court case, she and Ali went dancing in the covered market that an NGO had constructed in the center of the village. The sound of reggae, amplified by a PA system, went on until one in the morning. But when Ali ordered her to go home with him, well before midnight, she sent him back to the house and found someone else to dance with. "She calls him a bush person [fira morgo]," Sewa would tell me the following morning. "Ali needs to go to Kono to upgrade. But he better hurry. She's also in a hurry to upgrade. She wants one of those city boys!" And sure enough, Sayon spent the next day hovering around D.Y., clearly on the make. "Miss Kono," Sewa nicknamed her. And he called her Miss Kono to her face.

A few days later, Ali came by. I asked him how things were going with Sayon. "Everything is fine," he said. "Everything is smooth."

Was he putting a brave face on things, or had the marriage been salvaged?

THAT NIGHT, I WAS SITTING in the compound with Sewa. A full moon had risen in the western sky, a hand's-breadth from the evening star. Beyond the circlet of firelight in which we sat, the village was lost in darkness.

I could not see the girls on the nearby path, but I could hear their voices. "He's there," they whispered, "he's there by the fire." I knew then who they had come to see, and I goaded Sewa into action. "Come on, man, you can't just ignore them. Greet them. Call them closer to the fire. Ask them what they want!"

Emboldened by Sewa's invitation, the girls shuffled closer, nervously whispering among themselves.

"What is it?" Sewa asked.

"We have come to sing for you," one of the girls said. And she immediately broke into song.

Just as immediately, I was mesmerized. Of all the girls, she was the slightest. Almost frail. And yet her voice was as strong and thrilling as a woman's, and with a poignant beauty that took my breath away. Indeed, I was so entranced that I did not want to break the spell by going to my room and getting my tape recorder, much as I wanted to record the music.

The bigger girls chimed in, chorusing. But it was the small girl who carried the song, its words and sentiments as audacious as they were moving. Each line declaimed with finality and finesse. Echoed then by the other girls, before another line, equally uncompromising, began.

> I'll not accept this distance love
> No arranged marriage for me
> No matter how far away they send me I will not stay
> I'll only marry for love
> I will not marry an old man
> I will not marry for gold
> I will not marry for a big house
> I will not marry for diamonds
> I'll only marry for love.

I LOST TRACK OF TIME, as the girls sang other songs, clapping, chorusing, making their overtures to Sewa, D.Y., and Bockarie, waiting to be dashed. I distributed some 2000-leone notes among them and asked the lead singer her name.

"Sira Marah," she said shyly.

Sewa gave the girls some more money, but now the crowd had grown so much that everyone wanted to sing and receive money. Small boys complained bitterly that no one wanted to hear their song. Some girls who had arrived late on the scene argued for a share of what we had given the first group of singers. It was as though everything Fina had told me was being corroborated before my eyes—the fascination with love, the preoccupation with money, the competitiveness that had begun to undermine the spirit of cooperation and the pleasure of singing for singing's sake.

Sira was keen to sing and dance some more, but Sewa said, "Another night. We are tired now."

But I was not at all tired.

"Did you compose that song yourself?" I asked. "That song about not accepting distance love?"

"Yes. I have this natural gift. I sit, I think, it comes into my head."

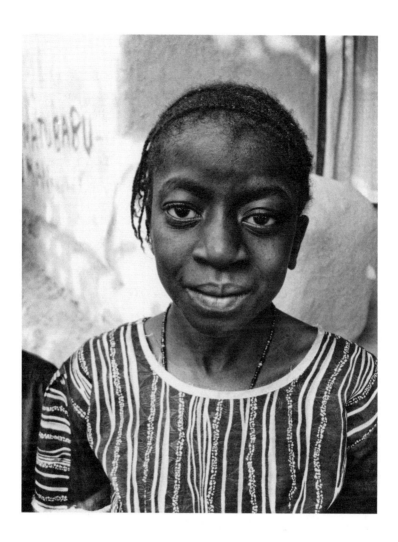

"How old are you?"

"I am not sure." I guessed her to be no more than nine or ten, though her mother would later tell me she was eleven.

"Where do get your ideas about marrying for love?"

"You understand me. You are like me, where you come from. You know."

"Because I am from overseas?"

"Yes. But if two people love each other, distance doesn't matter. It's only when there is no love, and you go to your husband who lives far away, then it is hard."

"Do your age-mates share your views?"

"Some do, some don't."

"Do others in your age-group compose songs like you?"

"We are about six, but I am the composer, the leader. The others give support, answering."

"You are very intelligent. I can see that. Do you go to school?"

"No."

"Why not?"

"Because I have only my mother to look after me. My father went away. He has been in Freetown for four years. I never see him. So I have no school fees, no way of getting them."

"How much would you need for a year's school fees?"

"I am not sure. But I went to school for two years. From class one to class three. I did well. I passed all my exams."

"Would you like to continue with your schooling?"

"Yes."

"Do you also compose stories?"

"Yes. I know many, and I have composed some too."

"I will come and see you tomorrow," I said. "Perhaps you can tell me one of your stories."

"I am there," Sira said.

Before turning in for the night, I asked Abdul to tell me about Sira. She was his granddaughter, he said, and it was his son Kome, "a good for nothing wastrel," who had abandoned his wife and daughter and gone to Freetown with his second wife. "But the mother is also useless," Abdul said. "She does not garden, does not make a farm, does not do anything to help herself or help her daughter. She only asks others for help. Only relies on others."

THE FOLLOWING MORNING I went to Sira's house with Sewa and Bockarie. The house had been burned during the war and only partly repaired. Crumbling mud brick walls eroded by rain. No shutters on the windows, and only one door. Sira's mother's only possessions seemed to be a mortar and pestle, a winnowing tray, a country pot for water, and a single fishing net. Seldom had I seen such poverty. We sat in the room where Sira and her mother slept. Sira sat on a bed that was propped up on mud bricks and covered with a floral cloth. Bockarie, Sewa, and I sat on mud bricks. Above us, the rafters were branches stripped of bark and blackened by wood smoke, and the thatched roof was full of gaping holes. Sira herself wore the same dress she had worn the previous night; she owned no sandals or shoes. But I noticed that her fingernails and toenails had been lacquered, though the red polish was now peeling and worn.

I was interested in something Sira had told me the night before about being able to divine, and I had asked if she would tell me and Sewa and Bockarie more about this gift, and whether it was like her gift for composing songs and stories.

Shyly, she answered my first question.

"Two djinn showed me," she said.

"What did they show you?"

"They showed me how to circumcise girls."

"But have you been initiated? Have you been through *biriye*?"

"No."

"Can you tell me more about these djinn?"

"They visit me every Friday and every Monday."

"Do they visit you at night, in your dreams?"

"They do not come in my dreams, but in daylight, in the afternoon."

"Can other people see them?"

"Only me."

"Can you tell me what they look like?"

"They are like white people [*tubabunu*]."

"Are they old or young?"

"Older. One is female, the other male."

"Where do they come from?"

"From the south."

"Do they resemble any white people you have seen?"

"No. They are not like real white people. The woman has long hair, down to the ground."

I wanted to ask if the female djinn was a *mamiwata*, but I could only think of the krio term—which Sira did not know—and neither Sewa nor Bockarie could help me remember the Kuranko word, though it came to me later—*ninkinanké*.

"Did the twin *nyenne* show you how to do anything else?" I asked.

"They showed me the leaves," Sira said, meaning that the djinn showed her how to collect medicinal plants from the bush and prepare herbal medicines.

"What illnesses can you treat?"

"Any. If a woman cannot get pregnant . . ."

"Have you ever helped a woman become pregnant?"

"Many."

"Can you read peoples' futures?"

"Yes."

"What of your own future? Can you see it?"

"You cannot see your own destiny."

"Do you use stones to divine?"

"Yes. The *nyenne* gave me the stones, but my mother threw them away. She was afraid the *nyenne* might take me away. So I use a mirror now."

"Did the *nyenne* also show you how to divine with a mirror?"

"Yes."

"And does your mother approve of you doing this?"

"Yes."

Thirty years ago I might have asked Sira to look into her mirror and tell me what destiny she saw for me, what sacrifices I should offer to ensure good fortune and avoid the bad. But no problems weighed on my mind, and I could not think of any plausible pretext for asking Sira to consult her *nyenne* on my behalf. But Sewa and Bockarie had questions to ask, anxieties to alleviate, and so I gave Sira 5,000 leones and watched as she drew a small mirror from the pocket of her dress and wiped the surface with the banknote.

"Bockarie first," Sira said softly.

She gazed down at the mirror, which she held in her cupped hands, resting in her lap. Her lips moved slightly. Again she rubbed the mirror with the wadded banknote, and turned the mirror around, or tilted it slightly, as if trying to catch the light, except there was little light in the room.

She continued to rub and turn the mirror around in her hands for several minutes, but from time to time holding it still and gazing into it. Bockarie leaned forward as if impatient to hear her prognosis.

"There is nothing amiss, nothing bad there," she said finally. "But you must be careful. Don't take anything for granted. You must take special care what you eat in places far from Firawa. And you must be prepared for bad news. Soon there will be news of another death" (indeed, within minutes of returning to Abdul's house, a group of

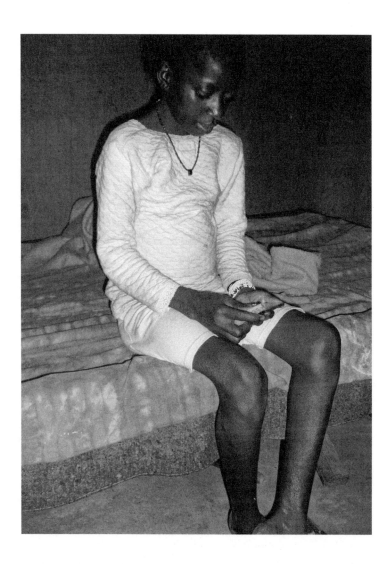

elders from the nearby village of Barawa Komoia would arrive,
bringing the grim news of a death that morning).

Sewa now gave Sira another 5,000 leones, and again she gazed
into her mirror, rubbing it, turning it, waiting for it to yield its message.

"There is nothing bad," she said. "But you should wear a country
cloth shirt with alternate white and red stripes. You should also give
red kola to a respected elder of your lineage. *Ara ban*—that is all."

I asked Sira what she saw when she gazed into the mirror.

"The twin *nyenne*," she said.

"Do they speak?"

"Yes."

"Why do you have to rub the mirror all the time?"

"Sometimes they fall silent and don't want to speak. Unless you wipe the mirror and turn it, you won't see them, or they won't say anything."

"Is the money a gift to them?"

"Yes. If I show them the money, they have to respond."

Half-teasingly—because of the fetishization of mobile phones in Sierra Leone—I asked Sira if the mirror was like a cell phone.

Her expression did not change. "It's different. The *nyenne* speak, not me."

"Are you tired?" I asked, "or could I ask you some more questions?"

"I am not tired."

"When I go back to my country, what would you like me to tell people about you?"

"That I want to be famous. That I have these gifts, of singing, of storytelling, of curing, of divining."

"What is the hardest thing in your life? What troubles you the most?"

"Especially in the famine time, the rainy season [when the granaries are almost empty and the next harvest is still several months away]. My father never sends us anything. My mother has to work for other people. We have no money. We have little food."

"What is the sweetest thing?"

"My mother's sister Fatamata once invited me to visit her in Kabala. I made some money there, divining."

Sira's mother unobtrusively entered the doorway, her face in shadow.

I greeted her and explained that I was interested in Sira's ability to divine. I then asked why she had thrown Sira's divining stones away. What did she fear might happen if Sira became a diviner?

"The *nyenne* would have taken her. She was too young to be doing that sort of thing."

"When Sira was small, did you know she had special gifts?"

"Yes. She had convulsions once. Her whole body was shaking [symptoms, it is often thought, of seizure or possession by a bush spirit]."

"Has anyone in the family been a diviner?"

"Yes. Her father. He was a *beresigile* [lit. 'one who sets down pebbles'[1]]. He still is."

"Did Sira observe him divining when she was a small girl?"

"Yes."

"Did she show any interest?"

"No, she never did."

"How did her father get his gift?"

"He was born with it, like Sira."

"Did he have twin *nyenne*?"

"Yes, but his were both female."

"White?"

"Yes."

"From the water or the bush?"

"The bush I think. I am not sure."

THAT EVENING, SIRA CAME TO Abdul's compound, wanting to organize more singing and dancing for us. I suggested that she wait. But perhaps she could tell me a story, one of her own.

"There was a man and a woman. They had a child. But the parents died when the child was very young, and the little girl was placed in the care of her mother's co-wife. This woman would prepare rice and sauce and put it on the same platter. All her children would eat from the same plate. But one day the woman divided the food into two portions. One portion was for her own children. The other portion was for her late co-wife's child. And into this portion the woman put poison. When the child ate this food she began to foam at the mouth, and she soon died. But after she had passed away she sent a dream to her mother's co-wife, saying that she knew about the poison, and how the woman had killed her. The stepmother woke up in dismay, saying, 'It wasn't me, it wasn't me. You must have eaten that poisoned food elsewhere.' The child said, 'All right, then; one day you will die and meet me here in *lakira*, and God will judge whose story is true.' After that dream, the child disappeared. She disappeared from this life."

This story was, in fact, familiar. I had recorded several versions of it in the past. But this only brought home to me the extent to which a sense of being unjustly excluded, discounted, or cut out pervaded the experience of many young Kuranko men and women. In an objective sense, the story was not wholly Sira's creation, yet it captured her experience so perfectly that it *became* her story, reforged in the fires of her own life.

IT HAD BEEN A LONG DAY, and as I wrote up my notes by torchlight in my room that night I wondered whether my accounts of Sayon and Sira—these glimpses into their lives, these Chekhovian slices or arrests—would speak for themselves, or would they demand annotation and interpretation. To what extent do we need science to decipher the human world for us, to divine its underlying meaning, to bring the hidden depths to light? And I asked myself whether or not I would need—if not now, then at a later date—to elaborate on the differences between the love Sayon sought and the love Sira imagined, or to point out that similar circumstances cannot explain the course of any two persons' lives. Would I need to spell out the reasons why Sira might fantasize "disappearing" from this life, when it was a life of poverty and limited opportunity, or why she should imagine, in a union with twin bush spirits—a man and a woman—or in love, or in education, an escape from a "poisonous" situation? Worse, would I be taken to task for describing the exploitation of villagers by traders or the plight of Sira without seeming to want to do anything concrete about it? How much can we leave to a discerning reader? How deeply is testimony compromised by explanation? And how much anthropological framing and theorizing can one leave aside without being accused of explaining nothing, of having nothing to say?

One answer to these questions is to shift our emphasis from explanation to comparison. Rather than find in a person's cultural milieu, early life, or adverse circumstances an explanation for their behavior or fantasies, one looks to *another* person's life for edifying comparison. So it was that I found myself thinking of my mother's subscriptions to women's magazines like *Ladies' Home Journal*, *McCall's*, *Women's Day*, *Women's Own* and my inability to understand why someone who loved great poetry and read the classics would waste her time reading photo-essays on the homes of the rich and famous or Mills and Boone romances. It took me many years to understand that she was not looking for love but for something amorphous for which love is but a metaphor. And this was also true of many Kuranko women for whom love affairs were, often as not, playful revolts against a male world that circumscribed their freedom on the assumption that they were intrinsically unable to govern themselves as competently as men. Inasmuch as men derided them for their emotionality and waywardness, women willfully became the creatures they were deemed to be, throwing back in their husbands' faces the stereotypes that men had imposed upon them. At the same time, love signaled a break from the bondage of marriage and the burden of one's duties. It implied the striking of a new balance between being an actor and being acted upon. Like the fantasy of being a witch, flying by night in another bodily form to far-flung places, a love affair was an imaginative strategy of being borne away from where one was stuck, put upon, and denied any freedom to move or maneuver. Paradoxically, then, love was not always a search for love; it was a hunger for something more, which was why, I suppose, Sira's hunger pangs seemed to weigh less on her mind than the prospect of losing her way in an arranged marriage.

Yet, as Judith Sherman once told me, remembering her time in Ravensbrück, "You must remember that sometimes bread is just bread."

So it is with rice, the staff of life, for Kuranko. During the hungry time (*same konke*, lit. "rainy season hunger") when rice is in short supply, people must have recourse to inferior foodstuffs such as yams, cassava, and sweet potatoes.[2] Without rice, people say, they starve. But hunger is also a metaphor. First, it is a metaphor for what is most difficult in life, and for the tenacity and strength of suffering. Hence the ironic response to the question "Are you well?" (*i kende?*) — *N kende i ko konde* ("I am as well as hunger"), meaning I am *very* hale and hearty. Second, the hungry time signifies any situation in which generosity goes by the board. It suggests an ethically compromised situation, characterized by self-interestedness and regressive behavior, when adults behave like children. "A hungry person does not think of tomorrow," people say, not only because hunger strikes at the moral core of what it is to be fully human — deferring instinctual or immediate gratification; it leads inevitably to death, in which case there *is* no tomorrow. Similar reasoning lies behind the giving of kola. Though its food value is minimal, its use value is immense. It was the first food in the world — the tree of life in the Garden of Eden. It is therefore the first food a child is given —

masticated and placed in the newborn's mouth. And it is kola that seals a betrothal. This is why kola is given to strangers: to incorporate them into the community, to signify a desire for their well-being and respect for their life. He who neither gives nor receives kola is "not a person." But chewing kola can stave off the pangs of hunger, and its two cotyledons, pressed together like yin and yang, provide a potent image of the consummation of identity in duality rather than singularity.

In understanding what it means to be well we must therefore take into account not only what we need as a bare minimum to survive but what we need for our lives to be worthwhile — for we do not live by bread alone, and well-being is never simply the satisfaction of biological needs, the possession of primary goods, or the attainment of personal fulfillment and happiness. Nor is it a matter of adaptation, since getting what we want invariably leads us to conceive of new wants, as if satisfaction is always a matter of possessing more than we have, even when we appear to have everything we could possibly wish for.[3]

Because human existence is nothing if not *social and ethical*, fulfillment does not lie solely in our freedom "to lead the kind of life [we have] reason to value";[4] it consists in our capacity to realize ourselves in relation to others. Amartya Sen's view that impoverishment is never simply a lack of income but a deprivation of opportunities to exercise one's ability "to achieve various valuable functionings as a part of living" is a valuable corrective to those who would reduce well-being to material circumstances or see it as a mainly clinical question of physical or mental health.[5] But the Kuranko emphasis would be less on an individual's situation than on the social weal. Impoverishment is therefore the absence of social harmony, the failure of a person to do his or her duty, or the use of scarce resources for entirely selfish ends.[6] As such, Sira's dreams of self-realization might be censured. But her choices would be approved, since in her stories and her singing she brings people together, symphonically and as a single body, just as her divination brings clarity and hope to those who have lost their way.

As an outsider, I tended to see her as someone thwarted in her ambition to be more than the person she would become if she remained in Firawa, without an education, without a firsthand knowledge of the wider world. But this implied that I, as a Westerner, had a monopoly on the truth of well-being—an assumption that has led many Euro-American feminists to criticize clitoridectomy as a barbaric practice that causes needless pain and medical complications while depriving young women of pleasure and thereby robbing them of the capacity to find complete fulfillment in life.[7] But such critiques see African women solely in terms of what they lack and, as such, are counterproductive, visiting anxiety and shame on people who are better placed than outsiders to judge how well-being is best fostered. My somewhat Eurocentric sympathy for Sira was also conditioned by the nineteenth-century "humanitarian discovery of hunger" as a trope for existential want—as when we speak of people in the poor world thirsting for knowledge and hungry for development.[8] A recurring problem is our persistence in seeing the lives of others as more problematic than our own, and of taking straitened circumstances and material poverty as signs of an impoverished humanity. Perhaps the most insidious corollary of these assumptions is the widespread view that poverty and powerlessness make people susceptible to irrational, magical, and occult behavior, while, by implication, wealth, education, and power make us more rational.[9] In this view, Sira's attraction to divination and fantasy is seen as a "weapon of the weak," a means whereby she accomplishes pathetically what she is barred from achieving in reality. But so-called occult, imaginary, or irrational strategies are present in all human thought, including the thought of wealthy investors and academics whose struggles for being, for love, and for existential satisfaction are no less fraught than they are for Sira Marah. And it must be pointed out that the occult was, for Sira, a supplement to rather than a substitute for a rational perspective;[10] rather than seek to escape from reality, she works creatively within the limits of what is possible, never losing sight of the difference between what Ernst Bloch called "abstract" and "concrete" utopias.[11]

For Kuranko, it is how one bears the burden of life that matters, how one endures the situation in which one finds oneself thrown. Well-being is therefore less a reflection on whether or not one has realized one's hopes than a matter of learning how to live within limits. Singing, like Sira, on an empty belly. This Stoic attitude makes a virtue out of accepting one's lot. To withstand disappointment and go on in the face of adversity imparts quality to life. One may dream of being rescued or saved from an unendurable situation, but fantasy is always tempered by common sense, and learning to negotiate the obstacles and uncertainties of everyday life is more worthy than the search for transcendence or escape.[12]

This ethical point is powerfully made in the following story that I recorded in Kabala in July 1970. The narrator, Denka Marah, had been blinded by a spitting cobra when he was a boy, so the story carries personal as well as cultural significance—alluding to how Denka's physical handicap had not prevented him from developing skills as a flautist, thinker, and storyteller.

A hunger came. It was a great hunger. Hunger become boastful. It said, "I will deal with the world this year." So cassava built a fence. Potato built a fence. Millet built a fence. Sesame built a fence. And groundnut built a fence. Finally, *suma* (rice) built its fence.[13]

I am now going to tell you how *suma* became known as *kore*.[14]

Whenever hunger came, it would say, "God willing, I will break down this fence. Give me two days, three days, and I will break it down." It went to millet. In seven days, millet's fence was destroyed. It went to potato. In eight days potato was finished. It went to cassava. In four days cassava was no more. It went to sesame. Three days and sesame was also finished. Then it came to groundnut. Groundnut said, "You will not break my defenses down." He tore a strip of cloth from his gown, wrapped it around hunger's neck, and threw hunger to the ground. Groundnut called to *suma*, "Elder brother, come quickly, come here!" When *suma* came, groundnut said, "Now we have caught it and have it in our power, let us cut its throat." But *suma* cautioned, "Let us not kill it lest in time to come there will be people who try to avoid hard work and who, in the absence of hunger, will become disrespectful of their neighbors. Let it live."

This is why we still have hunger in our midst. And why *suma* became known as *kore*, because he was so wise. So if a man quarrels with his wife, and she refuses to cook for him . . . hunger will remind him of what really matters. And if in times of plenty, people become lazy and quarrelsome, hunger will remind them of the need for people to work and live together in amity and solidarity.

Things Hidden Since
the Foundation of the World

IN THE DRY SEASON OF 1979, the elderly medicine master
Saran Salia Sanoh generously loaned me his house "for as long as
my family remained in Firawa," assuring me that he would move in
with his classificatory son Hassan, who lived on the other side of the
compound. I accepted Saran Salia's offer and set to work to make the
house more comfortable. Neighbors helped my wife and me resur-
face the walls and floors with white and gray clay and install a ceiling of raffia mats in the bedroom. Hassan loaned us a chair. Abdul's
wife, Tilkolo, with whom I enjoyed a joking relationship, brought
Pauline three hearthstones, and Abdul found us an old wire-wove
bed base to go with the straw and sacking paillasse we had carried
from Kabala. Finally, we made a back porch of mud bricks and dug
and fenced a pit latrine.

Before long, we had settled into a daily routine, with Pauline
home-schooling Heidi while I interviewed local bards and genealo-
gists on Barawa history. In the evenings I would sit on the front
porch, typing up my notes. It was rumored that I had a djinn working for me. A bush spirit was held captive inside my typewriter.
Some said that I too was a djinn who my friend Noah had somehow
persuaded to help him, though what *I* stood to gain by helping *him*
was anybody's guess. How could people know that without Noah's
help this anthropologist would have achieved little?

I left one room of the house as a storage space for Saran Salia, so
that his medicines would be safe from his classificatory sons, Hassan
and Lahai. The two Alhajis referred to these medicines as jujus, and
since returning from their hajj they had built a mosque, organized a
madrassa, and mounted a campaign to win converts and purge Firawa
of un-Islamic practices. Such practices had been Saran Salia's whole
life, and my keen interest in them angered the Alhajis, who saw my
friendship with Saran Salia as a challenge to their hold over him.

When Saran Salia was not fossicking among the cowries, mica flakes, fragments of tortoise shell, broken porcupine quills, and miscellaneous claws, horns, and bone in our back room, or doing his rounds of the village, checking to see that cooking fires were under control and small boys not getting into trouble, he would sit with me, sipping the sweet Pickwick tea I gladly brewed for him and recounting episodes from his life as a healer, as master of the Kome cult, and now as keminetigi—leader of the young men. But the Al-hajis were always on the prowl, reminding me that they had ordered Saran Salia to repudiate Kome, destroy his medicines, and embrace Islam if he wanted to be given a proper burial when he died and avoid eternal damnation.

One morning Alhaji Hassan brought his arguments to bear on me.

"Let me tell you of all that Allah made, and all that he did not make," Hassan began. "He did not make jujus, nor kola divination, nor the sacrifice of a chicken to a juju. What he did make was the seven levels of the sky and the seven levels of the earth. There is no pillar holding up the sky other than the truth of the words of Allah. You can begin building a house on a lie, but you cannot support the roof with a lie."

"What about people?" I asked. "Did Allah make us?"

"Did you make yourself or were you made by someone?" Hassan retorted.

"Neither," I said. "Just as a tree grows from a seed, so that seed grows from a tree. There is no original maker, no creator chief [dale mansa]."

"You see that mango tree over there?" Hassan said quickly. "Do you know of any medicine that could make it flower, bear fruit, and ripen the fruit, all in a single day?"

"No."

"You see. This shows that there is a creator chief. He made all people, including Jesus, son of Mariama. All these people were straight and true [latelan]. So Allah said, 'Because you are straight and true, I will never abandon you. But if you are not straight and true, I will not abandon you today though tomorrow I will. Allah also made two houses, Al-Jannah [the garden, heaven] and Jahannam [hell]. Whoever believes the words of Mohammed will go to heaven; he who denies the words of Allah, as transmitted through the prophet Mohammed, will go to hell. What is the price of heaven?

Fasting, sacrifice, alms, prayers, speaking the truth, giving to strangers. A child that loses its father at a very early age, you'll pity him and give to him. You'll give to the poor. Whoever does this will go to heaven. There are other good works, too. You go on pilgrimage, you build a mosque, you offer a lion, you undergo circumcision. This is the price of heaven. If one does these things, Allah will have compassion and send you to that sweet town. But if you deny Allah and the words of the Prophet, if you believe in none of these things but only in juju, if you believe in none of these things that you did not make but only in the things you made yourself, Allah will send you to hell. But Allah also said, 'Hnn, but let me show compassion. If it pleases me, I will rescue you from hell.' What does this mean? It means that a person could do evil when young but do good deeds as an adult. Allah will send that person to heaven. A person could do the good deeds as a young man and do bad things as an elder. If that person dies, Allah will send him to hell. Allah could forgive anyone and send him to heaven. He will do this just to show that he is the only chief."

"What of my fate?" I asked. "As an infidel?"

"You will go to hell. It will be like prison forever. Angels are there to lead and punish the prisoners. Do you believe this?"

"No."

"Then what do you believe?"

"I believe that when I die my life will go out like a light."

"Where will your life go then?"

"It is not a thing. It cannot go anywhere."

"In your country, do people dream of kinsmen who have died?"

"Yes. In fact I have often dreamt of my grandfather, who I loved."

"You see! This shows that your grandfather's life is somewhere in the world."

"No, it is only a memory that comes back to me when I am asleep. Like a tree you may remember from a place you visited long ago. But the tree may have been felled since you were last there. Thinking about that tree does not mean it is still there."

"But a person can dream of things he has never seen before. What of people who dream of Mecca before ever going there?"

Our argument was beginning to take on the overtones of Bishop Berkeley's *Dialogues of Hylas and Philonous*. The undecidable question of whether matter is a product of mind, or mind a product of matter. Had I possessed a better grasp of pragmatism, I might have been able to overcome this false antinomy of idealism and materialism and see that Hassan's position and mine did not necessarily imply fixed and opposing worldviews but potentialities, available to both of us, depending on the exigencies of the situations in which we found ourselves. I therefore found it both illuminating and ironic when Saran Salia later informed me that, despite the Alhajis' vehement arguments against jujus and magical medicines, Hassan secretly availed himself of them, hedging his bets, as people everywhere do when they fear for their safety or are unsure of themselves. "If Hassan offended a man who owned *korte* [the strongest of all the medicines]," Saran Salia wryly remarked, "and that man used *korte* against him, he would die just like any other man, unless the antidote was applied. *Korte* does not care where it goes when it dies! Heaven and hell are all the same to it!"

ISLAM BEGAN TO INFILTRATE the language and customs of West African societies as early as the mid-thirteenth century, when trade relations were established between the rulers of the Mande Empire and Arabia. But institutionalized Islam came but gradually to Barawa. Indeed, Kuranko long resisted Islam, escaping jihads on the plains of the Upper Niger in the early sixteenth century and seeking refuge in the West Guinea Highlands where they likened themselves to the kure tree, whose bark and wood are tough enough to resist even the sharpest axe (hence Kuranko, from *kure n'ko*, "Kure I say"). Despite the presence of Islamized and itinerant traders — mostly Mandingo and Fulani — in their midst, the first Kuranko convert from a ruling house may have been the Barawa chief Marin Tamba who, in the mid-eighteenth century, was persuaded by a visiting Fulani teacher by the name of Karakome Alpha Ibrahim to embrace the faith. But successive Barawa chiefs reaffirmed their *sunike* (non-Muslim) identity until Islam began to gather momentum in the 1970s, mediating relations not only with the afterworld but with the contemporary global world.[1] When I came back to Firawa in the dry season of 2007, Alhaji Hassan was the village imam, enjoying the same prestige as Saran Salia had enjoyed in his heyday as Master of Kome.

One morning I called on Hassan. His house was only a stone's throw from the mound of weed-covered earth that was all that re-mained of Saran Salia's old dwelling.

"Was it destroyed in the war?" I asked.

"It was destroyed long before the war came here. In 1985 there was a fire in the grassland on the hill. One hundred and fifty houses were burned to the ground, including Saran Salia's. But he was dead by that time."

Precisely the kinds of fires it was his duty to prevent, I thought.

I reminded Hassan of our conversations twenty-eight years ago and asked if he remembered trying to convert me to Islam or to his account of the origins of humankind—how blacks, whites, and Arabs had different ancestors—Hama the ancestor of the Arabs, Sama the ancestor of the whites, and Yafasa the ancestors of the blacks.

Not only did Hassan remember; he remembered my arguments that human differences were mainly superficial, and that all human beings shared a common ancestry and faced very similar issues in their lives. As for me, I recalled Alhaji Hassan's counterargument, pointing out that Noah, S.B., and Abdul were sons of the same mother and the same father, but all different in their behavior. "It is the same with the different peoples in the world," he had said. "Noah has become educated in the white man's schools, but would you say he is no longer a Kuranko man? And you. If you spent all your life here in Firawa, would you become a Kuranko man? No, you would not."

I had never dreamed I would see Alhaji Hassan again, let alone sit down with him and rehearse our unfinished conversation.

I asked him if I could return to that point where we had been at loggerheads.

He said that would be fine.

I told him of a rainy afternoon, many years ago, in the village of Fasewoia, when I had fallen into a conversation with a group of elders. One old man asked me if I considered Kuranko to be my kinsmen. Mindful of the connotations of the Kuranko term *nakelin-yorgonu* (lit. "mother-one-partners"), I shook my head and said no. But the old man had used the term in a moral and tactical sense to imply fellow human beings, and I was reproached. "Was I not aware that Africans and Europeans had the same ancestral parents, and that our grandfathers were brothers?"

According to the Fasewoia elders, the first people in the world were *bimba* Adama and *mama* Hawa—ancestor Adam and ancestress Eve. They had three sons. The eldest was the ancestor of the whites, the second the ancestor of the Arabs, and the third the ancestor of the blacks. The first two sons inherited book learning, but the last-born son—the ancestor of the blacks—inherited nothing.

It surprised me that the old men should imply that Africans were natively inferior to Europeans, and I asked them to explain why the last-born son was doomed to illiteracy.

"If you uproot a groundnut," I was told, "and inspect the root, isn't it always the case that some of the nuts are bad and some good?"[2]

"I have heard that," Hassan said. "There were three calabashes. Allah put the book of inventions under one, the Qu'ran under another, and groundnuts under the third one. The ancestor of the blacks would have taken the Qu'ran or the book of inventions, but the ancestor of the whites tricked him into taking the groundnuts."

I was aware of a similar Limba story in which deception figures,[3] but this was the first time I had heard of this motif from a Kuranko informant, and it led me to ponder the connections between notions of well-being, ethics, and natural justice.

HOWEVER ONE DEFINES POLITICS, it is so deeply rooted in our history and humanity that it is, in effect, "almost without origin." By this, Paul Ricoeur means that "there has always been politics before politics; before Caesar, there is another Caesar; before Alexander, there are potentates."[4] So it is with ethics. "Before the morality of norms, there is an ethic of the wish to live well."[5] That is to say, before the advent of any particular cultural, religious, or philosophical ethics, ethics has existed. Not as a unified, normative body of maxims, obligations, duties, or categorical imperatives,[6] but as a set of recurring quandaries and questions, *a sense of ethical anxiety or disquiet about the very possibility of achieving a good life, or of ever reconciling the ideals we espouse with the existential situations in which we find ourselves.* Although the origins of this proto-ethical sensibility cannot be pinned down, either in prehistorical or historical time, it is surely grounded in human sociality—in our awareness that our very existence is interwoven with the existence of others who are always there, as Sartre observes, even when physically absent, "in the form of some reminder, a letter lying on the desk, a lamp that someone made, a painting that someone else painted."[7] To this thought one might add Maurice Merleau-Ponty's observation that social exis- tence means that we are never quite at one with ourselves. Our per- spectives are never independent of each other; they have no definite limits; each "slips spontaneously into the other's," interweaving, merging, and in effect constituting "a common ground" that makes us "collaborators for each other in consummate reciprocity."[8] This conception of intersubjectivity as a mutually constitutive process of give and take also suggests, as Sartre argues, that a meaningful life cannot consist simply of a passive or slavish submission to the world as one finds it. One must have some sense of being an actor whose speech and actions matter or make a difference to the way things are. For Kuranko, custom is a given,[9] and when explaining the way the world is as it is, people typically fall back on such stock phrases as "That is how it happened" (*maiya ta ra nya na*), "That is how our ancestors let it happen" (*ma bimban' ya ta nya na*), or "That is what we encountered" (*maiya min ta ra*). Custom (*namui*) and law (*seria*) have been decided by others at other times. Nevertheless, the social order depends upon the capacities of the living to make that order viable. This means constantly adjusting to changing circumstances, adjusting one's own needs to the needs of others. But making the world existentially viable means going beyond what is given, *if only because the given always makes its appearance as a particular problem that does not admit any one straightforward ethical or political solution.* In other words, it is in the nature of life to continually interrupt and complicate the implementation of *any* system of abstract rules and to *appear* unprecedented.

In his *Essais sur le don* (1950), Marcel Mauss suggests that our most primitive sense of the ethical reflects the three obligations of gift-exchange, spelled out as the obligation to give, the obligation to receive, and the obligation to repay.[10] And it is to Mauss that we owe the insight that these basic modalities of exchange imply more than the trading of goods and services. Exchange is a "total social fact" with ethical and religious as well as material dimensions.[11] In other words, food, fertile farmland, money, blessings, honor, love, and recognition are all gifts of life, and exchange is, in effect, a way of distributing and redistributing the scarcest of all goods — life itself. But insofar as exchange presumes the possibility of equivalent value, it is ambiguous from the start. How can a material good be measured against a spiritual value? Does an adult life have greater value than the life of an unborn child, or does the life of a sovereign take precedent over the life of a subaltern? How can the gift of a bride be reciprocated in the giving of bridewealth? And how can money indemnify a grieving family for the life of a loved one, or an apology compensate for stolen lands or lost honor? Just as no economic calculus can unequivocally determine when a gift has been repaid, so no ethical system can ever unequivocally determine what is right or wrong. Ethics can only define a field of indeterminacy—of struggles and dilemmas that are born of human sociality itself, in which partial and temporary agreements are all that is possible, where incompatible viewpoints are the norm, and where scarcity is a permanent condition.

Consider Sira's situation. At first acquaintance it seemed so simple. She had not eaten for two days. She had no shoes. She needed money for food and for school fees. But then I discover that her father has turned his back on the family, and that her mother is incapable of providing for the children. These were the reasons why there was no food. Yet it was not the lack of food that Sira complained of, but the lack of love, of recognition, or of opportunity. And what of my response to her plight? Would enabling her to resume her schooling make a positive difference or complicate things further? Was raising her hopes of another life helpful or harmful? And who was to provide good parenting and love? Had she not already worked out a modus vivendi, within the limits of her situation, drawing on the imaginative resources of her culture—the power of divination, of the djinn? One can never know a situation so fully that one can judge how best to respond to it. We act with good intentions, but the road to hell is paved with good intentions. We think we choose, but our situations also choose us.

To speak of ethics as denoting a field of existential struggle where nothing can be confidently adjudicated or completely resolved leads us to a consideration of two complementary logics. First, one must give something up, give one's all to a task, or give something away in order to gain life. This is the logic of sacrifice,[12] which, while often purporting to be motivated purely by altruism—a giving up of one's own life for the life of another—in effect places the recipient of a gift under an obligation to the giver—as in the giving of hospitality, the giving of a wife, in the lavish giving of the potlatch where one is overwhelmed by gifts one cannot possibly reciprocate, in ritualized abstinence from sex or food, or in survivor guilt where one's life is owed to another—that one can never repay. In the logic of sacrifice the giver becomes *morally* superior to the receiver, even though the giver may sacrifice his life to this end.[13]

Consider the following myth (told by Fode Kargbo, a clan elder, in the village of Dankawali, January 1970) that explains the journey of the ancestor of the Kargbo clan from the Mande heartland, during which the life of the status superior—the Kargbo—is saved by the status inferior who thereafter becomes, in effect, an equal, since his *moral* superiority cancels out the *political* superiority of the other.[14]

What I know is this: my father told me that Bakunko Sise and chief Kama Kargbo left Mande and came to this country. Our ancestor came as a hunter, and the ancestor of the Sise clan came with him. On the journey from Mande they came to a river. Bakunko Sise could change himself into a crocodile so he crossed the river, but our ancestor, chief Kama, could not cross over. He became very hungry. He told Bakunko Sise that he was very hungry, and he asked how he was going to cross the river. Then the Sise ancestor cut off his calf and roasted it and sent it for our ancestor to eat. Then he swam across the river and came and took our ancestor across on his back. Our ancestor seven generations back [*bimba woronfila*, "ancestor seven"] came from Mande. I will now tell you how the crocodile became the totem of the Sise clan. This is what I heard from my elders. The Sise killed a crocodile. He ate it and died. His children decided that they should not eat the crocodile; it therefore became their totem. Then the Kargbo said, "Let the crocodile be our totem as well because the Sise ancestor gave part of the calf of his leg to our ancestor to eat, and he swam over the river and helped our ancestor across." So the crocodile became the totem of the Kargbo. Our own real totem is the *bilakunde* [a kind of amphibious reptile]; it is not found in this country. The second is the *lei*, a bird that eats rice. It lives in this country and eats rice by both day and night. These two are our totems. We inherited the crocodile through the Sise. Because the Sise ancestor cut off his calf, roasted it, sent it to our ancestor to eat, then swam across the river and carried our ancestor to the other side, because of this, our ancestor said that their totem should be our totem. If you notice the Sise and Kargbo calling each other *sanakuie* [joking partner] it is because of that journey from Mande. Because the Sise offered himself to us, to be a pathfinder and helpmate to our ancestor.

The second aspect of ethical struggle is as fundamental as the first. If sacrifice is a "giving up" of something of value, retaliation is a "taking back." But as a *re*clamation, retaliation is predicated on the conviction that something essential to one's life has been denied or wrongly taken from one. Phrased in ethical terms, the victim feels morally superior to the victimizer for as long as it takes for recompense or indemnification to be effected. Thus, the logic of retaliation,[15] like the logic of sacrifice, assumes that the one who has lost something of value to the other or freely given something of value to the other is "in the right" and "has right on his side." Inevitably, these logics impinge on each other, as when a person decides *not* to pursue a claim for compensation or an impulse for revenge. This is the meaning of forgiveness — the giving up of one's right to retaliate makes it possible to free one's own life from thralldom to the person who sought to take it.

It must also be remembered that both the logic of sacrifice (*sarake*) and the logic of retaliation (*talsare*) have conceptual and nonconceptual modalities. As Nietzsche observed, the impossibility of quantifying and controlling the kinds of gains and losses that occur in the course of human relationships means that the lived human body is often made the focus of ritual or legal redress and reordering.[16] Thus, in the past, Kuranko chiefs leaving their country to attend festivals or funerals in other chiefdoms might order the sacrifice of a pale-complexioned virgin girl for the safety of the country, burying her alive in a pit at the chiefdom boundary, her mouth filled with gold and her head covered by a copper container[17] — a practice whose logic is reminiscent of the large-scale sacrifices of young men in Western wars for the defense of a supposedly imperiled state, or Aztec sacrifice where the lives of women, captives, and children were ritually fed to the sun, their "vital energy transferred" to the cosmos as a kind of "debt payment to the hungry gods" for the expected regeneration of life on earth.[18] But whether we are speaking of life-giving resources freely given, gratefully received, or vengefully reclaimed, the overriding principle is life itself. Not the life of any particular person, but the life of a lineage, a community, a people. What augments life in the broad sense of the word is right, what diminishes it is wrong — sentiments, if not principles, we too espouse when in the face of loss we declare "Life must go on" or speak of "Life everlasting." For these reasons, the proto-ethical encompasses imperatives that many ethical *systems* abjure, such as sacrificing the life of an infirm individual in order to enhance the survival chances of his or her kin, or waging war to claim something that one's tribe or nation supposedly needs in order to live—*lebensraum*, oil, gold, fertile soil, water, or women, as the case may be. Nor are the logic of sacrifice and the logic of retaliation antithetical. But they do make ethics by definition ambiguous—a matter of choosing between courses of action that may enhance life for some, but at the expense of others (particularly life-forms that are classified as nonhuman). A matter of dilemmas that can never be resolved to the satisfaction of all parties concerned, *even when one is able to see the situation from the other's point of view.*

It is this reciprocity of viewpoints that accounts for the vexed nature of ethical conscience. But, to reiterate, this is a conscience that springs from the lived experience of intersubjective life, and is prior to any culturally elaborated ethical system.[19] This proto-ethical sense that what is given should be given back in equal measure,[20] and its corollary—that the well-being of one depends on the well-being of others—is nicely captured in the Kuranko phrase *nyendan bin to kile, a wa ta an segi*, meaning that when you walk along a path through the *nyendan* grass (used for thatching) it bends before you, but when you return along the path, the grass bends back the other way. Thus, greetings, goodwill, and goods and services move to and fro within a community, keeping the paths open, as Kuranko say, keeping relationships alive.

Mutual recognition—seeing the other as oneself in other circumstances—constitutes what phenomenologists call the "natural standpoint."[21] Yet this should not be romanticized, since mutual recognition may find expression in actions that appear to be altruistic, such as Kuranko clan myths in which an animal saves a human ancestor in distress, as well as in actions that take life, even though the taking of life may demand something in return.

Meditating on "the first and simplest operations of the human soul," Jean-Jacques Rousseau identified "two principles which are anterior to reason. One of them pushes us forcibly to consider our own well-being and our own survival, and the other inspires in us a natural repugnance towards seeing any sentient being, and especially our fellow-men, either perish or suffer."[22]

Consider the following examples of Rousseau's natural contract, and the "natural sentiment" of *pitié* or compassion that informs it.

First, a Kuranko myth that accounts for the origin of the Kuyaté clan's special relationship with its totemic animal.

The Kuyaté do not eat the monitor lizard [*kana* or *kurumgbe*]. Our ancestor went to a faraway place. There was no water there. He became thirsty; he was near death. Then he found a huge tree, and in the bole of the tree was some water left from the rains. The monitor lizard was also there. The ancestor of the Kuyaté sat under the tree. The monitor lizard climbed into the bole of the tree, then climbed out and shook its tail. The water splashed over the man. The ancestor of the Kuyaté realized there was water there; he got up and drank. He said, "Ah, the monitor lizard has saved my life!" When he returned to his hometown he told his clanspeople about the incident. He said, "You see me here now because of the monitor lizard." Since that time the monitor lizard has been our totem [*tane*, lit. "prohibited thing"]. If any Kuyaté eats it his body will become marked and disfigured like the body of the monitor lizard. His *sanakuie* [clan joking partners] will have to find medicines to cure him.

In her "Notes on the Deer Dance," Leslie Marmon Silko describes how, in the fall of each year, Laguna Pueblo hunters go into the hills and mountains to find deer. "The people think of the deer as coming to give themselves to the hunters," she writes, "so that the people will have meat through the winter. Late in the winter the deer dance is performed to honor and pay thanks to the deer spirits who've come home with the hunters that year. Only when this has been properly done will the spirits be able to return to the mountain and be reborn into more deer who will, remembering the reverence and appreciation of the people, once more come home with the hunters."[23]

This theme is echoed in Patricia Vinnecombe's compelling analysis of San art in Southern Africa. In *People of the Eland*, Vinnecombe argues that the naturalistic polychrome representations left by San hunters on rock shelters in the Drakensberg Range may be symbolic compensations for the killing of animals essential to San life—animals with whom people felt a close kinship, particularly the eland (in the south) and gemsbok (in the north). According to myths among Khoisan-speaking peoples, the ancestral shape-shifter, Kaggen, created and reared the first eland. When younger members of Kaggen's family killed his "child," Kaggen felt deep sorrow and bade the killer ritually atone for what he had done. This atonement involved "a ceremony *which brought the eland back to life*" so that now, whenever eland are killed, it is vital that the blood and heart fat from the eland are mixed with the pulverized ochers used to paint the eland's image on a rock face. "It . . . seems to be not improbable," Vinnecombe continues, "that many of the eland paintings, particularly those associated with over-painting and re-painting, are connected with an act of reconciliation and of reparation to atone for killing. By this means, dead eland would have been symbolically re-created in order to replace the life which had been taken, and thus to ensure their continued existence."[24]

Is the ethical difficulty of taking the life of a creature with whom one feels a profound identification grounded in a universal sense that one's own life is comparable to and connected with the lives of other living things such that killing *feels* wrong, as it were, even when it is culturally approved or ideologically justified? And is this ethical reasoning, which often emerges only as a vague sense of what is right or wrong, related to a deep sense of reciprocity or natural justice, so that we feel that we owe the world a debt when it has blessed us with good fortune and think that the world owes us a living when it has failed to show us any favor? Is there, in short, an ethics that foreshadows any specific ethical code — a morality before Morality based on the deep grammar of reciprocity?

Michel Serres argues that before there is a social contract there is a "natural contract of symbiosis and reciprocity" which finds expression in our sense that however much nature gives us, we must give that much back in return. While most social tracts, such as the Declaration of the Rights of Man, constitute the citizen of one's own state as the Legal Subject, excluding all those beyond the pale of reason — so-called savages, the insane, women, criminals, aliens, and animals — the natural contract encompasses all humanity and all life forms. Though we are socialized to play down our sense of owing something to the world at large, this sense of obligation, Serres suggests, is never completely extinguished in any society or any mind and haunts us.[25] "What do we give back, for example, to the objects of our science, from which we take knowledge? Whereas the farmer, in bygone days, gave back, in the beauty that resulted from his stewardship, what he owed the earth, from which his labor wrested some fruits. What should we give back to the world? What should be written down in the list of restitutions?"[26] To return to Alhaji Hassan Sanoh's explanation as to why blacks ended up as farmers and whites received the book of knowledge, may there not be in his embittered remarks and recourse to myth an understandable response to the gross inequalities of our contemporary world and a deep sense that these inequalities are neither natural nor justified, allowing us to confirm Anaximander's insight, which survives in only fragmentary form, that a thread of indebtedness and obligation runs through all life, so that "into that from which things originate, things also pass away, as is the nature of things, redressing imbalances and injustices, according to the ordering of time"?

The Reopening of the Gate of Effort

FROM OUR FIRST DAY in Firawa, Joshua and I were waylaid by small boys begging us to give them money, help improve their lot, and even adopt them. The plea "Take me with you . . . take me to America" became so familiar that Joshua asked me how he could respond without appearing unsympathetic and rude. Some of the appeals were written in scraps of paper torn from a school exercise book and folded to resemble an envelope — Ferenkay's letter, for instance, addressed simply to Mr. White Man.

> *Dear Sir,*
>
> *I hope my letter will meet you in good condition of health. My main purpose of writing you this letter is just to inform you about my problem. Please sir I wanted to let you help me. Because my father here old. Than my mother his die. After that I don't have any body to help me about my problem. So please sir help me. So in that matter I wanted to go with you please sir. So when me and you go together to your living home; so I wanted let you help me to give me a job. Please sir take me like you children. Mr. White Man I don't have any responsibility about me. When you help me I will like that like my life purpose. I like to work with you sir please.*
>
> *Just faithfully,*
>
> *Sisay Ferenkay.*

Born of a sense of desperation and isolation (all the notes Joshua and I received were from orphan children or children with aging parents) these hopes for a utopia, far from Firawa, were as unrealistic as they were compelling. For why shouldn't I, a man of means, be able to move heaven and earth and restore in some small measure the natural justice that seemed to have deserted the people of Firawa just as God once turned a blind eye or slept while a brutal war ravaged their homeland?

As with my conversations with Alhaji Hassan, Ferenkay's letter raised ethical questions. On the one hand, ethics reflects the interests of those in power who argue that the life of society itself depends on *their* well-being and therefore requires the subservience or sacrifice of lesser mortals. This is the distributive morality that makes worth relative to birth, wealth, or power. On the other hand, human beings everywhere acknowledge a *minima moralia* grounded in a sense of sharing a common humanity. Among the Kuranko, this ethic is expressed in totemic myths that recount how an animal once saved the life of a clan ancestor who was lost, famished, or parched in a wilderness. In response to this act of altruism, the ancestor decrees that the animal will henceforth become a totem (*tane*, lit. "prohibited thing"), to be respected and kept from harm. The totem later becomes adopted by clan allies, and over time a vast system of clan correspondences develops, encompassing the West Sudan, preventing the closure of each group, and promoting "an idea something like that of a humanity without frontiers."[1] This idea is also reflected in the social imaginaries of the young, who seek to escape the particular, confining world into which they were born and enter the global ecumene.

But the tension between a particularistic and universalistic ethics remains. And it is this tension that finds expression in Alhaji Hassan's juxtaposition of myths of ethnic difference and notions of Islamic *ummah* (community of believers), as well as in Ferenkay's letter with its assumption that the powerful owe it to the powerless to improve their lot.

I know of no better account of this tension between relative and absolute conceptions of right and wrong than Kenelm Burridge's description of a visit to the Melanesian island of Manam, during which local nobles revealed to the anthropologist their ancestral lore, contained in a "book" that was in fact a dusty collection of traditional objects made of turtle shell, hardwood, and stone. Taking the white man into their trust was but a prelude to asking him why the lore that made whites so wealthy and powerful had not been shared, and why the "message" Burridge supposedly carried, that "would straighten things out," had not been communicated to his younger Melanesian brothers. People were in tears as they spoke. But one impetuous young man did not mince words: "You see, this, the things you have seen [the ancestral lore], belong to us. They are ours, our own, and all we have. We think that white men have deceived us. So we are turning back to our ancestors. How is it that white men have so much and we have so little? We don't know. But we are trying to find out."

The anthropologist's response? "There was little for me to say, little I could say."[2]

Perhaps Burridge found himself in a similar quandary to mine. One is never quite sure how literally to read the overtures of others. Nor can one be sure how best to respond, given the extraordinary expectations and impossible demands. Perhaps such complaints are symptomatic of the mimetic desire that afflicts all human beings to some degree—the craving to possess what others have, simply because one does not have these things oneself, and the experience of this lack as an injustice, an affront. In shrugging off the young Manam man's demands, did Burridge feel something akin to what I felt, reading Ferenkay's letter—that if the plea was left unanswered and the expectations not met, no great harm would be done, no grudge borne? For we address the powers that be—whether these be gods, chiefs, potential benefactors, or men of means—*both* in the hope that some good will come of it *and* in the knowledge that our petitions may come to nothing. Our imaginations lead us constantly to try it on—an expression that captures the sense that life is a calculated risk, an experiment and a negotiation. Bloch's "spirit of utopia" suggests that the human imagination works largely outside the constraints and constancies of time, place, and personhood. It occupies a no-place (*ou-topos*), making us creatures of wishful thinking who opportunistically seek some melioration in our circumstance, some change in our vantage point, *while at the same time reconciling ourselves to our lot in the here and now, accepting the unlikelihood that our appeals will be heard or our wishes granted.* Hence the familiar rationalizations when our petitions fail, our gambles don't pay off, and our hopes are dashed—it's another day tomorrow, it was worth a try, I'll give it another go, someone's got to win. As Alain Badiou notes, hope does not necessarily encompass an expectation of improvement or justice; it is, in its most ontologically basic form, a kind of obstinacy, patience, or perseverance, warranted by the sense that one's subjectivity is ongoing rather than about to come to an end.[3]

IT WAS OUR FIFTH NIGHT in Firawa. A full moon. A fire in the compound. Sewa, American, Joshua, and I warming ourselves by the fire.

Musa Janneh came by for a chat. He was closely related to Alhaji Hassan Sanoh (the clan names Janneh and Sanoh are synonymous).

Musa had been a small boy when my family lived in Firawa in 1979, and a playmate of Heidi's. He remembered fetching water for us from the local stream, and Pauline paying him for his good work. And he remembered how Pauline fell ill and we had to carry her in an improvised litter from Firawa to the Seli river crossing and take her to Kabala hospital.

"Have you never left Firawa?" I asked.

"I have gone away, but I have always come back."

"The kids all want to go to America," Joshua said.

"It is true. Everyone wants to go overseas or to America. People say America is very powerful. If you're serious you'll make money there."

"Why do they want to go to America? What do they hope to find there?" Joshua asked.

"Well, one person goes and does well, so others follow. One succeeds, and builds a fine house back in his village, so others want the same for themselves. Look at your friend Sewa Koroma. Look what he has done."

"And you?" I asked.

"My hands are empty. I have tried, but I did not find diamonds, I did not find work, I did not find a way of going abroad. So I am here. Farming."

A young man who had been sitting unobtrusively in the shadows stood up and pushed forward toward the fire.

His name was Fasili Marah. He wanted to go "overseas." His father and mother were both dead. He wanted to go to America. Would I take him?

I was tired and asked Sewa to explain to Fasili that he was asking the impossible.

"He cannot take you," Sewa said. "He says you need a visa, and it is almost impossible to get a visa. Besides, life is hard in America. America isn't paradise. Many people are poor there. They do menial work. Working long hours. And still they do not earn enough to cover the costs of a room or food. And when they get ill they cannot afford to go to a doctor."

Fasili wasn't dissuaded.

"I will do anything," he said. "I am ready."

I listened as Sewa talked to Fasili about the hardships he had endured in London.

"I know it is hard," Fasili said. "People have taken the little money I have saved, promising to put me in touch with a white man who can help me. When I went to see the white man all I got was a packet of biscuits."

"What do you want most?" I asked.

"Clothes," Fasili said. He had borrowed a pair of plastic sandals in order to come and see me. His shorts were held up by a broken belt, and he wore a T-shirt with a faded American Express Card logo printed on it.

"Only clothes?"

"Also a car. And money. Take me with you. I will be loyal. I will work hard. If I do not get abroad my life is at an end."

"You have no life here?"

"Our lives are in the hands of God. *Koe be altal' lon*, everything comes from God, everything is destined by God."[4]

"Everything? Did God take your parents? Did God make you an orphan? Did God decide you should be poor?"

I hated the unkindness of my questions. And hated myself when I saw, in the light of the fire, that Fasili was crippled. His shin bones were grotesquely bowed, his feet splayed, his growth severely stunted.

"How old are you, Fasili?" I asked.

"I am twenty."

He had become crippled at age four. He fell from a bench. One minute he was normal, the next he was crippled. His mother told him it was witchcraft, though no witch ever confessed.

"But God is responsible for everything," Fasili assured me. "How we are punished, and how our destiny is made. God can make you rich one day and poor the next. You have to be patient. You have to accept that you must wait for God, and believe in God."

"But if the rebels came and said you could get anything you wanted—clothes, money, a vehicle—would you go with them?"

"Yes, right away. Definitely."

Given people's recent experience of war, in which Firawa was sacked and burned, young men and women abducted by the rebels, and many villagers murdered or maimed, I found it hard to understand Fasili's readiness to seize an advantage without much thought for the repercussions. But hadn't I been told that hunger gives no thought to the morrow, that there is nothing more tenacious than hunger? And wasn't Fasili's hunger for a better life so great that moral scruples were an unaffordable luxury?

To change the subject I asked Fasili if he would tell us his favorite story.

Fasili did not need to be asked twice, and he hurried through the tale almost without catching his breath.

"The animals formed a labor cooperative [*kere*] to dig a well. The hare [Fa San] was asked to pitch in and help.[5] But he pleaded sickness and said he could not work. The animals knew he was lying, and after they had dug their well they set the leopard to stand guard over it in case Fa San tried to take any of the water he had not earned the right to share. Sure enough, Fa San came to the well, bringing a sack of grasshoppers with him. 'Heh,' he said to the leopard, 'don't you know these people are using you? They've got you standing guard over the well while they eat. Have they brought you any food? I don't think so. But here, see what I have brought you to eat.' And Fa San gave the leopard the sack of grasshoppers and leapt into the water, which he spoiled by washing his dirty clothes in it. The animals, infuriated at having been tricked, set the bush cow to stand guard over the well, then lay in ambush in the bushes nearby. Fa San soon returned to the well with another sack of grasshoppers, confident he could fool the bush cow into letting him have access to the water. But the animals captured him, bound his wrists, and took him to a cotton tree where they intended to tie his legs together to stop him running away. But when the animals began tying Fa San's legs together, he cried out 'Heh, that is not my leg, it's a root. You're not tying my legs, you're tying the roots together.' And when the animals began tying their rope around a root, Fa San cried out, 'Heh, that's not a root, that's my leg. Don't do that. You're tying my legs together.' In this way, Fa San avoided having his legs bound, and was able to slip into a dark space among the roots of the great cotton tree and disappear. The animals now went to an old woman and asked how they might deal with Fa San. The old woman asked for food, and then told them what they needed to do. They should get their machetes and cut off his arms and legs. If he cries out, 'You're killing me, you're killing me,' this means that you are actually chopping the roots of the tree, but if he cries out 'You're cutting the root, you're cutting the root' this means that you are cutting him. And so the animals succeeded in getting rid of the deceitful Fa San."

I was stunned by Fasili's story. It was the first story of Fa San I had ever recorded (and I had, over the years, recorded thirty or forty Kuranko trickster tales) in which Fa San gets his comeuppance. What is more, this violent turning of the tables was reminiscent of the Revolutionary United Front who used machetes to sever the limbs of villagers who had allegedly betrayed them by voting for a government that enlisted the help of foreign forces to defeat the rebellion. And I did not have to think hard to recall the mango and cotton trees on whose long and buttressed roots the rebels laid the limbs of their terrified victims.

I was also mindful of the fact that the story Fasili had told was the original of the trickster story that survived the Middle Passage and entered the New World as one of the so-called Brer Rabbit tales, many of which were collected by Joel Chandler Harris and first published in 1868 and 1869.

Of the story from the New World that most closely resembles the Kuranko tale (itself widely known through the Mande-speaking area of the West Sudan), Charles Long arrives at this arresting conclusion: "Brer Rabbit is not simply lazy and clever; it is clear that he feels that *he has something else to do*—that life cannot be dealt with in purely conventional terms."[6] Although Long is interested in linking the trickster to the figure of the black preacher who "kept alive the possibility of another life" among an enslaved people, what struck me in talking to Fasili and other frustrated young men was the way they oscillated between a patient stoicism, declaring a person's fate to be ultimately in the hands of God, and an impatient and urgent desire for transformation, dramatically conveyed by the alacrity with which Fasili said he would not hesitate to join a rebellion if it would improve his lot.

"Were the rebels like Fa San?" I asked Fasili. "Did they use tricks to get their way?"

"Yes, all kinds of tricks."

Sewa knew them all. How the rebels would use all manner of cunning to cover their tracks, communicate with one another, and take their enemy by surprise. Identifying their comrades by taping red cellophane candy wrappers over their electric torches. Infiltrating towns, allaying suspicion, disguising their intentions, pretending one thing but doing another. But Sewa would not be alive had he not been able to beat them at their own game, outwitting them, making his escape. Not for nothing was he nicknamed Bonké, "slippery."

"Could you use the trickery of Fa San to get overseas?" I asked Fasili. "To get money?"

"No," Fasili said. "Trickery doesn't pay."

"And yet," I said, addressing Sewa, "you have used your wits, not only to escape the rebels when you were captured, but to get out of some tight corners in London."

Sewa agreed. But he had never broken the law, he said.

The line between social intelligence (*hankilime*) and trickery (*aliye*) was not, however, easy to draw. There was a gray zone — a zone of ethical ambiguity — in which it was difficult to decide if trickery was justified in retaliation for being tricked, or simply your best chance of survival in a situation where the odds were stacked against you.

Sewa had always reminded me of Fa San. Quick-witted, playful, street smart, smooth-talking, charismatic, and attractive to women, he was not above using his wiles to beat a rap or secure an advantage. But he was not a scoundrel.[7] He honored his ancestors as a source of life to the same extent that he sought to create a life for himself that had no ancestral precedent. As such, Sewa and Fa San are both refractions of the classical figure of Hermes, who stands on the boundary between strange and familiar worlds, god of the roads, of doors, of trade, and of craftsmanship, giver of good things, whose power comes from his contact with strangers and strange places "on the other side" from whence he brings, through trade, theft, and barter, the very goods without which his own community would perish or pale into insignificance.[8]

Clearly it is never easy to determine how far a person is justified in going in search of the "something else" of which Charles Long speaks—the lost portion that is owed you, the stolen lifeworld for which you should be compensated, the life or livelihood that are your due as much as anyone else's. For in securing a fair deal, or some form of natural justice, when do you draw the line between what is rightfully yours and what is not? And for those of us in the affluent West, who enjoy such privilege and power, when do we draw the line between what we feel we must give "to make a difference" or redress a historical wrong, and what we owe ourselves, what we must keep if we are to live? Such was the dilemma Joshua and I experienced, figuring how we could help people like Sira and Fasili in some small way without leaving ourselves with nothing, and that Sewa experienced with even greater intensity as he struggled every day to meet his family obligations yet retain some semblance of the identity he had gained in London.

But then, I asked myself: what if I had missed the point? What if Ferenkay and Fasili were not asking for fame and fortune but through these idioms asking to be taken care of, to be looked after, to be parented? Had they glimpsed in my close relationship with Joshua an image of what they, as orphans, had been denied? In which case their desire for money, for cars, and for utopia was nothing less than a longing for love, a hunger, like Sira's, for a home. And, in any case, isn't it true that all human fantasies of well-being as something that can be *acquired* echo an original state of being in which one was united with a parent body, protected, unconditionally recognized and nourished, so that utopia, in its most banal translation, means that there is no place like home?

[handwritten margin note: mis-recog. of well-being]

THE EVENING, I SAT IN THE compound with Joshua, helping him with his essay on the New Deal before spending an hour writing up my field notes—scraps of conversation and descriptive details surreptitiously scribbled in a pocket notebook in the course of the day. Later, Joshua and I shared with Sewa, D.Y., and American a meal of parboiled rice and groundnut soup that Manti—one of the late Yira Marah's daughters, now lodging with Abdul, her father's lineage brother—had prepared for us.

The fire burned. D.Y. and American played cards. In the darkness of the porch, Abdul sat alone and inscrutable. And while Joshua read by torchlight, I lay in the hammock looking up at the stars. Suddenly I realized it was Christmas Eve. How strange it was to be so far from Francine and Freya. When I told Joshua the date, he said, "I wish we could call Mum and Freya." But we were well beyond the range of mobile phones, electricity, and the digital world, in perhaps one of the few places left on earth where this was so.

Something's Missing

ACCORDING TO THE MANDE proverb *Allah ma ko kelen da*, God did not create anything single but only sets of relations: day-night, life-death, male-female, and so on. If reality is binary, and the world made up of pairs and opposites, then it is understandable that we should be fascinated by the nature of the *relationship* between these polar terms. Are they mutually arising or autonomous? Are they opposed or complementary? And how are we to understand the space in-between? Do we assign it a greater reality than the terms that frame it?

In Plato's *Symposium*, Aristophanes is concerned with the relationship between male and female. Originally, he says, human beings combined male and female forms, possessing two faces as well as four legs and arms. When the gods became alarmed by the strength, power, and ambition of these creatures, Zeus decided to weaken them by cutting them in half, "just as people cut sorb-apples in half when they're going to preserve them, or cut an egg in two with a hair." But because the very "essence" of these androgynous beings had been sundered, each half now missed its complementary half and sought reunion with it. Zeus now conceived the plan of moving their genitals from the backs of their bodies to the front, thus enabling these divided beings to enjoy sexual union and procreate their kind. "Love," Aristophanes concludes, "draws our original nature back together . . . Turbot-like, each of us has been cut in half, and so we are human tallies, constantly searching for our counter-parts."[1]

I recalled this myth of human origins the morning that five of Abdul's grandsons arrived in the compound, each holding a stave and dressed in a long blue gown in readiness for his circumcision. In the past, there would have been many more boys, and after their operations they would have spent weeks in a bush house,[2] subjected to such ordeals as *kinyale* (sleepless night) when chilis and green leaves are thrown on a fire to create a kind of primitive tear-gas and the boys beaten with switches by older men if they show signs of weariness and weakness. To become a man is to be "tamed" or "cooked"—images of domestication that suggest that childhood is a wild and unruly phase of one's life, dominated by raw emotions. Initiation separates one emotionally from one's mother and one's childhood and brings one's emotions—which are "feminine" and "hot"—under control. The removal of the prepuce is said to cleanse a young man of his vestigial "femininity" while the removal of the clitoris cleanses a young woman of her vestigial "masculinity," symbolically transforming an androgynous child into a man or a woman. Initiation creates complementary male and female identities and defines the limits of male and female domains, in much the same way that Zeus's violent sundering of an originally androgynous human being prepared the way for a social order based on sexual dimorphism.

Abdul bade me fetch my camera from my room. He wanted me to "snap" the *bilakorenu*. This was "culture," he said, and I should make a record of it. How ironic, I thought, that everything from local customs, country pots, country cloth, and locally made stoves—now called "culture stoves"—should be designated by an anthropological term whose analytical utility was as dubious as the term "race."

Though the *bilakorenu* supposedly did not know what was in store for them, I was amused to observe that three were holding their hands over their genitals, like footballers forming a wall. Yet all seemed calm and happy.

A lineage sacrifice of raw rice flour (*dege*) marks the last stage before initiation. Manti emerged from the house with a bowl of rice flour and set it down in the compound. Then, kinsmen of the boys—fathers, maternal uncles, and grandfathers—gathered around. The mothers stood some distance away, their faces grave. One woman was in tears, knowing what her son was about to go through. Indeed, this was such a wrenching moment for a mother that in days gone by her wrists would be ceremonially bound with a rope of woven cotton, and her hands left tied until a gunshot from the bush signaled that the operations had been brought to a successful conclusion.

As lineage head, it was Abdul's task to call the names of the dead—his father, his father's fathers, his maternal uncles and grandfathers—asking them to protect and bless the boys during the hours and days to come. As he called each name, we muttered *amina*, our hands outstretched toward the bowl of *dege*.

Now consecrated, it was distributed among those present, including the neophytes and the strangers—Sewa, Joshua, American, and myself.

Then the boys were led away.

An hour later, a gunshot from the bush told us that the local dispenser had done his job. The boys were now men.

Immediately, the mothers, older sisters, and paternal aunts, all of whom had been silent and doleful until this moment, broke into song and began to dance in a tight circle, celebrating the transformation that had taken place.

And we—Sewa, Abdul, and I—danced too.

But manhood, like personhood, is not achieved in a day. Indeed, it is an interminable project, never completely consummated or completed. A newborn child, for instance, is not considered fully in this world until it has been weaned. In a society with high rates of child mortality, even reaching puberty may be a cause for celebration, as when a parent declares, *a la ra beli* (lit. "he is grown"), expressing the relief and gratitude that his or her child did not die but lived

to become an adult man or woman. Even initiation is but a threshold, which is why there is always ambiguity over whether or not a particular child is physically "ripe" for *biriye*, as in the pun on the words "ripe" (*moi*) and "person" (*morgo*) in the phrase *a ma mor' we, a gberan lon*, "He is not ripe/person yet, he is still raw." For a young woman, full adulthood only arrives with the birth of children. And there are progressive stages of induction into the various women's and men's cults to which a neophyte is introduced during her or his *biriye*. But perhaps more important nowadays are other avenues for becoming a person of substance—acquiring money, getting an education, going abroad, entering politics. Indeed, many young people have adopted the idea of development not only as a national goal but a personal one.

That personhood is more fully realized in some people than in others may reflect differences in their natures. Of an incorrigible person (*morgo koron*), people might say *a ka tala, a soron ta la bole*, "He is blameless, he was born with it," or *a danye le wo la*, "That is how he is made." In other words, there are flaws and failings one can do little about, that one simply has to accept. Although initiation is a kind of second birth that creates a "new person" (*morgo kura*) blessed with "new understanding" (*hankili kura*), the transformation does not always succeed. There are always innate proclivities—generally known as "bad *yugi*"—that defy correction. Accordingly, life is a struggle between natural dispositions over which one has little control and the disciplines acquired during initiation that enable a person to master emotions, resist temptation, and sublimate self-interest to the common weal. Yet, for all this self-discipline and fortitude, life is hard; life tries one's patience, tests one to the limit, and sometime pushes one beyond it.

Indeed, it was the hardship I witnessed in Firawa—not the unavoidable hardships of bereavement and loss but the hardships that stem from poverty and marginalization, like Sira's struggle to make a life for herself, Abdul's struggle to hold on to the chieftaincy, Fasili's and Ferenkay's struggles to improve their fortunes, and Alhaji Hassan's struggle to come to terms with the cosmic injustice that allowed some people to enjoy great wealth while dooming others to

abject poverty—that brought me to ponder what it means to have a life, to feel that it is bearable and that, while there is always a sense of something more or something missing, one can say that one has enough to go on or work with, and that life is worth living. Like Ernst Bloch, I suspect that the human anxiety of "being not enough" and the search for a place where one is "secure and genuine" is always connected, albeit obliquely, not to anything as abstract as becoming cultural, as Geertz has argued, or even obtaining justice, but to the "inconstruable, absolute question" as to how we may come into our own *with others*.[3] It is for this reason that hope is predicated on the experience of being integral to the lives of others, one's own subjectivity coextensive with theirs.

"By ourselves we are still empty," writes Ernst Bloch, inadvertently echoing the social ethic best articulated in Confucianism.[4] But even without the Confucian virtues of caring for others, of filial piety and brotherly love, we can assert that no human being is sufficient unto himself or herself. We are never complete in our singularity. We need to augment, extend, enlarge, and complete our singular selves in order to be adequate for life—not simply to survive but to exist. But our bonds with others, as well as our attachments to things, are all paths—to use a Kuranko image—along which life ebbs and flows. Accordingly, understanding our relationship with our environments—social, physical, or natural—must begin with an understanding of the energy field of which we are vitally a part.

Consider the closely related Kuranko notions of life-energy (*ni*) and power (*fanka*). What ultimately defines a person, and gives him or her presence, is a capacity to generate life and create enjoyment—bringing children into the world, making a farm, feeding one's family, making light of hard work with music and song, recounting stories, resolving disputes, sharing knowledge, having networks of kin and contacts on which one can rely for assistance, or simply being able to make things happen. But this capacity is relative to whom one is with and what kind of situation one is in. During my time in London with Sewa, I had seen how instantly his confidence could be drained away by a racial slur, a neighbor's minatory look, an obstructive bureaucrat, an official form, a run-in with the police. Getting his stay papers had lifted Sewa's spirits. And he had earned enough money from his two jobs to buy a new cell phone, a wristwatch, fine clothes and shoes. The world was his oyster. He had it made. But in his struggle for legitimacy, he had been made to feel small many times, to feel ashamed, scarcely a person at all. And in telling me of his ups and downs he would often use familiar Kuranko metaphors, many of which had universal analogues.[5] Thus, wellness is likened to wholeness or wealth, a matter of being full or fulfilled (rather than empty), energized (rather than exhausted), moving (rather than stuck), having (rather than lacking). Other Kuranko metaphors require some unpacking, as when Sewa compared self-possession or self-confidence to a container (*miran*)—a house, a pot, a box, an article of clothing—in order to make the point that any disturbing and disorienting encounter (with a djinn in the bush, with a rebel soldier with an AK-47, or a policeman on a London street) could "take one's *miran* away," leaving you feeling like a dilapidated house, a broken pot, or a torn piece of clothing. Occasionally, he would compare the experience of living on the margins of an alien social world with being under attack from witches, his life-energy sapped, drained away, or consumed by a minatory force.

Any human world is a vital force field. But in this force field, life energy is always scarce, unequally distributed, and in flux.[6] Such was Spinoza's view. All living things seek to persevere in their own being—increasing their capacity for life while avoiding whatever diminishes that capacity.[7] It also finds expression in the second law of thermodynamics, which states that within an *isolated* system, energy dissipates and entropy increases. Although it is axiomatic that all living beings strive to conserve energy or, as Spinoza observed, to persist in their own being, all life forms are subject to enervation, wear and tear, aging and death. Nevertheless, these same life forms struggle, both literally and symbolically, against the loss of life, seeking to augment or increase life in whatever ways they can. This dialectic is captured in universal ontological metaphors of being up, high, or full (brimming with confidence, full of life, upbeat, enthused, exhilarated, inspired) by contrast with being down, low, or depleted (worn out, worn down, lacking energy, unmotivated, drained, diminished, dispirited, enervated, devastated, shattered, washed out).[8] We need to feel that we are on the move, getting somewhere, rather than stuck or bogged down. We expect to be able to look forward to something that is forthcoming, and to our efforts "paying off."[9]

This struggle for life against death, movement against stasis, holds true for individuals, societies, and ecosystems and may explain why personal, social, and natural *bodies* are universally seen as inextricably connected, the life of any one dependent upon a flow or transfer of vital energy within an interdependent and all-encompassing system. Ritual may be understood as the process whereby life-energy, in the form of fuel, food, labor, and generative power, is symbolically managed — amassed, increased, stored, shared, exchanged, and transferred. A singularly vivid ethnographic example of this is the Kung healing dance in which *num* or "spiritual energy" is activated in the participants and shared around, creating a synergetic consciousness in each dancer of being at one with others.[10]

But every human action, ritualized or not, discloses a central paradox of life: that we must both open ourselves up to and, to some extent, seal ourselves off from the surrounding world if we are to survive. While complete closure and fixity hastens entropy, absolute openness also increases the likelihood that life will be lost. Striking a balance between drawing upon the life around us and conserving the life we already have is, as Freud pointed out, the critical issue for every organism, from the lowly amoeba to Homo sapiens.[11] On this point it is therefore of some interest that for the Kung, the altered state of consciousness (*kia*) arrived at through the healing dance and the release of *num* is both exhilarating *and* extremely painful, liberating *and* terrifying. "The Kung must give up . . . their familiar identity," writes Richard Katz, "to enter the unknown territory of *kia*. They must experience death before they can be reborn into *kia*. *Kia* remains an experiential mystery; it demands a truly frightening passage into the unknown."[12]

WHEN I FIRST LIVED and worked in Firawa the sources of life-energy and power lay within the village as well as in the bush. As with men and women, so with town and bush — *both* were necessary to the generation and maintenance of the human lifeworld. The same was true of secular rulers and the masters of the bush cults. While the power of chiefs depended on the blessings of their ancestors, the power of the cult masters and the spirits of the wild was a vital supplement to secular power. And whenever one found oneself in difficulties, one could ask a diviner to tap into and see into a zone that lay beyond one's immediate comprehension and control and so discover how one might find a way out of an impasse. Wild energies of the bush thus supplemented the bound energies of the village. But they also *compensated* for what one could not find and accomplish within the compass of social space. Sira's discovery of such oracular power within her, and in her relationship with twin bush spirits, was typical of what the orphaned, the disadvantaged, and the dispossessed have always sought — not just imaginary friends but real allies. Even Hassan's Islam needed the abhorred jujus to supplement it. And there were always shape-shifters and witches, able to leave their bodies and enter the body of an animal, traveling vast distances within the space of a night to accomplish their nefarious ends.

But nowadays the power once associated with the bush and the djinn resides in gold, diamonds, money, mobile phones, education, politics, and the "new" religions of Islam and Pentecostalism. And witches travel to New York and London in witch airplanes to acquire stylish clothing, electronic equipment, gold and diamonds. These are therefore the foci of the contemporary imagination; these are the things that bolster life and make a person feel alive.

For years I had watched village boys build skeletal vehicles from beaten tin cans, twisted wire, or even raffia palm wood. They trundled their trucks around the village or whipped a hoop into life with the same zeal that they sketched images of djinn in the dust or told tall tales of fortunate encounters with them. I coined the term "migrant imagination" to capture the way human consciousness involves a constantly mobile, opportunistic search for an object that will bolster one's sense of self, increase one's energy, raise one's spirits, and carry one into a new and more fruitful relationship with the world.[13]

In Firawa, symbolic mobility seemed the key.

Early one morning, Sewa told me a story he had heard the previous night. Knowing my interest in such stories, he thought it might amuse me.

It was a riddle story (*sosogoma tilei*[14]) and, as it turned out, familiar to me.

There were two men. The first man went to his mother-in-law's farm to do his bride-service. He dressed in his finest clothes and carried his work clothes in a bundle on his head. But it had been raining, and walking across a muddy patch of the path he lost his footing. Before he hit the ground he changed from his good clothes to his work clothes. The second man was making a mat in his compound. Several chickens were pecking at the ground nearby. Suddenly a hawk (*tamba koroma*) fell from the sky, but before it caught its prey the mat-maker had gone to the bush, cut raffia, made a chicken coop, and put the chickens safely inside it. Now tell me, which was the fastest man?

I told Sewa I had no idea. "Why not ask American?" I said. American had just taken a seat in the hammock and had heard the end of Sewa's story. "American drove us from Freetown to Kabala in the fastest time. He's an expert on speed!"

American laughed.

"Sometimes it is good to slow down," he drawled. "Sometimes you want to get somewhere in a hurry."

"Why do they call cell phones 'mobile phones'?" I asked. "Is it because you can carry them around with you or because they make it easy to move around the world, getting in touch with people. Maybe the fastest man is the man with a mobile phone. In the time it takes to hit nine buttons, he's talking to someone in London or New York."

"You're right!" said American, suddenly excited. "Here in Firawa, without communications, we're dead. Communications is life."

Bockarie and Sewa had gone to Barawa Komoia two days before on Bockarie's motorcycle. They had climbed the inselberg behind the village, from where it was possible to make a call to Kabala. Sometimes, if the reception was good, one could reach Freetown. It was the only place in the chiefdom where a cell phone worked.

"Why is communications life?" I asked American.

"If I had communications here I would know what is happening to my family in Freetown. I would not be so cut off. In Africa, we have many kin—cousins, brothers, sisters—scattered everywhere. Without communications you're moving like a blind man. What if your father died and no one could communicate the news to you? When my father passed away I knew immediately. They phoned me and I went at once. Without communications you'll miss these things. When you've got communications, the whole world is in your palm. Everything is easier. If I want to call my brother in the UK I can call Sewa, communicate with him, ask my brother 'Are you well?' He can ask me, 'Are you well?' The mobile phone is one hundred percent nice for Sierra Leoneans."

"How did you manage before?"

"Before?"

"Before there were cell phones in Sierra Leone."[15]

"We would write letters. Give them to someone to deliver. But it was slow, and some people were not reliable. They would not deliver the letter, or they would open it to see if it contained money."

Later that day, when Joshua was working on an essay and I had time to write up my morning's notes, I went back to some of the observations I had made in Kabala, before coming to Firawa.

I had been fascinated by the ubiquitous advertisements and slogans of the two major cell phone companies in Sierra Leone. *Africell* — "Bringing People Together." *Celtel* — "Making Life Better." Their offices and booths were everywhere, selling phone cards and "top up" services. But what is it, really, that people seek to have "topped up," bolstered, improved upon? What is the link between the crude spam messages that promise a man an enlarged penis, Mohammed Fofana's self-transformation into an elephant,[16] a Bangladeshi migrant in London who finds herself longing for the presence of people, "just people,"[17] the Evangelical churches that offer

West Africans "supernatural abundance" and "deeper life," the cell phone advertisements that promise a "better life," Sira Marah's spell-binding song about the power of love, Fasili's fetishism of America as a land of money, fine clothes, and the talismanic Mercedes, and American's remark about communication being life? Are all these objects symbolically equivalent—alternate ways in which we imagine how we might gain existential potency and consummate a life that we feel is somehow wanting or on the wane? Is it in our nature to desire more than we have, to be more than we are, to do better than we are presently doing, to be perennially dissatisfied? And is even the writer—of fiction or of anthropology—whose task it is to explore the human condition, inevitably carried away by the same desire "to see people not only as they are but as they might be."[18] Henry James was "haunted by incompletion." In truth, he writes, "everyone, in life, is incomplete, and it is [in] the work of art that in reproducing them one feels the desire to fill them out, to justify them, as it were."[19] In this same vein, Jean Duvignaud argues that the sociological imagination is utopian. It is an attempt to realize Mauss's ideal of a "total social phenomenon"—a complete picture of a social world, of a living whole.[20] But is this not a fiction? And do we have to invoke a postcolonial or postmodern condition of dismemberment and fragmentation to explain why Mauss's vision is empirically false? Even if the lifeworld of Firawa, let alone the Kuranko-speaking area as a whole, were, or had been once, internally coherent, the lives of no two individuals would run an identical course and the experiences of no two persons would be the same. Accordingly, even the most sensitive ethnographer finds himself or herself in a paradoxical situation—for in seeking to do justice to the infinite, if small, differences between people, he or she hesitates to make the generalizations, conflations, and idealizations that have traditionally given anthropology its identity and authority.

The Politics of Storytelling

ABDUL HAD DRAWN A BLANKET around his shoulders, and I was wearing Joshua's Red Sox jacket to keep out the cold. The sun was a blemish, a gobbet in the mist. The village bandaged in gray gauze, the hill all but invisible.

Abdul's grandson brought coals on a piece of roofing iron, and a handful of grass. He nudged these under the logs from last night's fire, crouched down, and blew. The grass smoked furiously before catching fire. A minute later, I lowered a blackened country pot onto the logs and sat back, waiting for the water to boil.

A rooster crowed, desultory and hoarse.

Abdul's grandson had been sent by his father to sell rice. Abdul had told him he had no money to buy rice. The boy called him a dirty and grumpy old man. "This is how grandchildren and grandparents joke together," Abdul explained to me.

Years ago, Abdul was indifferent to my ethnographic work and, at times, appeared suspicious of my motives. Now he took pains to spell out everything to me. *Mamane di den ko*, he said, (The grandchild is sweeter than the child). "Just as when you plant a tree and the tree starts producing fruit, so when you have a child and he starts producing, the fruit of that one will ensure that your name will not be lost. That is why the grandchild is dearer to you than your own child."

"I know," I said. "Heidi gave birth to a son last year. My first grandchild."

When the water boiled, Abdul handed the thermos to his grandson and ordered him to fill it. I then made coffee, let it stand for a few minutes, and poured two mugs for Abdul and myself.

"Michael," Abdul said, "I want to warn you. Don't trust some of these people you talk to. You can't trust what they say."

"Who?"

"The man who looks after that boy Fasili. He is my enemy."

"Your enemy?"

"Today I will explain everything to you. You will bring your notebook, and we will talk about it properly."

I KNEW WHAT THE ISSUE WAS. It had hung over the house like the dank early morning mist from the day we arrived, never lifting. Different people gave me different versions of the story. That Abdul was biding his time was, perhaps, because he wanted me to hear these stories before putting me straight, having the last word.

Karifa Jawarra was a young man that Abdul had raised as though he were his own son, so Karifa's account of events carefully avoided any details that might impugn his mentor.

"The problem of the chieftaincy," Karifa said, "goes back to 1992, the year Tala Sewa died."

But beginnings are one thing, origins another.

In the late eighteenth century, Barawa was ruled by Marin Tamba Marah, a warrior chief whose nickname, Sewa, meaning "happy," was an allusion to the elation of a conquering hero as well as his people's happiness, knowing their lives were in safe hands. But when Barawa was invaded by Fulani and their Sulima allies, Marin Tamba, devastated by his failure to protect his country, declared, "Take my body too," and withdrawing into his house he plunged his war sword into his belly.

The Fulani were soon defeated by a Sankaran warlord called Konde Braima, and in Barawa the chieftaincy devolved to Marin Tamba's eldest son Morowa. When Morowa died, he was succeeded by his younger brother, Balansama, whom the Scots explorer Alexander Gordon Laing met on October 2, 1822. Laing described Balansama as "the king of Northern Kooranko" and was impressed "with a display of awkward pageantry and African pomp exceeding any thing of the kind that [he] had yet seen."[1] Balansama had traveled from Kulokonko to Kamato expressly to see the explorer and to negotiate the opening up of trade routes to the coast. He arrived accompanied by three hundred armed men and nearly as many women, and his cavalcade was preceded by drummers, xylophonists, and other musicians blowing on elephant tusk horns. When Laing espied three kettle-drummers dressed in brand-new uniforms of the 4th West India Regiment and the Royal Africa Corps, it was immediately evident to him that he was dealing with a polity with extensive trade connections, and Balansama's motives became clearer when the ruler made a gift of gold earrings to the explorer, sacrificed two bulls, and urged Laing to take one of his wives for his pleasure, a request Laing politely declined. After three days of feasting, dancing, and amusements, discussions began. In return for allowing people from the Sankaran to pass freely through Kuranko country, Balansama asked Laing to help open the road to the sea so that Kuranko could exchange rice, gum-copal, and camwood for salt and cloth.

After Balansama's death, the chieftaincy passed to the late Morowa's son Fayira, thence to Fayira's younger brother Faramata Morowa. But after Faramata Morowa's death, the chieftaincy returned to the junior line of the late Balansama where it remained for the next one hundred years. This rivalry between the two lines—the senior Morowaia and the junior Balansamaia—resurfaced whenever the chieftaincy was contested, and for many generations the descendants of Morowa agitated and conspired to have the chieftaincy restored to them.

In 1992, Tala Sewa, a direct descendant of Balansama, died, and the old feud might have caught fire again had war not engulfed the country. "For ten years," Karifa told me, "we were hostage to the rebel war. Many of our elders fled to Freetown. Tala Sewa's successor could not be decided."

To fill the power vacuum, a trusted associate of the late Tala Sewa was made interim chief.

Konkoro Marah was considered neutral. Though he hailed from Musudugu, a town in Mongo chiefdom, he had lived in Barawa for many years and been Tala Sewa's spokesman and drum-beater.

The trouble was, Karifa said, that Konkoro was a close friend of a certain Alhaji Suleiman Faroh, also from Mongo, and despite the fact that the Alhaji had no customary right to contest the chieftaincy in Barawa, Konkoro schemed to have him appointed over Abdul, despite Abdul's status as the only legitimate candidate from within the Barawa ruling house.

Karifa's loyalty to Abdul was so unwavering that had I relied solely on his account I would have been left mystified as to why anyone in Barawa could seriously consider backing a rank outsider for the chieftaincy, and thereby breaking with a tradition that went back hundreds of years.

What Musa Janneh confided to me was, therefore, not without interest.

A few years ago, Musa said, some local alluvial gold-panners discovered a nine-carat diamond. Abdul got wind of this and went to the stream where the diamond had been found. Although Abdul tried to keep the find secret, word got out and several men from Barawa lodged a formal complaint with the district officer, claiming that Abdul was cheating them.

When I later asked Karifa about Abdul's attempt to keep the discovery of the diamond to himself, Karifa laid the blame on Konkoro. In order to clear the way for his friend, Alhaji Suleiman Faroh, Konkoro had spread lies about Abdul, telling people not to support someone who did not have the well-being of the chiefdom at heart.

Yet, from what I learned about the Alhaji, *he* was not averse to using underhand means to secure an advantage. His father had been a mori-man and leader of the witch-finders (*Gbangbane*) in Mongo. Whenever people were slow or reluctant to throw their weight behind him, the Alhaji threatened them with his inherited powers of witchcraft and sorcery.

But if the struggle for Barawa echoed an age-old struggle between sacerdotal and secular power—the power of Islam or the djinn versus the power of chieftaincy—it also echoed equally longstanding tensions between local and central government.

When Abdul had asked me to leaf through the official papers in his briefcase, I had been somewhat baffled. Now, however, I realized that Abdul's older brother S.B. had used his influence as member for Koinadugu South, leader of the House, and close friend and brother-in-law of the president (Tejan Kabbah) to have Abdul appointed section chief of Barawa. In a letter to the D. O. in Kabala, S.B. asserted that the interim chief, Konkoro Marah, "has been doing things inimical to the chiefdom of late and I have therefore thought it fit to have him replaced with immediate effect to help ease the chiefdom administration as tradition in my land demands." When S.B. died suddenly in 2003, the paramount chief of Nieni Chiefdom, of which Barawa was a small section, launched a public campaign against Abdul's appointment. Sending money to Konkoro and demanding that the drum of chieftaincy be returned to Konkoro, the Nieni chief did everything in his power to undermine Abdul and thereby avenge himself against S.B., with whom he had old scores to settle.

And thereby hangs another tale.

Musa Janneh began with a Kuranko adage: the lenke tree scatters its seeds all around, but its seeds never fall underneath the tree. "S.B. raised up the Kuranko in the world, but he did not do much for his own kith and kin. Many people in Barawa remember this. Though he was in government for many years, S.B. did very little for his own people."

The explanation lies in Barawa's vexed relationship with the larger chiefdom of Nieni to the south into which Barawa was assimilated in one of the amalgamation acts of the 1940s. Like many colonial decrees, this one was as insensitive to local realities as it was blind to history, for in the early 1860s the Barawa people had been driven into exile after a devastating invasion by the Kono, allegedly abetted by the Nieni ruler Yelimusu Keli Koroma.[2] In an echo of what would unfold a century later, thirty-four of Barawa's forty-three towns were plundered and burned, and it was not until the British established their administrative headquarters in Kabala in 1904 that the Barawa exiles were able to return to their natal country and rebuild their towns.

"We have passed through three ages," an old man once told me in Kabala. "The world began in Mande. We then left Mande and came to this country. Then began the age of the white man's rule. Yesterday and today are not the same, but whatever sun shines, that is the sun in which you must dry yourself."

All his life, Abdul's father, Tina Kome Marah, was regarded with ambivalence by many of his countrymen. In 1907 he enlisted in the West African Frontier Force and saw action in the Cameroons and Nigeria during World War I. For many of his kinsmen, Tina Kome's decision to join the army was tantamount to "cutting his mouth off" from his own people. He had "thrown his life away," they said, "and become a child of the white men." After the war, Tina Kome joined the Court Messenger Force and rose to the rank of sergeant-major. But his ability to read and write, the value he placed on education, and his close association with the British were deeply troubling to many people in Barawa. One year, when the British were short of district officers, "Sergeant-Major"—for this was how people now addressed Tina Kome, his wives included—was appointed acting D.O. People called him a black district commissioner, recognizing his power to collect taxes but unsure if it was compatible with chieftaincy. His children had become white men, some said, meaning that they were receiving an English education. His wives are not Kuranko, said others. If we follow this man our children will never succeed. When Tina Kome made his bid for the Barawa chieftaincy in 1946, following the death of Tenaba Sewa, the then district commissioner, Victor Ffennell-Smith, and the Sengbe paramount chief, Denka Marah, both advocated his election.[3] But Barawa gave him no support, and when he lost the election he rebuked his people. "Ah, you Barawa, I've worked for you and helped you but you do not know it. But tomorrow, you will."

A generation later, in 1964, Tina Kome's son S.B. contested the staff of Nieni. Again, Barawa gave no support, and the unforgiving S.B. punished those who had failed his father and failed him in turn, declaring that thenceforth he would help his own immediate family in Firawa but not Barawa. "You may see an airplane fly over Barawa," he declared. "But it will never land here."

It is clear from Laing's account of his meeting with S.B.'s ancestor Balansama in 1822 that Barawa had long sought trade with the outside world, an open road, access to markets, and an improvement of its standard of living. But in making such gains, it did not want to cede power to another polity, be it Nieni or the colonial government. Given these imperatives, S.B.'s words were like a curse, dooming an already remote chiefdom to isolation and backwardness.

Abdul's struggle for the chieftaincy had taken place in the shadow of this history. His father's dreams and his older brother's decisions set the limits of what he could and could not do.

IT WAS THE MIDDLE of the afternoon. The village was still. People had gone indoors or sought some shade in which to wait for the cool of the evening. As Joshua worked on his math homework at a small table under the mango tree, I listened to Abdul's own account of Barawa's troubled history.

Abdul began with the years immediately after his father's retirement in 1942, when Tenaba Sewa was still chief of Barawa. After almost two decades in the Court Messenger Force, Tina Kome was ready to return to Firawa and insisted that his firstborn son accompany him, even though Kulifa was at that time a student at Bo Secondary School for Boys. Kulifa refused on the grounds that he wanted to finish his secondary schooling and did not want to live in the bush where there were no schools, no hospitals, no decent houses, and no amenities.

Abdul threw his hand back over his shoulder to describe the ritual gesture of disowning one's child.

"It was like a curse," Abdul said. "Our father turned his back on his eldest son. He did not care about him now. He told him he would suffer in life."

"Because he could no longer expect the blessings of his patrilineal ancestors? Because he was now outside their protection?"

"Exactly."

And Kulifa did suffer. He went to America and remained there for thirty years without any communication with his family until, in his dotage, he came back to Sierra Leone. I still retain a vivid image of him standing under the mango trees beyond the perimeter wall of S.B.'s house at Thompson's Bay, dressed in a navy blue suit, white tie, and braces and wearing polished black shoes. "A clown," Rose called him. "S.B. will not let him in the house. Even the mother has said she will kill herself unless he stops bringing shame on the family." Kulifa threatened to blow open the gate with dynamite. And as he shouted slanderous comments, loud enough to be heard by all the neighbors, Rose encouraged her kids to shout back. "You useless beef!" they cried. "You teef-teef [thief]." The kids then ran terrified and tittering from the balcony. It was not long before the slanging match was over. Kulifa began his slow walk back up the lane, a small boy toting his suitcase as Rose's kids took their parting shots. "Send sweet for me. Send chocolate for me!" "He *don* shame," Rose said. And later I learned that he had been arrested, manacled, and taken to Kissy hospital for observation. He died a few years later, a half-crazy beggar on the Freetown streets, still shunned by his family.

"I did not want to go to school if it meant leaving Firawa," Abdul said. "I wanted to stay and take care of my mother. In fact, I am the only one who has remained rooted in Firawa. I have never regretted this. I am proud of it."

"Do you mind me asking," I said, "why Barawa refused to vote for your father in 1946?"

"The eight heads of the main clans voted against him. As the only literate Kuranko man in Koinadugu people identified him with the British. One time, he brought picks, shovels, hoes, and handcuffs to Firawa to make farm work and grave-digging easier, but rumors spread that if he was elected chief people would have to work for the British, making roads in addition to their farm work. So they voted for Pore Bolo. My father was bitterly disappointed. He left Firawa and rebuilt Kurekoro. Pore Bolo went to him there and begged him to return to Firawa, saying there were no hard feelings, that he had nothing personally against Tina Kome. But my father refused."

Recalling this moment, Abdul was fighting back tears. The shock of his father's political defeat, the misinformation and misunderstanding that led to it.

"You see," Abdul said, quickly recovering his equilibrium, "it was the same then as it is today. What I am going through now is nothing new to me."

"How old were you at that time?"

"I was born in 1935. The election was 1946."

"So you were eleven."

"I was initiated in Firawa during the dry season that followed Barawa's amalgamation into Nieni. I was the head of the *bikakorenu*, the young boys. And I was a great wrestler—"

"*Kin gbilime*" (heavy-foot), I said, moved by how easily even Abdul's imperturbability had been undermined by the memory of his father's defeat so many years ago.

"The past is heavy," Abdul said. "It cannot be moved easily. You cannot easily put it behind you."

"That dry season," Abdul resumed after a long pause, "I led a group of the other *bilakorenu* on a tour of the newly amalgamated chiefdom, paying our respects at the chiefs' compounds, visiting kin and notifying them of our forthcoming initiations. Everywhere we went we were given hospitality and small gifts.

"My father had given me a gun. And the *keminetigi* (leader of the young men) who accompanied us had two small drums. Whenever we approached a village or town where we wanted to show our respects, I would fire a shot to announce that we were coming and the drummer would beat his drum. You had to show off a bit. Dancing. Singing. Showing people how happy you were that you would soon be a man. We went from Firawa to Momoria, to Bandakarafaia, Kondembaia, Yifin. At Yifin I spent a night and a day, lodged with the chief. Then we went on to Alikalia to see my father's sister. As we neared the compound I fired a shot, careful to point the gun away so that its back blast did not hit the house. People asked, 'Who is that?' Someone said, 'Sergeant-major's son from Barawa. The one that betrayed us.'"

"Why did they say that Tine Kome had betrayed them?"

"Just as I told you. They thought he had the interests of the British at heart. They did not see that he was trying to improve the well-being of his own people. But before Barawa was brought into the amalgamated chiefdom of Nieni, my father argued against this, saying that we would lose our traditional right to rule, and that Nieni would dominate us, as it had in the past. And you know how rumors spread like a grass fire. Once they have started you cannot stop them."

"I was taken with the other five boys to chief Da Bonso, who poked at our heads and verbally abused us. I was frightened. But I knew I would have to master my fear and speak out. So I asked if I could speak.

"I told the chief that my father had sent me to pay my respects. I had not expected Alikalia to arrest me.

"There was a big crowd now. Word had got around that the gunshot was some kind of sacrifice, and this was why I had been arrested. I was told that pretending to fire a gun was all right, but it was a crime to actually fire one in the village.

"I pleaded that my father was a man who knew the law. Therefore I knew it was no crime to fire a gun. What is more, I had fired the gun and we had beaten our drums in many villages since leaving Firawa."

"I was detained. The chief allowed people to abuse us verbally but not physically. So there we were, for a day and a night, unable to leave. But the chief's daughter was a friend of mine, and though the chief had refused to allow us food, she managed to smuggle some to us.

"Early the next morning, an old man with a walking stick came to the compound and ordered the chief to release us. We were not to blame for the quarrels caused by the amalgamation acts and the struggle of each chiefdom to maintain its own traditional right to rule. 'We're all in the same struggle together,' he said. 'When there is a problem you don't molest the messenger. These kids were paying their respects before their initiation. The gunshot was part of their way of celebrating, that's all. We have problems, certainly, but let us not take them out on these boys.'"

The palaver went on for some time, with the old man's view vying with old suspicions and rumors. Finally, the boys were released. They finished their tour, but did not dare fire their gun or beat their drum again. When they reached Kulanko and told their story, word went ahead of them to Firawa. "Barawa was much feared in those days," Abdul said. "We still had a reputation as warriors. If anything had happened to us, the initiations would not have taken place. Who knows what else might have happened . . ."

Abdul paused and looked me in the eye. "You know, Michael, I cannot believe that with all this history, people have not learned the lessons of the past. They listen but they don't understand. That is why I shed tears before. This trouble between people. These misunderstandings. The way politics affects ordinary people, who become enemies and betray their leaders. But you know, we have that saying, 'A palm wine tapster may have a dog with him, but that doesn't mean that the dog drinks palm wine.'"

I must have looked mystified.

"Those who follow a chief cannot become chiefs," Abdul said.

LATER, PONDERING MY CONVERSATION with Abdul, I thought long and hard about the tragic ironies and echoes with which the story of Barawa was replete. Tina Kome's rejection of his firstborn son, for example, and the repercussions of that irreversible gesture, not only in his son S.B's act of turning his back on Barawa, but in S.B.'s coldness toward his own sons because, like Kulifa, they chose to follow their own destinies rather than respect their father's wishes. This conflict of interests has its origin in the rule of primogeniture, since the birth of a man's first son not only foreshadows his own demise but is potentially a bone of contention among his other sons. "The eldest son is looked upon as the father's rival," Noah once told me. "So in public they avoid all contact and familiarity." That the father is publicly critical of and hostile to his firstborn may be seen as a magical stratagem for denying the ultimate succession and at the same time disguising the power inequalities among his sons. But these fault lines between father and firstborn, and between siblings, are universal, suggesting perennial and possibly unresolvable differences between the rule-governed, established order we associate with the old, and the vital but unregulated energy we associate with the young. How this energy may be controlled and stabilized on the one hand, but released and celebrated on the other, is a central problem of social existence.

Abdul's allusions to Oedipal rivalries put me in mind of a passage in Meyer Fortes's essay on the firstborn where he speaks of the widespread assumption "among tribal and oriental peoples" that "there is underlying and essential to parenthood a fund, but only a strictly limited fund, of male vitality and female fecundity, which is partly physical but largely metaphysical . . . which must be transmitted to the filial generation to ensure the proper continuity of the family and thus of society *but which can only be transmitted at the cost of the parental generation*. There is no alternative for parents but to sacrifice themselves for their children."[4]

This implies an ethical tension between the life of any particular person or creature and Life itself, for life in this broadest sense of the word — the life of one's lineage, community, or nation, or life everlasting — is often seen as the greater good to which lesser goods must be sacrificed *and to which we must ultimately aspire*. It goes without saying, however, that the gift of life is for the individual to surrender; it is not something that a cause, or another, can simply take.

Doctrines of reincarnation spring readily from this notion that particular lives flow into and out of the stream of life itself.[5] By this reckoning, death is never final but simply a stage on the way to becoming another form of life — albeit a form of life predefined by tradition.[6]

If Tina Kome judged his firstborn harshly, it was because Kulifa was acting for himself and by implication had elevated his own particular life to the status of the greater good. And yet Tina Kome had passed, in his own lifetime, from honoring his own lineage and his own chiefdom as the greater good to embracing the higher ideals of Islam.

This was poignantly brought home to me when Abdul recounted the story of his father's final days.

He never became chief of Barawa or Nieni. But the British regarded him as an able man and backed his appointment as court president at Yifin [the main town of Nieni]. But even then, Barawa whispered that the government favored him. That he was their puppet. It was the stress of fighting these rumors that brought upon him the illness that killed him. I was in Firawa in the time and he had gone to a council meeting at Yifin. When my father fell ill, Paramount Chief Kali Koroma decided that he should be carried back to Firawa. The journey took two days, and news of his illness went ahead of him. My mother and my twin sisters left Firawa and met him at Yankakoro. They were there when he died. His last words were these. He opened his eyes and said, "Manse" [chief]. My mother asked him, "Which chief?" She thought he might be referring to chief Kali Koroma. He said, "No, I am calling God the chief."

The Road to Kabala

TO SOJOURN IN ANOTHER SOCIETY is to become susceptible to its imagery and preoccupations. The night before we left Firawa, I had a strange dream. Of dark amber water and dead leaves in sandy shallows. Of the leaves suddenly coalescing into a female form. Of this half-naked, alluring woman, her skin dark green, rising from the water, attired with overlapping leaves, before gathering me sensuously to her and bearing me upward into the night. Later, when I shared my dream with Sewa, he said that I had been visited by the Mamiwata. That she had appeared to me was a great honor. Now I would have to find a way of responding to her overtures.

Unable to get back to sleep, I began packing in the dark—taking down the mosquito nets, working around Joshua's sleeping form, filling our suitcases with folded clothes, enamelware, books, and blankets.

At first light, Abdul joined me in the compound and nursed the fire back to life. The compound had been a stage. Every morning for ten days, I had taken my seat and waited for some new drama to unfold. I would miss this open-air theater, this stream of life eddying and flowing around me.

When I pressed money into Abdul's hands as "my respect"—my thanks for his hospitality, asking that Manti and her co-wives be given their fair share—Abdul responded by saying he expected nothing of me. I had spent a small fortune coming all the way from America; that alone conveyed my respect for Barawa.

"But I gain far more than I ever give," I said, reminding him that I would likely write another book on the strength of my return visit to Firawa. I also asked if he would ensure that the money I would send for Sira's schooling found its way into her hands and not someone else's.

"That too is your respect," he said. "Telling the world how life is here."

He extended his left hand to me—a Kuranko way of signifying one's desire that a departing friend quickly return. I took his hand, not knowing when or if we would see each other again.

As we made ready to leave, Abdul returned to his chair on the porch. Sewa supervised the loading of our suitcases, American checked the 4Runner's oil, water, and tire pressure, and Bockarie sat astride his moped ready to go. Joshua and I then shook hands with the people who had come to see us off and climbed into the backseat of the vehicle.

At the last minute, Bockarie's sister asked for a ride to Kabala. Bockarie could not refuse her and asked me if it was possible. I had a sudden flashback to thirty-seven years ago when Noah ordered me to stop my Land Rover on the road to Koinadugu. A lineage sister had flagged us down, and Noah dared not risk her curse by refusing her a ride. It was my first lesson on the hold a sister has over her brother (who is symbolically if not actually indebted to her, since he marries with bridewealth brought into the family when she marries). So I assured Bockarie I understood his situation, and asked D.Y. if he could make room in front for the young woman.

Though we made good time, I was loath to be leaving Barawa behind, and when, just out of the village of Bambakoro, we were stopped by a huge acacia tree that had fallen across the road, I read it as a sign that we were leaving too precipitously, that I needed time to take stock, that I was not yet ready to return to Kabala, let alone Freetown.

It seemed that old age had brought the tree down. And from some boys already at the site, we learned that it had fallen only half an hour before our arrival and that ours was the first vehicle to come along the road that morning.

I sat on the side of the road while Sewa walked back to Bambakoro to get help. I was thinking of the blocked road. How it summed up so much of what I had seen in Firawa. From Balansama's determination in 1822 to have Laing help "open up a road" from Barawa to the coast for purposes of political alliance and trade, to people like Fasili and Sira, determined to leave their isolated village and seek their fortunes in the wider world. But what does one do if the road is blocked, one's movement impeded, no means at hand to attain one's goal, no opportunities forthcoming? And considering the tree across the road, should we endeavor to clear it away ourselves, wait for it to be cleared by someone from Bambakoro, blaze a track around it, or return to whence we came?

I watched with fascination as the situation resolved itself. Someone from the village owned a chainsaw. The sawyer arrived on the scene, surveyed the task at hand, and discussed with his sidekicks the safest and most efficient way to attack the problem. Someone now turned up with a can of petrol, and ten minutes later some oil appeared on the scene. But the sawyer could not get the chainsaw started, and after several unsuccessful attempts he engaged in more palaver with the now-swelling crowd as to what might be causing the problem. An adjustment to the carburetor was suggested. After further palaver, everyone agreed that such an adjustment was necessary. But a spanner was needed, and so a young man was sent back to the village to get one. When he returned there were further delays. It was a shift spanner and would not shift. A few drops of oil did the trick. The carburetor was adjusted, the chainsaw sputtered into life, and the sawyer, stripped down to his jeans, set to work lopping off smaller limbs and working his way back to the main branches. Various people toted away the lengths of sawn wood, dumping them in

and beyond the ditch alongside the road. Within an hour a space had been cleared, and we were free to continue our journey.

As we drove on, Sewa said, "You never know from one day to the next, one hour to the next, what will happen. You can't plan. Life is full of surprises."

"You're right," I said. But I was also thinking how different Sewa's attitude was from my own. I came from a world where one found it hard to abandon one's carefully laid plans, to accept blocked roads or sidetracks, to make detours, or reconcile oneself to the situation in which one finds oneself, shelving the dreams on which one has set such store for so many years. And I thought, too, of the difference between Joshua's situation and Sira's—Joshua born into a world that made it likely that he would realize his dreams—through travel, through education, through work; Sira cast into a world where the chances of her fulfilling her desires—for education, for recognition, for love—were less assured. What enabled Sira to endure her situation was patience—a stoic attitude that parents both exemplify and teach to their children from an early age. Life is hard. You must accept your lot and show forbearance. Above all, you must wait for blessings to find you. You cannot go out into the world and wrest good fortune from it. You cannot force your time to come. You must wait upon God's good time and graces. Everywhere in a poverty-stricken country like Sierra Leone you see people waiting. Yet the anxiety that we associate with waiting for someone to turn up, or for a message that we have been told to expect, or for a scheduled event is absent here, for the time we disparage as "African time" is never unstructured and uneventful. Men take up their positions on a porch at daybreak and sit there until well after dark, watching the world go by, greeting a friend or neighbor, waiting for food to be brought to them, observing the comings and goings of everyday life, its minor changes, its pedestrian events, its unexpected visitations. This is not absolute inertia, for by sitting *outside* one is immersed in the stream of *social* life, participating in local gossip and palaver, involved in family crises, attuned to ritual and seasonal cycles. And for those who appear to drift through the streets or sit around idly talking, playing draughts or drinking, one hesitates to speak of killing time, of aimlessness or hopelessness, since in the enjoyment of being-with-others a situation of unemployment and lack of opportunity is transformed from futility to fulfillment. At the same time, despite the appearance of being at a standstill, a person's imagination is ceaselessly at work, grasping at straws, glimpsing possibilities, interpreting events, relishing a minor epiphany, tying up loose ends.

In *A Midsummer Night's Dream* (5.1), Theseus speaks of the imagination as a capacity for "shaping fantasies, that apprehend more than cool reason ever comprehends." So when Sira finds herself with few reasons for hopefulness, she has recourse to an imagination that "bodies forth the forms of things unknown," turning them to shapes and giving "to airy nothing a local habitation and a name." In her visions of the twin *nyenne*, her story of the malevolent stepmother, her songs of true love, her power to heal, and her dream of schooling, she gives voice to a nebulous longing to be more than Firawa and her family situation allow. It may be a cognitive "trick," as Shakespeare suggests, when the imagination transforms the mere apprehension of joy into a figure capable of bringing joy, just as, at night, it is easy to suppose a bush a bear, but it is through such "tricks," whether of "the poet's pen" or the occult imagination, that life becomes bearable. And were we to press the modernist claim that recourse to the imagination, to art, to the occult or religion was simply a pathetic attempt to compensate oneself for what could not be gained through realistic and reasonable action, thereby advocating a social order in which dreams came true and governments provided raisons d'être for their citizens, we would, ironically, be as guilty of wishful thinking as the people whose fantasies we decry as mere opiates.

My train of thought did not, however, weaken my resolve to do everything in my power to help Sira get an education; it simply placed in perspective a Eurocentric idealism that celebrates action over inaction and sees the realization of dreams and the gratification of desire as the consummations of the meaning of life. In fact, what passes for life in the America of Fasili's fantasies are, in Pascal's words, forms of *divertissement* that spring from "the natural unhappiness of our condition which is weak, mortal and so miserable that when we think about it clearly nothing can console us,"[1] and so people throw themselves into media amusements, gambling, games, drugs, affairs, and vain pursuits to stave off the anguish and tedium of existence.

Still, the question bothered me: what if Sira's and Fasili's fantasies *were* realized? Would they find that they had replaced one set of limiting circumstances for another, discovering that the attainment of what they thought they needed had failed to provide fulfillment or compensation for the life they had given up in order to pursue their dream?

If anyone understood this quandary of getting what one wants but not what one needs, it was Sewa.

His life in London had gone well for him. He had earned good money. He had married. He had his residency. He had good prospects. But he was losing touch with his homeland. He had gained a future at the expense of his past. Then he returned home. I remembered our excitement in London as Sewa, Joshua, and I prepared for our journey. And though Sewa's spirits were dampened in Freetown by the importunate pressures of family and friends, they were not crushed. In Firawa, he bounced back, ironically finding respite there from the consumerist ethos that people like Fasili craved to embrace. But even in Firawa, Sewa could not escape the negative repercussions of his ostensible success.

On our last night in the village, Sewa and I were sitting with Abdul. We were all but invisible to one another. But our conversation penetrated the darkness and drew us together. Making small talk about our journey the next day, our hope for an early departure, our plans for Kabala and beyond.

We were interrupted by a visit from Saran Marah, an elderly widow with whom I had spoken from time to time and had helped with small gifts of money. Saran had heard we were leaving and had come to say goodbye. But she had kept count of the number of times she and I had conversed, and reckoned that I had not paid her for one of these occasions.

Abdul was irked by her insinuation that I owed money to everyone with whom I had talked, but the old woman persisted in pressing her claim. Her son went away to Guinea forty years ago, she said. She now wanted to go and find him. I could help her find the money she needed to make the journey.

Also irritated by Saran's demands, Sewa said that his own mother's firstborn went to the United States twenty years ago and "got lost." He had not communicated with his family in all this time. No one knew if he was dead or alive. What person would let all contact with his family lapse? Sewa asked.

Sewa's remark worked on the old woman like a spell or curse.

At once venomous and furious, she accused Sewa and one of his cousins living in London of having conspired to steal the elections in Koinadugu South earlier that year.

Sewa's reaction astonished me even more than Saran Marah's accusation. Profoundly offended, he got up, left the porch, and took refuge in the 4Runner.

Over the next half hour, Abdul, Bockarie, American, and I took turns to calm Sewa down, to bring him back from the place his anger had carried him. But he was not open to our words for a long time.

Even when I coaxed him out of the vehicle and walked with him to the outskirts of the village, hoping the star-filled night and the empty grasslands would restore him, his explanations for his outrage came in fits and starts.

"Bockarie in London does not even speak Kuranko! He has no rights in Barawa! He has no knowledge of culture, let alone the responsibilities of chieftaincy . . ."

Inconsolable, Sewa said he would not remain in Firawa another minute. He would pack his bag and walk to Barawa Komoia, sleep the night there, and meet up with us in the morning.

"Don't take Saran Marah's remarks so personally. You have nothing to reproach yourself for. She is angry at me for not giving her more money, and angry at you for supporting me. She can't take out her anger on a white man, so she's taking it out on you. Everyone knows you here. We know you would never do anything underhand."

"We must complete our mission as we planned it," American said, bringing the impartial voice of the military man to bear on the problem. Besides, Rugiatu, his superior officer's wife, had made him accountable for our welfare. "The road is not safe at night," he said. "If anything happened to Sewa, I would be held responsible. I would blame myself."

I agreed with American. "Don't go," I said to Sewa. "We must stick together. We started this trip together; let us end it the same way."

But it could not end as it began. Life is not like that. Things seldom come full circle. Every event gives birth to something new, something that cannot be foreseen or avoided. We are thrown off course. And Sewa had suffered this more than I had, leaving Sierra Leone, creating a life for himself in London only to lose touch with the life he knew before. And the more he struggled to keep these worlds in balance within him, the more desperate he became. "Stressed," as he would say, by all the pressures and demands. He had, I think, hoped to return home as an admired hero. But he had encountered not admiration but suspicion, envy, and resentment. And every gain had been accompanied by loss, so that, in drawing up a balance sheet, it was sometimes impossible to say that his dreams had paid off, his journey had been worthwhile, the game had been worth the candle. Indeed, if Sewa's dilemma found expression in myth it would resemble that ubiquitous folktale motif in which the elixir of life is located on the far side of a narrow portal that closes behind the traveler to prevent his return so that, though one gets the elixir, one cannot bring it back to the world of mortal men.[2]

FIVE MILES OUT OF KABALA, one of the 4Runner's rear tires punctured, and again we found ourselves sitting on the side of the road, working out how best to deal with the situation. Should Bockarie tie the tire to his moped, ride on to Kabala, have the puncture mended, and return? Or should we try to fix the puncture ourselves? As luck would have it, a passing cyclist resolved the situation. He was not only happy to help but had a puncture repair kit he had put together himself—with a bush glue made of vine sap, patches of rubber cut from an old inner tube, and a scraper made from a piece of tin through which nail holes had been hammered.

As the cyclist went to work, American engaged me in conversation. He was a believer. I was not. And he found it difficult to accept that a seemingly decent person like myself could be decent without a doctrine to guide his behavior, to keep him on the straight and narrow. "You must believe in something," American insisted. "What about the djinn? Do you believe in them?"

I didn't want to forestall further conversation, so I said, "I am not sure about the djinn."

Sewa now joined us. He reaffirmed his belief in the ancestors, in the dead, and reiterated his faith in the sacrifices he offered his late and beloved father every morning.

"Are you not blessed?" American asked me.

"I am. I am blessed with a happy family, a fulfilling job, and good health. I have the means to travel here. What else could I want?"

"But who has given you these things?" American asked. "Is it not God? And if it is not God or the ancestors, is it not a djinn?"

I had reached this kind of impasse with Kuranko friends many times before and was well aware that, for them, belief was less a matter of inner conviction based on empirical evidence than of accepting the taken-for-granted assumptions of one's community. You paid lip service to ancestral values, or placed your trust in the prevailing worldview, because to do otherwise would be to ostracize and alienate yourself from the very world that gave you life. So, rather than press my case, I hedged; the last thing I wanted was to risk offending American, whom I had come to admire and like.

"I cannot say. Perhaps God is a word we use when we don't know exactly who or what is the source of our fortune, good or ill. But when I first went to Firawa many years ago, some people thought I was a djinn, and that I would bring good fortune to Noah because of my special powers. Others thought I had a djinn working for me, helping me type, powering my Land Rover, giving me money."

At that moment, Sewa reminded us of the story of Lake Sonfon.

Sonfon is an "intermittent" lake, which means that it rises in the wet season and falls in the dry. But it is also symbolically intermittent, as Sewa explained.

The first Koroma to enter the region around Lake Sonfon found it inhabited by the Tegeré and Seko (both Kuranko clans). These autochthonous people begged the Koroma to settle among them, hoping they might mediate trade relations with the coast. This is how the Koroma came to settle in the vicinity of Lake Sonfon and build such towns as Gbesenia, Kamaron, and Diang Sukurela. But for many generations no Koroma would build or farm near the lake that, according to the Tegeré, was owned by powerful djinn. The djinn would one day raise the lake level, thus joining its waters with the ocean, and white men would follow, bringing wealth and benefits to Diang.[3] It was then that Manti Fila Magba Koroma, founder of Diang Sukurela, decided to offer sacrifices to the lake in order to receive these blessings. Legend has it that he gave 100 cows, 100 sheep, 100 people, 100 of everything that possessed life. After making his offerings to the djinn of the lake, he explained his motives to them. Unfortunately, the chief's wife got wind of what her husband was doing and communicated this to his praise-singers (*jelibas*). So the next time the chief set off for the lake, the *jelibas* followed him, singing his praises, playing their xylophones, clapping their hands. Hearing this commotion, the djinn took fright and withdrew into the water. Despite all the chief's appeals and sacrifices, they could not be persuaded to emerge again. And so the lake, whose waters would have extended as far as the open sea, allowing white men's ships to sail inland as far as Diang, stopped growing. Yet, even now, people fill calabashes with rice flour, food, and offerings, and push these offerings out into the lake. There will be a sudden whirlpool and the calabash will be drawn down, only to bob to the surface minutes later, empty. The gold that has recently been discovered near Lake Sonfon was also put there by the djinn. Apart from token payments to the Diang chief that were not shared with the people, all the gold goes abroad.[4] Had the chief's wife not betrayed the secret of the lake to the *jelibas*, the djinn would have seen that the gold was shared among the people of Diang, and the chiefdom would have become like countries in the developed world, and people would have been rich.[5]

With our puncture mended, we continued on our way. I looked into the bush, reluctant to be leaving it behind. But I was also remembering something Abdul had said about the first time he went to Kabala from Firawa as a boy. "In those days, to visit Kabala was like visiting overseas. You didn't want to just go and come back straight away." And hadn't Sira described going to Kabala as the sweetest time in her life?

I too had experienced this yearning to get away. A child in a backwater New Zealand town, lying awake at night, listening to the whistle of a freight train in the hills, dreaming of glittering and distant cities where I might find the fulfillment I could not find at home.

Who does not have his or her private Lake Sonfon?

Their Eyes Were Watching God

I WOKE TO THE SOUND of a neighbor bellowing at someone. "You work now. I swear to God, you do the work! Before God. You *work*! Light the fire! Bring water!" Was it a child he was berating so raucously with this inane mantra? Or was his wife bearing the brunt of his bad temper? I heard no voice raised in response. Only the soft sobbing of a child. And then the call of the muezzin in the dark. The man fell quiet then. I imagined him going off to mosque, washing his hands of home, attending to higher duties.

THE EARLY LIGHT FILTERED into the room. Outside, a bucket was scraped across concrete and lowered into a well with a muffled splash. I smelled wood smoke. Heard voices. Wondered whether to wake Josh, who was still sound asleep beside me.

There was a 2007 Star Beer calendar on the wall. The calendar picture was a crude reproduction of Leonardo's *Last Supper*. The caption underneath read, "Sharing a bright moment with Star." Again, I thought of waking Joshua and sharing the unintended joke with him. But instead I fell to thinking of the link between advertising and magical thinking—the associational logic that entices us into buying the beer held out to us by a radiantly healthy young woman, the Coke that "adds life," the Guinness that "reflects the power in you," the cell phone that "exceeds expectations" or promises to "make life better." Frazer's principles of sympathetic and contagious magic—the first assuming that one can make something happen by manipulating a homologue of that thing, the second assuming that something that has been in contact with a person may give one power over that person—are truly illuminating; his only error was to see these modes of thought as unique to "primitive" people.

I dressed and headed out into the street in search of fresh bread.

On the dusty and eroded road to the market, I took note of the litter of shredded plastic, bottle tops, squashed soda or beer cans, discarded footwear, orange peel, rice husks, groundnut shells, candy wrappers, and meanders of filthy water, as if everything had the same symbolic value as the Star beer calendar. And as I crossed the culvert and walked beside deep roadside ditches filled with slime, rank weeds, rubbish, and stagnant water, I suddenly recalled something that American said in Firawa about the way all human beings seek to improve their lot and how "helping others comes after."

In 1979 there was only one guesthouse in Kabala, and my wife, my daughter, and I were staying there after our months in Firawa. Sitting on the porch of the guesthouse one morning, I watched a pariah dog limping along the roadside.

It shared the color of the laterite road: a reddish tawny pelt with black moles and pale pink patches on its belly. It was so gaunt that its ribs showed clearly, a bony cage. One ear, lacerated in a fight, had festered. Pus exuded from the blotchy pink flesh, and flies clustered on the wound.

The dog did not see the lurching truck that bore down upon it. Without even a surprised whimper, it was suddenly gathered up in a cloud of dust and trapped beneath the chassis. The truck did not stop, but two men clinging to the tailboard shouted back at where the dog had been, as if to admonish it. On the canopy of the truck, I made out the motto "Look Road for 'Power-Man.'"

The dust settled. Little shivers and spasms tugged at the dog's body as it were invisibly wired to the world. Then it fell utterly still.

Women were now filing along the road toward the market, carrying on their heads wide enamel basins filled with groundnuts, rice, bananas, sweet potatoes, and cassava leaf. Each group of women stopped when they came to the dog, peering at it as if to see whether it was really dead before they went on.

A group of children came down the road. One boy was bowling along a bicycle wheel, hitting the rim with a stick. His companion was wheeling a toy truck fashioned out of wire and controlled by a long wire handle connected to the front wheels. When the boys saw the dog they slowed, and came up to it warily. The boy with the toy truck picked up stones from the road and lobbed them at the dog. When it did not stir, the boys muttered amongst themselves and continued down the road. The skeletal hoop and toy truck left three thin lines in the dust.

At the culvert, a group of washerwomen bashed their sodden bundles against the concrete, wringing out the suds into the slimy water of the near-stagnant creek. None of them glanced up at the passers-by.

As the morning wore on, the dog seemed to stiffen and sag. Its belly became bloated and the scruffy skin puffed out until the ribs were no longer visible. The dog's lips shriveled, exposing a snarling line of small, sharp teeth. A trickle of blood from its broken hip went black in the sun. Flies hovered above the wound, ignoring the festering ear for more fertile ground.

A hen stepped gingerly onto the road and was making toward the dog when it suddenly flapped its wings and scampered into the grass. Two vultures clumsily swept down and, like a couple of broken umbrellas, folded their shabby wings and took up vigil on the ridge of the Guest House roof. From time to time they shifted about, scratching their claws on the roofing iron, but making no move to descend to the dog.

Through the noonday and into the afternoon, the vultures kept watch. People passed down the road. Some stopped for a moment to look at the dog. Some discussed briefly how it had been killed. Trucks swerved to avoid running over it. Young men on their Japanese mopeds tooted it.

It was now swollen, and its bony legs stuck out from its body. Its teeth, bared in an inane grimace, were covered with flies trying to find their way into its mouth.

In the evening it began to stink, and the foul air carried to the Guest House. I went out and picked up the dog from the road and hurled it into the long grass.

The dead dog was like the war. Something you threw away. Or like farming, a life you sought to leave behind. In early 2002 the market was in ruins. No sign of anything that could be traded. Now it was a hive of activity—traders hanging lengths of cloth from the rafters of their stalls, setting out shoes, secondhand clothes, enamelware, and cosmetic products on flimsy tables. How determinedly life goes on, like a river pushing its way around a submerged boulder or fallen tree.

After buying several sticks of bread from the Fulani baker, I threaded my way through the crowd and back to Paygay's where Joshua and Sewa were awake and waiting to hear what plans I had for the day.

I needed to buy Sira's school supplies, I said. The green and white cloth for her uniform, sandals and shoes, satchel and exercise books, pens and pencils. When that was done, and the supplies sent back to Firawa, we would be free to head south to Kondembaia, Sewa's hometown.

SEWA MADE NO EFFORT to hide his ambivalence about going home. It seemed that wherever we went he was besieged by demands or reprimands, and on the road to Kondembaia he shared his worries with me. "All the young men from Diang want money from me. And last night, my elder sister was asking me why I didn't come and greet her before I went to Firawa. She's always been like this. Expecting we the younger ones to do things for her. 'You see me no greet me? You don't greet me? Why you no greet me?' Like that, all the time. Even in London sometimes, I can't get away from it."

Sewa spoke of an altercation at the Wandsworth Cinema where he was working. A Sierra Leonean woman and her child had presumed that they could bring food and drink into the cinema. Sewa explained that this was permitted only if the food and drink were purchased at the cinema shop. He was happy to put her soda, hamburger, and chips in a safe place until later, but she could not take these things into the cinema. The woman saw the name Koroma on his ID and asked in krio if he was Temne. He said no, he was Kuranko. The woman then bawled him out, declaring that she would report him to the Sierra Leone Immigration Department where she had good contacts. "Next time you go back to Sierra Leone, they will deal with you!" She then reminded Sewa that her party had just won the elections, so he better watch out; she had friends in high places, and he did not.

The road was as rough as the road to Firawa. And when we reached Kondembaia I could not get my bearings. Where, thirty years ago, the great cotton trees had towered over a street of mud-brick and iron-roofed houses, they now stood in the middle of a cleared space on whose perimeter some new houses had been built. One of these was the house of Sheku Magba Koroma III, the Diang chief, and the focus of an ongoing controversy as to whether he was fit to rule.

When Sheku Magba Koroma II died in 1995, his son and namesake was living in Washington, D.C., where, for fifteen years, he had allegedly been studying mechanical engineering. Sheku returned home in hope of succeeding his father as paramount chief and was elected in June 1996 after a rancorous campaign in which the two rival lineages of the ruling Koroma clan were pitted against each other. Sheku quickly became as divisive as he was unpopular, and because of his lack of respect for his section chiefs and elders, and his decision not to rebuild his father's house (burned to the ground by the RUF in 1998), some villagers took the view that he smoked too much marijuana, others that he had been in the USA too long, and others that his father had pampered him too much after his mother died when he was four. Sheku was Sewa's brother, and though Sewa was loyal to the chief, he shared his countrymen's wariness of him.

Toward the end of 2005, politically well-placed members of the opposing lineage began agitating to have Sheku Magba III removed from office. In Diang, people offered a sacrifice of rice flour (degé) to the ancestors, swearing that they would accept death if their complaint against the chief was groundless or if they reconciled themselves to his continued rule. Responding to these events, as well as pressure from the chief's most vocal critics, the president ordered Sheku to vacate the chieftaincy and initiated an inquiry into his alleged abuses of power.

But here he was, back home from his temporary exile in Freetown, warmly welcoming Joshua and me, American, D.Y., and Sewa into the well-furnished parlor of his house. At least one person has profited from the gold of Lake Sonfon, I thought, as we settled into one of the massive armchairs, upholstered with dark brown velveteen, that formed a square around a heavy, varnished coffee table in the center of the room.

Though I had met Sheku in 2002, I felt uncomfortable in his presence. Something did not feel right—like the combination of the dark brown material that covered the chairs and the ultramarine paint on the plastered walls. And it quickly became clear that Sheku was not altogether at ease with me, either, no doubt because he knew that Sewa would have provided me with a full and probably unflattering account of his tribulations.

Sewa soon found an excuse to leave the house, taking Joshua with him. I remained seated, making small talk with the elders around me, dutifully putting in as much time as custom demanded before I came up with my own pretext for leaving. I was eager to greet Keti Ferenke's family, I said at last, hoping that Sheku would remem-

ber how I used to come to Kondembaia to record *tilei* from the renowned storyteller, and not assume that I had clandestine business
with the Ferenkes—the rival lineage.

I found Sewa and Joshua beyond the cotton trees. The trees, I
noticed for the first time, were dying. Where their great canopies
once cast burly shadows onto the street was now a sketchy cartogra-
phy of dead limbs. Then I recognized the old chief's house. Though
the superstructure had been destroyed by fire during a brief RUF
occupation of the town in 1999, and saplings and grass were growing
through the cracked concrete floor, I recognized the rain-blackened
concrete of the balustrade and steps where, on so many occasions, I
had paid my respects to Sewa's father, Sheku Magba Koroma II. The
old chief's grave was slightly behind and to the side of the ruined
house, and Sewa showed me the plaque he had placed there. Nearby,
and facing the compound and the cotton trees, was the house Sewa
and his sisters were having constructed. Although only the mud
brick walls and the pan roof had been built, I could admire the large
window spaces, the carefully shaped Middle Eastern arching over
the front porch, and the generous dimensions of the rooms. "Next
time you and Joshua come to Sierra Leone," Sewa said, "the house
will be finished, and you will have a place to stay here."

But even as Sewa said this, I sensed his ambivalence. Though his
dream was to one day occupy the same position his father had once
held, today's world and his father's world were not the same, and
nor was he. He would return, certainly. But would he ever return for
good?

We passed through the half-finished house and back toward the
cotton trees. Sewa wanted to show Joshua the two concrete-edged
graves of the forty men, women, and children who were murdered by
the rebels during the 1999 incursion. He then showed us the gnarled
root that ran from the huge buttressed foot of one of the trees and
out into the compound. It was here that drug-addled rebels placed
the limbs of their terror-stricken victims, chopping and severing
with machetes. I recalled Fina Kamara's description of the fear and
panic of that terrible day, as sporadic gunfire signaled the arrival of
the rebels. People cried, *Yuge bi nala* (Badness has come), and later,
as word spread of what was happening, *Ma faga yo* (We are being
murdered), *A bi na faga* (They are killing us), *Ma bin na faga* (We
are all dead). And then, *Allah ma ma dembe* (God help us), *Kele na l*

bama (The world is coming to an end).[1] Here, Fina Kamara watched helplessly as her daughter Damba's arm was hacked off before she, in turn, had her own arm amputated.

As we walked away I told Sewa that I now understood why the cotton trees were dying. It was not old age. It was from what they had witnessed.

"We think of the trees as husband and wife," Sewa said. "You see. The larger man is the male, the smaller one is the female."

Keti Ferenke Koroma had died before the war came to Kondembaia, so I never got to ask him if his stories, which often made reference to the cotton trees and to violent acts of eye-gouging and vengeance, echoed the violence of the past or even fed the violence of the RUF. Are stories, for all their dramatic and terrible excesses, just stories, separate realities?

But I did ask Kuna, Keti Ferenke's fifth-born son, whether the events in his father's stories ever actually happened. Animals that acted ethically and could speak. Djinn who helped orphans get a better life or saw that an aggrieved person got justice.

"The *nyenne* can actually help people in that way, though I know of no one who has received such help," Kuna said. "But the imams don't like this devil business. Islam has changed people."

"So if a person wants to improve his life, what do the imams say?"

"They speak not of this world but the next."

"Do you know any of your father's stories. Can you remember any?"

"Yes, I know them."

"What is your favorite?"

Kuna laughed, and the small crowd that had now joined us on his porch also found my question amusing.

"Why do you laugh?"

"We do not tell stories in the daytime."

Presuming Kuna to be referring to the Kuranko belief that telling stories in the daytime can bring about the death of a parent, I reminded him of the reason his father used to give for flouting this rule—namely, that his parents were already dead.

"That is so," Kuna said with great gravity.

"So would you tell me a story?"

"*Awa.* There was once a man and a woman. The man was called Ferenke. His wife was called Mariama. They were old and gray-haired, and had no children.

"Then God made it possible for the woman to conceive a child. But when she announced that she was pregnant, people accused her of lying. They said she was ill, not pregnant. How could an old, gray-haired woman give birth to a child?

"The child was born. The woman said, 'Since God gave me this child I will call him Alama [lit. 'Of Allah'].'

"Alama grew up. But his father was very old. One day he called his wife to him and said, 'Mariama, we have only one child. And because I never learned Arabic and you never learned how to pray, we should send our child to a karamorgo [lit. 'learned person,' i.e., an Islamic teacher]. Do you agree?'

"They gave their child to the karamorgo, who said, 'This is good. I will take your child and teach him the Qu'ran.' The woman asked how many months her son would be away. 'Do not ask how many months,' her husband said, 'ask how many years.' The karamorgo then told her that her son's education would take seven years. 'But during this time, who will take care of us, who will feed us? And how will we be able to pay you the gift of a cow that I am told we must

Their Eyes Were Watching God 129

pay you at the end of our son's time with you?' The husband said to her, 'I cannot read and write and you do not know how to pray. We will benefit from sending our child to this karamorgo. We should not be thinking of how long he will be away from us, how we will live, or how we will pay this karamorgo.' The woman said, 'All right. Since the day I married you I have never argued against you, and I will not do so now.'

"Life was hard. The thatch on the roof of their house rotted away, and the man and the woman were unable to mend it. But they did what they could. The woman fetched water from the stream or pounded grain for people in return for small portions of rice. And the man planted tobacco, which he sold in the market. This went on for seven years.

"The boy now reached the last stage of his education, and the karamorgo brought him back to his parents' village. The karamorgo decided not to lodge with the boy's parents because their house had a broken roof, so he lodged with the chief. The chief then summoned the man and his woman to his compound. 'Your son's education is finished,' the chief said, 'and his teacher has come to receive his due. You must repay him the cow and the sheep he sacrificed when your son passed the penultimate stage [*yasi*] of his education last year.' The man agreed, for it was still his hope that his son would bring blessings to his elderly parents. But he insisted the karamorgo lodge in his house, despite its broken roof. The karamorgo agreed to this.

"The man's wife prepared thirty-six basins of cooked rice. The karamorgo ate well. He had not expected such hospitality. The following morning, the man gave the karamorgo a sheep. He said, 'This is your gift.' Next day he gave the karamorgo another sheep, in payment for the sheep that the karamorgo had sacrificed when his student passed the *yasi* stage of his education. And the day after that, the man brought a seven-year-old bull. He said, 'Here is the bull I promised in payment for my son's education.' The karamorgo was very pleased. He said, 'I have forty-six students. I will send them to re-thatch your roof.' Then he turned to the boy. 'I have one thing more to tell you,' he said. 'Your father and mother do not know how to pray. When you go to pray, take them with you. Write your suras on your slate and teach them to your parents. This is all they need to know.' Then the karamorgo went away.

"Three days later, the man sent his son to his farm, which happened to be on the site where he made his farm the year his son was born.

"On his way to the farm the boy passed three wells. The first was at a place like Kondembaia here. The second was at a place like Koinadugu. The third was at a place like Yogomaia [on a map, the three towns form points of a rough triangle]. The water from the well in Kondembaia flowed into the well in Koinadugu, and the water from this well flowed into the well in Kondembaia. But no water flowed into the third well at Yogomaia. The boy saw this, and was mystified.

"He went on and saw a bush cow that was so old that one side of its body was putrefying and covered in maggots. The other side was healthy. The boy saw this, and was mystified.

"As he went on his way he encountered a group of monkeys. They were praying. The boy saw this, and was mystified.

"When he arrived at the farm, he saw a young woman standing there. She was pale-complexioned, like a European. The boy was afraid. He thought she was a djinn. Just as he was about to run away, the girl said, 'Come here. I am your wife. But if you want me you will have to catch me.' The man took off his cap, held it in his left hand, and pursued the woman for many hours. But he could not catch her. He then decided to return home.

"After praying with his parents, he told his father what he had seen on the farm and how it had confused him. 'Can you explain these things to me?'

"His father said, 'All right. Tell me what you saw.'

"The boy described the water flowing between the two wells, and the third well into which and from which nothing flowed.

"His father said, 'My son. Although you are learned and I am not, I still have the intelligence I had when you were a small child and I sent you away to get an education. I can therefore explain what you saw today. You saw that wealthy people look after their own interests and neglect the welfare of their kinsmen. Their kinsmen become very poor.'

"The boy said, 'Father, you have spoken the truth.' He then described the bush cow with one side putrefying, the other side healthy.

"His father said, 'Well, my son, the bush cow is the head of the family. The head of the family endures many hardships. There are so many brothers who do nothing to help him. They refuse to work, they don't give him clothes, not even a cap, and yet, when they fall on hard times, they ask the family head to help them and accept responsibility for their welfare. The distress of this is what you saw on the putrefying side of the bush cow. The healthy side of the animal is a sign that the brothers are respectful of the family head, and helping him.'

"The boy now told his father about the praying monkeys.

"His father said, 'Yes, that is a sign that in time to come, Muslims will say to people, 'Embrace our faith and we will help you become chiefs.' But people should do what they have to do without being bribed. You have to work to get a wife, to get food to eat, to get clothes to wear. God may give you life, but that life is for you to make something of. God cannot give you everything.'

"The son asked, 'Was that why I could not catch the pale-complexioned virgin?'

"'Exactly. Good fortune will always elude us when we seek it on our own.'"[2]

WRITING UP MY NOTES that night in Kabala, I already knew that the events of the day would constitute a chapter in my planned book. Yet did these events possess any narrative or intellectual coherence? The story of Alama envisaged a society where patterns of life-giving exchange were in jeopardy.[3] It echoed memories of a war that had been fought largely to seize or plunder wealth wrongly withheld from the people. It connected obliquely with the dying cotton trees in Kondembaia, my memory of a dog run over in the street twenty-five years ago, and the political intrigues in Diang that preoccupied my friend Sewa. Juxtaposed in a text that preserved the sequencing, interruptions, and distortions of lived time, these episodes did not amount to an essay in understanding. And yet, the associational logic that gathers together events, memories, and emotions so indiscriminately brings us back to Ricoeur's notion of the origin. Any one element echoes others, even though there is no discernible causal link between them and the only hub seems to be the consciousness of the observer. What binds things together, then—whether we are speaking of cultural traits from very different regions of the world, or events occurring in the space of a single day—is the active imagination of the person whose consciousness encompasses these things. Here, as in dreams, the disparate detail is subject to a perpetual and largely unconscious process of combination and recombination—similar to what Lévi-Strauss called bricolage and Jung called "the acausal connecting principle" of synchronicity. As with a kaleidoscope, the semblance of a pattern will always be present, yet the pattern changes from moment to moment, depending on a slight movement of the observer in relation to the observed, but leaving no possibility of a final pattern that consummates *the* truth that lies within that cylinder of entrancing glass debris.

Albitaiya

MY DAUGHTER HEIDI WAS BORN during the rainy season of 1970 when many bush roads were impassable and villagers were living on remote farmsteads with little spare time to satisfy the insatiable curiosity of an ethnographer. And so I spent less time in Firawa, preferring brief trips to more accessible villages like Kamadugu Sukurela.

When I returned there in 2008, it was mainly to see an old informant, Morowa Marah, who had also assisted the Swedish anthropologist Chris Coulter during her fieldwork in 2003–2004.

Our arrival provoked the usual excited response in the village kids who milled around, wondering who we were. Most, I later discovered, had presumed we were aid and development experts, bringing yet another project to the village. But soon I was shaking hands with the newly elected town chief and the local imam and elders and taking my seat in the shade of an orange tree in the chief's compound while people hurriedly improvised gifts for a more formal reception.

With Sewa's help I explained that I had come to pay my respects, and to see Morowa. But there was no need to explain. Someone had recognized me and everyone now knew that I was Chris's "uncle" who used to lodge with Bundo Mansaray in the village many years ago and had been the first person to drive a vehicle over the newly made road from Fasewoia. A child had already been dispatched to fetch Morowa from his house on the other side of the village.

And so we sat, waiting for Morowa to join us, as word was spread of who I was, who Joshua was, and how Sewa was related to me.

Then Morowa was striding toward us in black Wellington boots and farm clothes.

"Michael!" he exclaimed.

As we embraced, Morowa explained that he had been about to go to his garden to supervise the six or seven workers he had hired to clear a larger area for planting pineapples.

"We will talk soon," I said, aware that the town chief and imam were impatient to begin proceedings.

Imam Janneh was elderly now, dressed in a long sky blue jellaba, and with a white beard not unlike my own. When he gave me kola, one red, one white, I reciprocated with 20,000 leones. Respect (*gbiliye*) was thus given and returned.

Imam Janneh now presented Joshua with a red chicken.

"We are so happy to see you again," he said, looking first at me. "That you made such a long journey to come back. That you brought your son with you. You belong here. But your son is our stranger.[1] So let him take the chicken. We deeply appreciate your coming here. We remember—we old ones—how you were the first person to drive a vehicle into Kamadugu Sukurela. The entire town gives you respect. The Mammy Queen sends her respect.[2] The town elders give you their respect. The town chief. Everyone. This chicken is our respect, especially to Joshua and Sewa. We are happy to see them here with you."

With the formalities concluded, Sewa, Joshua, and I accompanied Morowa to his garden about half a mile beyond the village. It was uncannily familiar—the mango trees along the local stream, the cool shadows, butterflies catching the light, the worn path through brakes of elephant grass. Morowa led us past a grove of young oil palms, cassava, pineapple, and cowpea gardens. We stopped at a small thatch-roofed shelter where several of Morowa's grandchildren sat each night by a fire, taking turns to catch some sleep and keep marauding black colobus and red patas monkeys from the crops. I was impressed by Morowa's enterprise.

"It is hard," Morowa said. "I am too old to do the heavy work myself, so I have to hire labor. And brushing an upland rice farm is too much for me now. So I exchange palm oil for rice. One tin of oil for twenty-five pans of rice.

"What of your sons?"

"They are in Kono, prospecting for diamonds. Except the diamonds are finished now. There is nothing there for them."

When we returned to the village we sat on Morowa's porch, eating parboiled rice with a cutting-grass stew. Not far away, across the compound, was the house of the Kometigi who was killed by sorcery in 1972 and whose death had haunted me ever since.[3] In the adjacent compound was Bundo Mansaray's house, where I used to pass the evenings playing wari with Bundo — or, to be accurate, where I used to be soundly defeated by Bundo despite his best efforts to make me a more adroit player of the game. After lunch, Morowa showed me the room in Bundo's house where I used to lodge. The concrete floor now broken, the ceiling mats in tatters, the place oppressive, so that I soon led the way back to Morowa's compound.

Morowa's room was at the end of the porch. After he had shown me photos of Chris Coulter with her husband Michael Barrett and their two children, I asked Morowa what changes there had been since I was last in the village in 1972.

"Islam," he said without hesitation. "This is why Kome [a men's cult association], Gbangbe [a men's witch-finding association], and bese koli [medicines associated with sorcery] have gone underground."

"Are you a Muslim?" I asked Morowa.

"Yes."

But it was clear from his next remark, that Morowa was nominally a Muslim and, like many other villagers, had simply gone along with the turn to Islam.

"There were Christians before," he said, "but it is Islam that people turn to now."

"What other changes?"

"Money. You saw for yourself when I took you to my garden. I am paying seven workers 2,000 leones a day to clear new garden land for me. Everything now is a matter of money. Having money."

"What about education?"

"You have to have money to send your child to school. To buy what they need. Nowadays, the kids insist on going to school. That is why they are against the idea of kinship marriages and arranged marriages. They want more choice in the direction of their lives."

"And the war?"

"They burned the entire town. Killed sixteen people. God alone protected us. I was captured, but a rebel from Kono recognized me. He said I was a good man (*morgo nyuma*), and begged the other soldiers to spare my life."

"What would you say has been the hardest thing in your life? And what has been the sweetest?"

"Michael, that is easy. The hardest thing was the war. The sweetest is the peace. But, you know, one of the sweetest was your coming here years ago, and your 'niece' [i.e., Chris Coulter] coming here more recently. We are poor, but we are at peace."

"I read something recently," I said to Morowa, "that claimed that most people who suffer traumatic losses not only recover, but actually claim that their lives were improved by the experience. We seem to have a happy knack of seeing the positive side of even the most terrible events."[4]

Oppressing me, however, was an event I had never been able to see in a positive light.

"I must tell you, Morowa, that for all these years, since I first came to Kamadugu Sukurela, my heart has not been at peace. And I want to tell you that the hardest thing for me, when I was here with you all those years ago, was the death of that young Kometigi, and what happened afterward. Do you remember?"

In February 1970 an epidemic of insect-borne encephalitis had swept through the village. There were many deaths, including the chief's brother. The village was under a pall. After much discussion, the chief and elders sent for the men's witch-finding association, Gbangbane, from the village of Farandugu, four miles away. That night, as we huddled indoors, the Gbangbane moved among the houses. Its ominous, muffled voice, the shuffle of feet in the darkness, the staccato of wooden clappers — *gban gban, gban gban* — infected us all with deep disquiet.

My field assistant Noah Marah and I spent several days in the village, thinking we might be of some use, but there was little we could do and we returned to Kabala. A couple of weeks later we came back and sought out Noah's friend Morowa and asked him to tell us what had happened in our absence.

The witch-finders had diagnosed the cause of one's man's illness as witchcraft and promised to deal with the witch before returning to Farandugu. According to Morowa, Gbangane had told the chief and elders that the offending witch would fall ill with chest, neck, and head pains and be unable to control her bowels. The following day the sick man succumbed and died, just as Gbangbane had predicted. Eight days later his sister fell gravely ill. In her pain and distress, she confessed that she had killed her brother by witchcraft. "I was hunting him for a year," she said. "The first time I tried to kill him was when he went to clear his farm, but I missed him. The branch only knocked out some of his teeth [such an accident had occurred]. But this year we [her coven] lay in wait for him on the path to his palm wine trees. We beat him up and injured him. Then he fell ill." The woman also explained her motive for wanting to kill her brother. She had once asked him for some rice and he had refused her. But why she had had recourse to witchcraft, rather than cursing her brother, as is a sister's right, was left unexplained. Then, as the woman lay ill inside her house, Gbangbane came again and ordered that she be buried at once. Men bound her hands and feet and dragged her to the outskirts of the village. There they dug a shallow grave and buried her alive. Banana leaves and stones were thrown in on top of her. During the entire episode, all the women and children of the village remained indoors.

When Morowa finished his account I found it impossible not to accuse him of being accessory to a murder. My outrage astonished him, and he tried to help me understand.

"If it had been my choice," he said grimly, "I would have had her thrown into the bush without burial. But we buried her in the grassland beyond the Mabumbuli [stream] so that when the grass is dry we can set fire to it and turn her face into hell. A witch deserves no respect. A witch is not a person."

I knew that Morowa and his wife had lost children as a result of witchcraft; I also knew what appalling tension the community was under. But the image of a woman being buried alive poisoned my feelings toward Morowa and, for a time, toward all those who shared his view. In short, I had come up against the limits of my cultural and moral relativism; I had discovered the limits of my ethnographic openness to a culture not my own. But there was some consolation in knowing that no one kills another human being—even when he imagines the victim to be *inhuman* and undeserving of life—without paying the intrapsychic cost of creating and recreating self-protective rationalizations and repressing remorse. And I discerned in Morowa's report that shortly after the murder (for I could not think of it otherwise), the witch's shade or *pulan* haunted him, evidence that his cultural explanations did not altogether eclipse his human unease at what he had done.

It is said that the *pulan* resembles or assumes the form of a small lizard, and a *pulan*-catcher may show people a lizard wriggling inside the bag in which he has allegedly caught the witch's shade. A *pulan*'s power enables it to lift country-pots or oppress people in their sleep. So terrified do people become that they will be paralyzed and have to be straightened out in the morning. If it does enter an unprotected house it counts off people in pairs, declaring "this and this are all right, this and this are all right," until it comes to a single and therefore vulnerable person, when it declares, "this and myself are all right." Since a *pulan* cannot attack two people at once, one may take precautions against *pulan*-haunting by sleeping in pairs.

As Morowa slept, the *pulan* settled on his head. He opened his eyes but could not cry out. He lay in terror as though an immense weight were pressing down on him. Other men in Kamadugu Sukurela were also afflicted. The *pulan* terrorized the village. Finally, the chief and elders summoned a *pulan*-catcher (*pulan brale*) from Bambunkura, a village twelve miles away. This man, Musa, bagged the *pulan* in the form of a lizard in the dead woman's house. However, her son, distressed by the awful circumstances of his mother's death, refused to accept that the lizard was his mother's shade. Piqued, Musa went back to Bambunkura and the son was ordered by the chief and elders to pay the eight-leone fee as well as apologize to Musa for doubting his skills. Musa then caught the *pulan*, again in the form of a lizard, and killed it.

Morowa confirmed the accuracy of my recollections and said he remembered these events as though they had happened yesterday.

"These things troubled me deeply," I said. "They weighed on my mind, just as that *pulan* weighed on yours. For me, that woman imagined she was a witch. But she was a person."

"I know what you thought. You said these things at the time. But it is our custom here. A witch is not a person. She had to die."

DRIVING BACK TO KABALA, Sewa was playing the video he had made in Firawa of the reception we had been given the day we arrived there. The jelimusu singing his praises and his father's praises. The jelibas with their xylophones, playing Sewa's father's favorite songs.

"This is the sweetest thing for me," Sewa said.

"And the hardest?" I asked.

"Having to dash everyone. Everyone demanding some favor from me. Threatening to badmouth me, to spoil my name if I don't give them what they ask. That is hard."

Yet every day, Sewa dressed to impress. A diamond-studded wristwatch that he would rarely wear in London lest it attract thieves. A silver chain around his neck. A diamond ear stud. Carefully pressed, white clothes. Everything about him advertising city boy. Repudiating the bush, farm work, and dirt.

"If you didn't dress up you wouldn't draw so much unwanted attention to yourself," I said. And then the instant echo: *if the witch had not confessed she would not have been killed.*

"But I want people to see how I have succeeded. (*Just as the witch wanted people to know how she had suffered.*) You have to dress up. Tomorrow, we will all be in our best clothes for going up the hill. Even you!"

EVERY NEW YEAR'S DAY, thousands of visitors arrive in Kabala for an annual "pilgrimage" to the top of the inselberg that overlooks the town. But even before year's end, processions are the order of the day. A band of neophytes, accompanied by drummers, moving from house to house in Yogomaia. A group of ten young women in green hats and pleated skirts, white stockings and blouses, and black shoes, followed by twenty-five young men wearing black suits, white shirts, ties, and academic gowns processing through the dusty streets to the beat of kettle drums, tambourines, and a bass drum and led by a tall bony girl in a blue uniform twirling a baton. They were chanting "We're educated, we, we're educated, we" and singing the praises of education, "the royal road to salvation and progress." I learned that they were all from Koinadugu, and recent graduates from a Freetown business college. They wanted to inspire the local kids with their example.

On New Year's Day, everyone was dressed in his or her best clothes. From the foot of the hill, I watched as they wound their way in single file up the steep slope before spreading out, silhouetted on the ridge, like a broken comb. I could not get the story of the Pied Piper of Hamelin out of my mind. This image of an enchanting stranger leading the burghers' children into a mountain where, except for a single crippled boy who could not keep up with the others, all would be entombed. Whether it was a matter of politics, education, or religion, people sought to move as one, to move in the same direction, to be swayed by the zeitgeist, to go with the social flow. *Be minto i le ti i ban wo ma?* people would ask rhetorically, "If everybody is where you are not, would you remain apart from them? Would you want to be the subject of resentment [*Ke i ma gboiya*]?"

"Why the turn to Islam?" I had asked Sewa on the way back from Kamadugu Sukurela.

"The chiefs embraced it, and the people followed," Sewa said. And he added that some of the first Muslims in Koinadugu were Mandingo traders, and that locals thought that Islam would bring prosperity. Hence the labor migration to Kono where diamonds might be unearthed, the dream of education or overseas, and the European as a Pied Piper, drawing a flock of children in his wake, all chanting *Waitman, Waitman* (Whiteman, Whiteman) and clamoring to be taken to America.

Ironically, the leitmotif of the mountain maw also had its local analogues. Only a few miles north of Kabala, in the fastness of the Wara Wara Hills, a legendary inselberg towers 2,000 feet above the once stone-built village of Kakoia. High in the granite wall of the mountain is an inaccessible cave inhabited by a guardian spirit (*krifi*, or djinn) of the Limba people. The djinn are said to gather up the spirits of the dead.[5] Echoing the legends associated with Sinke-konke (gold mountain) in Barawa chiefdom, it is said that when a man of a ruling house is about to die you will hear the creaking of great granite doors opening to receive the departed spirit, the bleating of animals as they are prepared for sacrifice, and xylophone music borne on the wind.

That I choose to remain behind when Sewa, D.Y., and Bockarie set off to scale the mountain was not merely because I had no head for heights; I was held back, I think, by my aversion to the *pensée de survol* that sets more store by a bird's-eye view (or should one say, a vulture's-eye view?) than the view from the ground up. I had climbed hills in search of clarity and distance, to be sure, but not in order to be the monarch of all I surveyed. The Archimedean stand-point did not come naturally to me. I was more at home within the practical, physical, sensible space of an immediate lifeworld. Rather than a "nowhere" transcending time and circumstance, my ethno-graphic instinct was to seek displacement—a vantage point "else-where" from which to re-view what I had previously seen solely from my own cultural or personal perspective.

One afternoon in Firawa, Joshua had asked me to take him up the hill. It was an ironic moment, for in *Paths toward a Clearing* (1989) I had argued against my impulse, when I first lived in Firawa, to dis-tance myself from the village, to take panoramic photographs from the hill, to map the layout of the compounds below me. In trying to gain insights into the organization of village space I lost touch with the village. Ten years later, I took my daughter Heidi up the same hill and found the gnarled and charred lophira tree where I taken my photographs of Firawa in 1969. I asked Heidi what she thought of the view. "It's all right," she said, "except you can't see anyone in the village." And sure enough, there was no human movement visible; only the smoke from cooking fires.[6]

When I told Joshua this, his wry comment was, "I am glad you brought me here too."

I could not have hoped for a better comment—for it reminded me that getting above or away from the world is not always a bad thing, for it may put you in touch with what you had not noticed, or ne-glected, before.

And so the hill was many things, not one.

For Barawa exiles in the late-nineteenth century it had been a refuge. Hence the name given to the high point of the inselberg, Albitaiya, meaning "Under the protection of Allah." This history was repeated in 1994, when the RUF invaded Kabala and people took to the hills, seeking refuge among the boulders and rocky niches of the Wara Wara range.

For the Limba people, the hill was where dead chiefs began their afterlife.

For many contemporary Sierra Leoneans, it was also a symbol of constancy. Bearing on its flanks the claw marks of centuries of rain, Albitaiya had remained untouched by war, as if impervious to change, the one thing you could count on, coming back, to be the same as it was when last you saw it. For others it was a place of renewal. One traveled here at New Year and joined thousands of others, not to dismiss the past nor to embrace the future but to enjoy that liminal moment of being out of time, out of mind. Here, you could forget for a moment the feuds at home, the corruption in government, the hassles and hardship of everyday life, and experience a kind of transcendence — the world at one's feet, people like ants in the dust, houses reduced in scale, and the township itself rendered remote, in a sea of grassland and the haze of the harmattan. For some, for whom this experience was not intoxicating enough, there was beer and Guinness. One inebriated man, Sewa would later tell me, fell hundreds of feet from the summit and had to be carried off the mountain on a stretcher. He showed me photographs he had taken on his cell phone. People sitting together on the rocks, drinking, eating, laughing. Others strolling around. The sky blue. The spaciousness of it all. As if everyone had been momentarily gathered into the palm of the hand of God.

We are afforded such moments out of time whenever we play a game, begin a ritual, recount a story, or create a work of art. For in these simulations of lived reality, our subjective experience is translated into "objective correlatives," reduced in scale and pared down to a handful of manageable features.[7] Persons are transmuted into counters, ciphers, or pieces. Words stand in for the world. Physical landscapes symbolize a social field. Climbing a mountain gives us a momentary sense that we have transcended the difficulties and confusions of our everyday life. Playing a game of draughts on an improvised board, with bottle caps as draughtsmen, distances us from the hurly burly of life, allowing us to feel that it is within our grasp and our goals are attainable. A sports arena serves as a rule-governed space where we can vicariously resolve rivalries and frustrations. A story becomes a stage on which we recast and replay the real-life dramas that defeated our best attempts to bring them under control. In all these forms of symbolic subrogation, an artificial field—a board game, a playground, a story, a theatrical or ritual setting—becomes the locus and focus of vicarious action that helps us reorient ourselves to a reality we cannot directly manage. Though the course of life, like true love, never runs smooth, art makes it appear otherwise. Random events, bad decisions, and inept actions are replayed in the imagination in ways that satisfy our craving for order, for justice, for closure, and for control. Just as a story conjures the illusion of symmetry and natural progression, so a painting, a play, a poem, a sculptured form, a religious vision, a theoretical treatise or a mathematical model may restore our faith that the world is intrinsically coherent. But more important, perhaps, than the "magical" potentiality of art, narrative, and ritual to switch our consciousness from the immediate face-to-face world in which we so easily lose our way into an artificial or imaginary space in which we experience a sense of security, purpose, and design is the existential transformation that takes place within us—from feeling that we are at the mercy of forces beyond our comprehension and control to feeling that we actively participate in shaping those forces in ways that we decide. In her memoir of her unhappy marriage to Jack Kerouac, Joyce Johnson writes: "If time were like a passage of music, you could keep going back to it till you got it right."[8] But insofar as a passage of music is an analogue of life, it does enable us to vicariously replay the events that befell us and bestow upon them the sense that we, in some small measure, have a hand in determining and understanding our own fate. In art, as in games, we are given a second chance, a sense that we are not stuck, that tomorrow is another day. Unlike the game of life, which we are bound to lose, a game is something we can return to endlessly in the belief that we will one day win. Unless we take seriously these symbolic and imaginary strategies for playing with reality we cannot even begin to understand our human capacity for well-being.

The Year of Supernatural Abundance

AS WE DROVE PAST One-Mile I peered through the mango trees, hoping for a final glimpse of our old house. But Josh was directing my attention to the Africell sign and the slogan *Your chance to win a dream house*. He wanted me to see for myself what he had been telling me about yesterday — that the cell phone companies ran many of the lotteries in Sierra Leone. Realizing that my mind was elsewhere, he asked, "What are you looking for?"

"I was saying good-bye to our old house," I said, trying to hide my tears.

All the way south, there were new mosques, churches, and school buildings. And as we got closer to Freetown, signs for Ahmadiyya and Christian Mission schools were interspersed with signs for Evangelical, Pentecostal, and other churches — Seventh Day Adventist, Church of Jesus Christ of Latter-day Saints, New Apostolic Church, Bread of Life Church, Holy Ghost Redemption Church, Victory Evangelical Church, Faith Liberation International Ministries, Living Springs Ministries, Deeper Life Bible Church, and so forth. Logos emblazoned on cars, taxis, and trucks also suggested a renewed and pervasive interest in religion, including the "religion" of football and of material prosperity. Over the last forty miles, I recorded these logos in my notebook.

> In God We Trust
> God is Great
> Allah is One
> Justice
> Thank the Lord
> Man. United
> Arsenal
> Real Madrid
> Nar God Go Gree [God Willing]

Be Honest
Look For Me
City Boy
God Bless
God Go With You
Loose You Face [Cheer Up!]
Patient Blessing
Believe in God
Judgement Day is Coming
God Bless Islam
Wait For God's Time
No Justice For the Poor
Power Vision
Allah is My Provider
God's Time is the Best
Jesus Reigns
Patience is a Virtue

I was struck by the readiness with which Islamic terms were sub-
stituted for Christian terms and vice versa, as well as the pragmatic
and syncretic spirit that pervades West African thought. This has
also been the case historically, despite fundamentalist objections to
the opportunistic ease and hermeneutic openness with which African people adopt "foreign" beliefs, ritual practices, and medicines
without repudiating their own traditions.[1] At least in popular religion, questions of faithful adherence to dogma and true belief are
clearly less important than practical appeals to whatever sources
of well-being happen to be available to a person in dire need. I was
equally fascinated by recurring allusions, in these logos and slogans,
to a logic of sacrifice—in which one gives up striving, submits to
a divinity or spiritual guide, attaches oneself to a football team, or
buys a lottery ticket, then waits hopefully for a windfall or deserved
benefit. One might be forgiven for concluding that an entire society—despite the energy and effort expended on driving a truck-
load of farm produce, charcoal, or firewood one hundred miles to a
Freetown market, or on toiling to make a farm, raise a child, study
for a school exam, build a house, or simply engage in banter or palaver with a neighbor—was fatalistically resigned to the very real possibility that none of this effort would necessarily pay off, and that

if it did this was less a result of one's labor than of God's arbitrary beneficence. Indeed, this notion of God as the ultimate arbiter of human destinies recalls E. E. Evans-Pritchard's famous account of the Zande granary that collapses and kills someone. The proximate and obvious cause that Zande refers to as the "second spear" is termite damage. It made the granary prone to collapse. But the ultimate cause—the "first spear," in Zande hunting parlance—was malevolent human agency. And I thought back to our departure from Kabala that morning, when I had impressed upon Bockarie the urgency of getting Sira's school supplies to her. I was Sira's "good cause" (*sabu nyuma*), the person on which she had pinned her hopes. But Sira's mother, Sira's teacher, or a perfect stranger might cause my gift to fall into the wrong hands, go astray, or be forgotten. Perhaps, then, it is reasonable to qualify all our actions and decisions with a fatalistic appeal to, or recognition of, powers that lie completely outside our control, so that we never lose sight of the fact that even our best efforts may be in vain, or have unforeseen repercussions, or be nullified by the efforts of others.[2]

But this is to forget the principle of hope. The necessary illusion that justice will be done and everything work out for the best.

I have always liked Woody Allen's ironic way of making this point. "We have to accept that the universe is godless and life meaningless, often a terrible and brutal experience with no hope, and that love relations are very, very hard."[3] Such an acceptance does not mean, however, that we live without hope or meaning; it places the onus on us for finding a way, even under the most appalling or limiting conditions, not only of coping but of leading a decent and moral life.

In fact, I like the idea that value derives not simply from the pleasurable and the good but from the adverse and difficult. There is no experience that does not have its value, and judging from the stories we like to tell, tragic stories are more edifying than happy ones.

At the end of Woody Allen's *Annie Hall*, Alvy (played by Woody Allen) has just had lunch with his old flame Annie, who he has not seen for some time. After bidding Annie goodbye, shaking her hand, and kissing her "friendly like," Alvy walks slowly down the street. And as he thinks back to the good times he and Annie shared, an old joke drifts into his head. A guy goes to a psychiatrist, and says, "Doc, my brother's crazy. He thinks he's a chicken." The doctor says, "Well, why don't you turn him in?" And the guy says, "I would, but

I need the eggs." Then Alvy muses, "Well, I guess that's pretty much how I feel about relationships. You know, they're totally irrational and crazy and absurd . . . but, uh, I guess we keep going' through it because, uh, most of us need the eggs."[4]

But how can the ethical imperative to live a decent, moral life—albeit for the "eggs" rather than any just reward, fairytale ending, or divine compensation—be reconciled with the dream of a better life?

That Kaimah found his situation so oppressive was, perhaps, because he had not yet discovered the sense of irony and humor that his cousin Sewa possessed in abundance, and that had enabled him to surmount enormous difficulties. But to acquire this levity Kaimah would have to learn to overcome his *fear* of the people who allegedly blocked his path, and the *hope* of a benefactor who might smooth his way. Like the sick man, of whom Ernst Bloch writes, who "has the feeling not that he lacks something but that he has too much of something,"[5] Kaimah would need to let go of his view that everything and everyone was conspiring against him.

Kaimah called at my hotel the morning after my arrival from Kabala. Over breakfast, I had watched CNN, with news of Barack Obama's win in the Iowa Democratic primary. The "audacity of hope"—for old divisions transcended and "change we can believe in"—was therefore on my mind before Kaimah and I set out along the beach road to Lumley to buy some bread and fresh fruit.

I began by telling Kaimah about my fieldwork in Firawa. How it had prompted me to ponder the question of well-being—the various things that people need to make their lives complete, worthwhile, or at least bearable. How I had been led to wonder to what extent the past—in the form of ancestral custom, war trauma, power struggles, or family feuds—so constrained our present actions that they effectively denied us any future.

"The war is not on people's minds these days," Kaimah said abruptly. "The problem is poverty."

But poverty—as a condition and a concept—was a European invention, reflecting the Enlightenment view that human inequality is not the will of God or the ancestors but the work of man. "People did not complain of poverty forty years ago," I said. "If there was inequality between men and women, rulers and commoners, elders and juniors, it was seen as being in the nature of things. Now it is thought to be the fault of those in power, who have become wealthy at the expense of others."

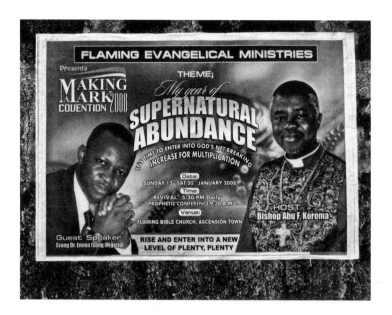

"That is true," Kaimah said.

"What interests me," I said, "is that people look to God as much as to the government for a fairer deal. But they do not look for a fairer distribution of wealth; they seem to seek windfalls and benefits solely for themselves."

I mentioned to Kaimah the numerous religious slogans I had seen in the streets of the city. The beaming, chubby-faced preacher, usually depicted with his equally chubby wife, promising everything from a "deeper life" to "miraculous prosperity." "Jesus the Impossibility Specialist," one flier had read, while another announced "The Year of Supernatural Abundance."

"Most of the ministries are run by Nigerians, or by Sierra Leoneans who have trained in Nigeria," Kaimah said. "When the war ended and the Nigerian ECOMOG soldiers went home, several of them left the army and returned to Sierra Leone. I knew one retired lieutenant. His name is Ibrahim Godfather. He told me that Sierra Leone was 'virgin land,' and he began a vehicle spare parts business, though most of the spare parts are cheap fakes. Many Nigerian traders also came to Sierra Leone, selling medicines that do not work, and passing off counterfeit 100,000-leone bills. As for the pastors and reverends you were talking about, they build mighty churches, able to accommodate two or three thousand people. But let me tell you, Mr. Michael, they are all drug dealers. Even my friend Ibrahim Godfather. During their crusades at the National Stadium they smuggle drugs in with the musical instruments they use to entertain the crowds . . ."

"What kind of drugs?"

"Cocaine, brown-brown, anything at all. They distribute it to their agents here who sell it on the street. It's a big problem now. Many young boys and girls are in the habit of taking these drugs as a form of social life and high meditations. But they steal in order to buy the drugs, and many have got mental problems now and are in the Kissy Mental Home."

We were strolling along the narrow dirt path beside the beach road. The mangy grass was littered with plastic, soda cans, cigarette packets, and old shoes. A sordid image of globalization, I thought, knowing that the cocaine in West Africa came from Colombia, destined to be sold on the European market.

I did not want to argue against Kaimah's benighted view of the Nigerian ministries; I wanted to hear what he had to say, and understand the source of the vehemence and bitterness behind his words.

"Do you belong to any church?" I asked.

"I am a Muslim. The only Christian churches I trust are the Catholic, Presbyterian, and Methodist churches. The older established ones in Sierra Leone. They help people with clothing, micro-credit and schooling. They try to improve people's lives. But these new Nigerian ministries are out for their own fame and fortune. They tithe people. They are based solely on making money for themselves. And they are devil worshippers. They practice human sacrifice. You have to give human flesh, human blood, to get fame. And the ministers use human body parts to make medicines to give people more power, more life, better chances. Depending on what you ask for, you have to give to God something of equal value. In many cases this is the life of one of your children. You'll have to sacrifice your child for a chance to go overseas, for prosperity."

 I was intrigued by this strategy of seeking gains through giving up. This ethic of living within limits rather than struggling to transcend them. Of surrendering one's freedom in order to be free. Of subtracting rather than adding. The underlying reasoning seemed to be that no matter what earthly goods we crave — more money, more love, more freedom, more power — access to such tangibles depends on intangibles, variously imagined as luck, fate, fortune, or spiritual powers. In other words, the world in which we actually move is encompassed by a force field that lies beyond our empirical comprehension and control. Accordingly, our despair at being able to lay our hands on the goods that our social world has to offer may bring us to a point where we give up striving and place ourselves at the mercy of extra-social forces in the hope that subjecting ourselves to them will prove more efficacious than struggling to act upon them. As a corollary, any successful action *on* the world requires a reciprocal act of submission *to* the world, a giving up that will compensate for what has been received. In ethical terms, one cannot expect to get something for nothing, though by dispossessing oneself of all that one has one may stand to gain more than one could ever have hoped for.

This logic of sacrifice is ubiquitous. In Sierra Leone, it is the same ominous and unforgiving logic that underlies the widespread belief that in return for a favor bestowed by a djinn one must be prepared to give up the life of a loved one. However, the logic of being born again, like the logic of sacrifice, cannot be understood quantitatively in terms of what one hopes to gain by giving up something vital to one's current life. Renunciation is *in itself* fulfilling, because it involves an emptying, exorcizing, or opening that automatically makes one receptive to *a new form of life*—being filled with the holy spirit, entering into a caring community, or coming into a fortune.[6] Paradoxically, however, it is not the attainment of such goals that consummates this sense of being renewed, but a sense of release from the past, one's moral debts cleared, one's errors forgotten, one's old ways no longer an impediment to forging new relationships with the world, and finding a new path.

Kaimah, however, saw renunciation as an invitation to the demonic and spoke of the Charismatic and Pentecostal ministries as an "underworld" whose "evil works" were done clandestinely. "They perform cleansing ceremonies at night in the hills, rivers or sea. Sometimes in the forest. They use lime, black soap, red candles, kola nuts, alligator pepper, perfumes, and Surrine [a kind of baby oil] from Nigeria. The black soap, lime, and water are common among the Burning Bush churches and the Allajobie churches. They wear white, with a red robe, and walk barefooted with a bell on their hands, preaching the word of God and at the same time predicting events that will befall the land. And they instruct people in the sacrifices they have to make in order to avert problems in the future."

"What kind of problems do people bring to them?"

"Many women who are barren go to them. Women who cannot find husbands. People who are not prospering. People who want to block someone else's chances of progress. People seeking political office or employment. People who want control and command over others."

We had reached the end of the beach. So focused had I been on Kaimah's account of Freetown's occult economy that I was startled to see that the ocean was pouring ashore, tongues of salt water licking the white sand, as innocent as ever.

"How far to the bread shop?" I asked.

"It's not far now. Are you tired? Do you want to wait here while I go on to Lumley and buy the bread?"

"I'm fine, Kaimah. But let's rest a little. I want to take some notes so that I can remember all the details of what you are telling me."

When we walked on, I asked whether these new religious practices were essentially different from the old practices of Muslim alphas and mori-men.

"It's all the same," Kaimah said. "It is all based on sacrifice. Like in the gospel of Luke. 'To whomsoever much is given, of him shall be much required.'"

"'And to whom men have committed much, of him they will ask the more,'" I added.

Kaimah was not amused. "To get a better opportunity in life, you have to offer money. Sometimes you have to offer your child. Sometimes you have to pay up front; sometimes you pay only if the work is successful. We Africans are of the conviction that all of these supernaturals have an element of truth. They are not strange to us. Most alphas or pastors have snakes or devils or evil spirits to whom they pledge their loyalty in order to get fame and fortune. This is why they do their work at night, in the sea, hills, or forest. We Africans find it hard to succeed because so many people here are full of envy, grudges, and jealousy. Always trying to block your progress in life. You are trying to achieve something, but other people with evil intentions are fighting to block your progress and ambitions. It is very common in polygamous households where every woman is fighting for her own son or daughter to achieve fame. Some go the extra mile and visit alphas or mori-men, looking for a way of spoiling the chances of their co-wives' children."

"Was this an issue in your family?"

"My father's second wife never liked me. Even now she makes things difficult for me. The very day you left Freetown for Kabala, she came to my house and said that Ibrahim [Kaimah's 'half-brother'] had phoned her from London. He said that you were going to help me go to London and continue my studies. She asked me if this was true. She sees me as a threat, because I am better educated than Ibrahim. This is why I never confide my plans to anyone. You never know what people might do to spoil your plans. I don't say a word about what I am planning to do, except to my friends. Friends you can trust, but not family."

We had reached the bread shop, owned by a Fulani baker, and I bought several sticks of bread and a bunch of bananas.

Walking along the eroded edge of the road back to the beach, I asked Kaimah if he believed all the things he had told me about the increasing use of lethal medicines and illicit drugs, the human sacrifices, the Nigerian crime networks, the corrupt churches.

Kaimah immediately recalled an incident in his early childhood. He had traveled with his parents to his mother's natal village in Temneland. On their first night in the village, Kaimah fell ill. He was so weak he could not even get out of bed. After much discussion, it was decided that Kaimah was bewitched. A local woman, with shape-shifting powers, had transformed herself into a night owl. She had perched on the roof of the house where Kaimah sleeping and consumed his blood. But on the second night, the villagers caught the owl and beat it to death. The witch, now weakened and seriously ill, confessed to her crime and explained how she had assumed the form of an owl in order to attack Kaimah. Perhaps she bore some grudge toward Kaimah's mother, Yebu. Her exact motive was never known, for she died soon after confessing.

Kaimah's second story was hearsay. A certain man with witch-craft powers was able to appropriate his wife's genitalia and pregnant belly. Leaving his own sleeping body at night, he would then move around the village as a pregnant man. One morning, just before first light, he found himself unable to reenter his own body. He was discovered, struggling and writhing, with the swollen belly and genitalia of a pregnant woman. He died soon after. As for his wife, she woke that same morning no longer pregnant.

"These things are strange," Kaimah said.

I did not comment. For me it was not a matter of *what* had occurred but *how* it was interpreted. There is no mystery in the oneiric experience of journeying to other places, of flying, of bizarre encounters and metamorphoses. Nor is it mysterious that human beings should nurse resentments, or bear malice toward a kinsman or neighbor. But where I was inclined to see misfortune as the fallout of historical events or global socioeconomic forces, Kaimah suspected foul play, conspiracy, and greed—in a word, witchcraft.

But what of his allusions to siblings trying to impede his progress, spoil his chances, and deprive him of the blessings or bounty he had sought through higher education and hard work? Was there any truth to these assertions or were they also fantasies, borne of his frustrations in getting a job, in improving his situation, in finding the wherewithal to marry? At one point, Kaimah touched on the vexed issue of his uncle S.B.'s legacy. It was rumored in the family that when S.B. passed away, a considerable amount of money was left in trust, but that S.B.'s widow Rose or one of S.B.'s most favored children was contriving to prevent this legacy being equitably distributed. Kaimah was convinced that this was the case. It was, as he put it, another sinister example of how people will "go the extra mile" in securing a scarce resource for themselves and disinheriting anyone they dislike or consider to be "distant kin."

Passing the gray concrete shell of a new beachfront hotel under construction, Kaimah said it was being built with money earned overseas by the famous Sierra Leonean footballer Mohamed Kallon. Kallon had been signed recently by AEK Athens, but earlier contracts with French and Saudi professional clubs had made him a lot of money. "But he's the younger brother," Kaimah said, "and his older brothers have squandered much of his wealth. Fortunately, this hotel is in the hands of a private contractor. It is a fixed asset, so he can protect it from the vultures."

What truth there was in Kaimah's story I did not know. But like his other stories, it gave me glimpses into what it feels like to be marginalized, to be "cut out"—as his father Noah often said of himself, comparing his desperate situation to that of his elder brother, S.B. There is historical, even contemporary, evidence of human sacrifice and the use of human body parts in producing empowering magical medicines.[7] But the force of these grim images mostly derives not from empirical evidence but from their metaphorical weight. As Derek Hughes puts it, human sacrifice is "a metonym for all transactions in which life is the currency."[8] In existential terms, material scarcity translates into a sense of being socially *without* — outside the pale, lacking the recognition that one's life has the same worth, the same potentiality, as any other life, and lacking the luxury of ever being able to take for granted that the life-energy one has today will be sufficient to see one through tomorrow. It is this constant anxiety that the scarce resource of life itself will be drained from you, sapped by the ill will or negligence of others, or from underhand dealings of which one can never be aware. One is gradually worn down by the lack of any reciprocity between what one reasonably expects from one's environment, the energy one expends in improving one's chances of "progress," and the corrupt and corrosive forces that deny one any advantage. One is sometimes driven to countermeasures, simply to survive — seizing the symbolic capital, the wherewithal for life, that has been unfairly withheld. And in this dialectic, images of eating give objective form to an inchoate sense of being deprived (one's life stolen or overwhelmed by another) or of being re-empowered (literally through getting one's own back).[9] It is a dog-eat-dog world. Either one's life energies are consumed by others or increased through the acquisition of consumer goods — from imported commodities to symbolic substances such as the blood of others — that effectively transform one's external world into an *inner* world of strength, personal solidity, and vital power. It is this experience of empowerment through the ingestion of life energy that underpins the social institution of exogamy (guaranteeing the life of a lineage by incorporating childbearing women into it), finds expression in cosmologies that assume that the social order can avoid entropy by tapping into and domesticating the "wild" powers of the bush, feeds the notion of economic increase through migration and "development," and generates images and fantasies of human sacrifice (in which the flagging powers of the old are reinvigorated by eating the vital organs of young victims). But the line between actual and imaginary strategies is never clearly drawn, and the *logic* of human sacrifice never *necessarily* entails the *practice* of human sacrifice. Nor, for that matter, do people necessarily turn to the occult when deprived of real avenues for self-realization. Indeed, I was often impressed by how faithfully Kaimah stuck to a secular agenda, despite his embrace of Islam, his belief in witchcraft, and his stories about the machinations of his kinsmen.

For him, the gospel of prosperity, the talk of righteous riches and of health and wealth, was hollow; he had placed his faith in education, and in going abroad to widen his horizons.

"You should talk to Sewa," I said. "He will tell you that the streets of London are not paved with gold *or* knowledge, but with a lot of human misery. You should know what you are getting into, exchanging Sierra Leone for England."

"I know it will be hard," Kaimah said. "But it will be worth it."

"Yes," I said. "It will be worth it." For hadn't I once left my own homeland with exactly the same dreams? And had anyone tried to dissuade me from my course with talk of expatriates returning home with empty hands, ending up in a local mental asylum, exhausted by the cumulative impact of family intrigues, malicious gossip, endless demands, and envious criticism, would this have held me back?

Nevertheless, as I had misgivings about helping Sira, so I wondered what destiny I was visiting upon Kaimah by helping him go to London. Although Kaimah had painted a grim picture of African sociality as claustrophobic and depleting, it seemed to me that the ebullience, laughter, and energy generated in face-to-face relations with others was precisely what compensated people for the lack of work, the lack of money, even the lack of food on one's table. But who was I to romanticize a lifeworld that so many saw as an obstacle to their self-realization?

That evening, walking alone on Lumley beach, my thoughts turned to well-being as the possession of existential power. To some extent, this power lies within, manifest in the conviction that one has what it takes to endure one's lot, survive a setback, improve one's fortune, or turn one's life around. But existential potency is equally contingent on one's relationships with others, and on what the world affords one as opportunity or possibility. These entwined motifs of internal and external potentialities are central to Kuranko notions of well-being. Empowerment comes from a combination of innate giftedness, acquired social skills, inherited status, luck, ancestral favor, and powerful connections. Although money, migration, education, and development are now fetishized as avenues to well-being, a viable life depends on commanding as many resources as one can legitimately locate and exploit. It is not that God, the ancestors, and djinn have ceased to be sources of earthly well-being; rather, that blessedness now depends on other factors as well—

though the same reasoning governs attitudes to the new as to the old. Just as sheep, goats, cows, rice flour, and kola are ritually given to the ancestors and to God, so now, in the new churches, money is prayed over, blessed, and purified in the hope that it will, once given, pay dividends or protect the giver from predatory strangers. However, occult economies do not generate wealth. They magically redistribute what already exists. This is why the gains from occult practices are always mixed blessings. One person's windfall entails another person's loss. And those who are blessed must pay a price for any improvement in their fortunes—the death of a loved one, the alienation of close kin, or the loss of the lifeworld that shaped their identity.

Strings Attached

SPINNING, WEAVING, BINDING, THREADING, braiding, and knotting are not only some of humanity's oldest techniques; they are among its oldest metaphors. In societies throughout the world, human relationships—including relationships with gods and spirits, with material possessions, and with abstract ideas such as history, society, fate, and destiny—are conceived of as bonds, ties, or strings, while wider fields of relationship are compared to networks, webs, and skeins, or the warp and woof of woven cloth. Even anthropologists have had recourse to such images in their analyses of social relations. One reason for the ubiquity of these images may be that spinning and weaving are closely associated with clothing, which is itself a core metaphor for social being, as in the cognate terms "costume" and "custom." That these same metaphors are commonly used of luck or fate also suggests an intimate link between a person's destiny and his or her primary relationships with parents and close kin, a link that begins with the umbilical cord, through which nutrients flow from the mother to the fetus, and which continues as a symbolic "tie" or attachment after the cord is "tied" and severed after a birth.[1] Among the Yaka of southwest Congo, the person "is seen as a knot of kinship relations."[2] Becoming a person (*wuka muutu*) involves "tying together or interweaving" the various forms of exchange that transmit life, emotions, energies, and knowledge among agnatic and uterine kin, as well as between the living and the dead, human beings and nature spirits, people and nature.[3] Among the Kuranko, a person's most immediate social field is compared to the network of ropes that is placed over a rice farm when the crop is nearing maturity. One end of the main rope is tethered to the foot of a high platform on which children sit with slingshots to scare birds away from the ripening grain. When this rope is tugged, the tributary strands shake, frightening the scavenging birds away. So it is said that "one's birth is like the bird-scaring rope" (*soron i le ko yagba-*

yile), or "one's birth is like a chain" (*soron i la ko yolke*) since one's fate is inextricably tied to the fate of others. Alluding to kinship relations, it is said that the main rope is the father, its extension is the mother, and the children are the secondary strands. Kuranko also share a well-nigh universal belief that kinship, fate, spells, curses, and duty are binding. Such bonds often derive from one's birth. They are in the nature of things. They cannot be revoked. "One's duty (*wale* also means "work") is "that which you have to do"—the actions and obligations that are alleged to follow naturally from being male or female, chief or commoner, father or mother, firstborn or last born, and so on. But while Kuranko invoke the notion of innate essences to explain why certain roles are binding and inescapable, classical Indo-European thought takes the notion of human bonds more literally. In Homer, for instance, fortune is "a cord or bond fastened upon a man by the powers above."[4] At birth the gods or fates spin the strands of weal or woe that a man must endure in the course of his life as invisible threads.[5] And man is bound to die. Comparable images appear in Norse mythology, where the gods are called "the Binders" and the Norns spin, weave, and bind the fates of men at birth.[6] For the Anglo-Saxons, too, fate was woven, while pain, age, and affliction were spoken of as bonds.[7] Yet in all human societies we find a dramatic contrast between necessity,[8] conceived of as that which a person is bound to do or that which is bound to happen, and freedom, construed as the possibility of loosening, unbinding or escaping the constraints placed upon a person by virtue of his or her birth and situation. Intersubjectivity is vexed and unstable—a matter of both bonds and double-binds, of fulfillment and frustration— a point that Kaimah had driven home in his conversations with me. Even hospitality comes with strings attached, and promises may be broken. Indeed, to break a promise and disappoint a friend is compared to the way beads fall from a broken string—*baiya*, referring both to the threaded beads that girls wear around their waists and to a compact or promise. Kuranko also liken human relationships to paths (sing. *kile*), so that the give and take of everyday social life is said to open paths between people, ensuring that these paths do not die (*kile ka na faga*). But relationships are often strained, in which case "the path between is not good" (*kile nyuma san tema*). Of a person who betrays a friend, it is said, "he did not walk on the good path with his friend" (*a ma kile nyuma tama a bo ma*). To extend this metaphor, one might say that paths are never made by a single crossing of a field; they are gradually worn into the ground by the traffic of human interactions over time — visiting, greeting, exchanging, commiserating, cooperating, helping, *but also feuding, refusing help, and failing in one's duty.* For even a breakdown of communication, a loss of contact, a violation of trust, and an absence of love are elements in human bonding, as Aristotle reminds us, citing Heraclitus's adages that "it is what opposes that helps" and "from different tones comes the fairest tune" and "all things are produced through strife."[9]

"WHAT IS THE WORST SITUATION you could imagine?" I would sometimes ask my Kuranko informants. To be alone, they would answer. To be cut off from family and friends. To die without issue. To be nursed when you are ill by people you do not know. To be at the mercy of strangers in a strange land. Social death and the radical disruption of social bonds seemed more awful to contemplate than one's own physical annihilation. Reflecting on his fourteen months' solitary confinement as a political detainee in 1974–75, my friend S. B. Marah once told me that the worst of it wasn't the physical deprivations he endured—the unpalatable food, the polluted water, the threat of execution. It was "not being with my family, not seeing my children." In his idle hours S.B. would close his eyes and imagine running through the streets of Freetown, "running in my mind's eye, going home to my wife and my children." Or he would sing Kuranko songs quietly to himself, telling his mother to pray for him, assuring her that he was bearing his hardship as his father had borne his. He would not disappoint his forebears. Despite his isolation, increasing ill health, and almost no contact with his fellow detainees or the outside world, he would not yield. In Kuranko villages, people would speak in a similar vein, of the horror of being estranged or cut off from kith and kin. Even though neighborliness was not always "sweet" and families were often riven by competitiveness and ill will, conviviality remained the ultimate good. To be healthy and to live long were desirable, to be sure, but what good were health and wealth if you had no one to share these things with? Both the pain and wonder of life lay in the systole and diastole of intersubjectivity, for no matter how difficult social life was — with its mismatched and messy relationships, its conflicting agendas, divided loyalties, betrayals, and miscommunications — it alone could provide that sense of fulfillment that comes from being more than merely oneself, of being a part of a greater whole.

I HAVE DESCRIBED ELSEWHERE my experiences of returning to Sierra Leone in January 2002 as the decade-long civil war was coming to an end, and my conversations, in the Murraytown ampu- tees camp in Freetown, with a young Kuranko woman from Kon- dembaia who had, like her six-year-old daughter Damba, suffered the amputation of her hand and lower arm during a rebel attack on their village three and a half years before.[10]

In the course of our conversations, Fina Kamara told me that Damba had been taken to the United States, ostensibly for specialist medical treatment. But Fina had no idea if or when Damba would return to Sierra Leone. All she knew was that eight to twelve chil- dren had been taken from the Murraytown camp, and that the man who organized their trip to America went by the name of Uncle Joe.

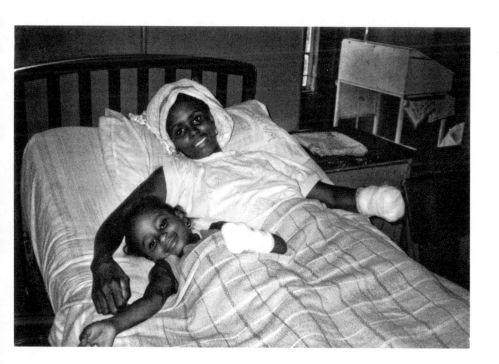

After two years of inquiries, during which I wondered how this unidentified agency had justified such a prolonged separation of mother and daughter, I discovered that the child amputees, including Damba, had been flown to New York by a nonprofit organization called Friends of Sierra Leone.[11] Its "Gift of Limbs" project had been cosponsored by the Rotary Club of New York, and its purpose was to fit the amputees with prosthetic limbs and provide physical therapy. Damba, I discovered, was subsequently placed in the care of an expatriate Sierra Leonean family living in Virginia.

Between 2002 and 2003, Damba's "guardian," Amina Jah, phoned Fina on three occasions, twice sending $200 money grams to help her with medical expenses. Damba also phoned, saying she missed her mother and could not wait to see her again.

As baffled by the events that had led to the loss of her only daughter as by the unspeakable events that had reduced her to the status of a refugee, Fina nonetheless accepted that her daughter would have opportunities in the United States that she would never have at home. Her only hope was that the Jah family would not change Damba's last name, and that Damba would return to Sierra Leone and meet her real family.

Fina's rationalizations reflected the widespread West African custom of fostering—placing one's child in the care of kinsmen in order to give the child a better life (especially through schooling), "loaning" a child to a needy or childless couple, apprenticing a child to a Qu'ranic teacher, or even "pledging" a child to work off a debt.[12] The radical departure from traditional practice in Fina's case was that Damba had not been freely given but taken and kept without full disclosure. I had the impression that Fina's separation from Damba was like another amputation. The phantom pain from her severed hand was now compounded by the loss of her daughter.

In mid-2003, Fina Kamara moved from Freetown to an amputees camp in Kabala so she could be closer to her home village and extended family. When I passed through Kabala in January 2008, I wanted to visit Fina, to see how she was faring and to ask after Damba, but time ran out and it was not until I was back in the United States that I learned, through Kaimah's mediation, what had happened to Fina since we last met in Freetown in January 2002. I e-mailed Kaimah, giving him guidelines and questions for an interview I wanted him to conduct with Fina Kamara in the Number

Three Amputees Camp in Kabala. The following passages contain transcribed portions of this interview, which Kaimah conducted in Krio.

Kaimah began by asking Fina if she was well.

"I am alive, thank God, though I still feel pain in my arm and my health is poor. It is very hard for me, and I have difficulty taking care of my children."

"How many children do you have now?"

"Magba, my firstborn, is in the Ahamadiyya Secondary School. He is in form three. Abdulai and Kunnah both attend the Ansaru Primary School. Abdulai is in class five and Kunnah is in class one."

"How do you manage to pay their fees?"

"The NarSarah clinic pays Magba's fees.[13] I pay for the other children."

"And Ferenke, is he there?"

"Yes, but he is still too young to attend school."

"What about your husband, is he there?"

"He is in Kondembaia. But he is old. He used to farm, but now he is unable to work. He lives with his other wives. I have to be father and mother to our children. I barely survive. The government provides shelter for us, nothing more. We depend on those who come to our rescue. It is really hard. My left hand is gone, so I cannot do farm work. I do a little soap making and *gara* dying. And I took out a micro-loan from the NarSarah clinic for 68,000 leones [$25]. I used the money to pay other farmers to clear a farm for me, so I could plant groundnuts, peppers, onions, and rice. But the interest after six months will be 1,500 leones [$5], and this will be hard for me to pay."

After a long pause, during which Kaimah switched off his tape recorder and gave Fina the money I had sent her, Kaimah inquired about Damba.

It seemed that when Fina left Freetown in the rainy season of 2003 she lost all contact with Damba and her "guardians" in Alexandria, Virginia.

"Was this because you had no way of communicating?"

"I had no cell phone, then. They could not call me, and I could not call them."

In 2006, Fina was invited to the United States, all expenses paid, for a reunion with Damba on the *Oprah Winfrey Show*. It took the show's producers four months to locate Fina, secure a visa for her (in Guinea), and make the necessary travel arrangements. It was an extraordinary story, and it was not until I had done some research on the Internet that I fully understood what had happened.

In 2006, Damba was fourteen and attending the Francis C. Hammond Middle School in Alexandria, Virginia. She sang alto in the choir, acted in school plays and excelled in her academic work. She was also an anchor on the school's daily newscast. But she had never explained to her classmates why her left arm was missing. One morning she aired a video of herself in which she recounted the story of how rebels invaded Kondembaia in August 1998 and her "peaceful and normal life" came to an end. Men, women, and children were rounded up and made to stand beneath the two great cotton trees in the center of the village. Even though she was a six-year-old child, Damba was one of those selected to pay the price for those who had, in the rebels' view, recently voted into power a government that had vowed to destroy to them. She was forced to the ground and her arm pinioned to the root of one of the cotton trees. "I could not hold the fear in me," she said. "I was cold and terrified. I felt a sharp pain running through my entire body. I was overwhelmed, and my whole body was shaking. When my mother asked if she could pick me up and tie my bleeding arm, the same rebel who had cut off my arm ordered her to lay by me, and he cut off my mother's left arm."

A school friend sent Damba's video to Oprah Winfrey, and in October 2006 Damba was invited to travel to Chicago and appear on Oprah's show. Oprah had told Damba that she was going to help her "dream come true," and Damba assumed this meant she would be going back to Sierra Leone to see her mother. Instead, Fina was brought to America and on November 7, when the show aired, Damba found herself reunited with her mother and holding her baby brother Ferenke in her arms in front of a television audience of several million. Damba was in tears, unable to find words for the happiness she felt. As for Fina Kamara, she thanked Oprah, Oprah's mother, and the Jah family, and expressed through an interpreter her appreciation and joy.

IT IS IN THE NATURE of media spectacles, as it is in the nature of stories, to conjure the illusion of moral closure. And there is always a heroic agent or supernatural helper, like Oprah, who effects the closure, and whose benevolent power makes possible the reunion, the happy ending, the miracle. But such stage-managed moments of truth may easily blind us to the vexed world in which we actually live, and to which we return when the story has been told, the carnival over, and the spectacle done.

"So much happened to me in America," Fina said. "People were so friendly when they found out that I was Damba's mother. I was so happy when I met my only daughter again. Now I am praying that with the help of God, my other children will go to America too. My husband is too old to take care of them, and I believe that if my sons go to America all my difficulties, stress, and poverty will be over."

"But would you want to live in America?"

"I worried a lot when I was there, because my children were back here. There was no one to take care of them in my absence. That is why I wanted to come back as soon as I could."

"Do you know who Oprah Winfrey is?"

"She is a South African lady who took pity on Damba. She arranged for me to travel to America to meet Damba. Damba cannot travel to Sierra Leone because she has no Green Card. That is why I had to go there."

"Did Oprah offer you any help with your children's education, or with your health problems?"

"She paid for my trip, that was all. I hoped someone would help me, but no one did."

I could not help but think that had Oprah funded a visit home for Damba, far more might have been accomplished than this brief reunion between mother and daughter before an audience of strangers. Damba could have spent time with all her siblings and restored a sense of continuity with her natal community.

"Where did you stay in America?" Kaimah asked.

"Amina Jah and her husband took care of me throughout my one-month stay. On Sundays they took me to their church to pray. I visited Damba's school, and her friends and neighbors."

"Are the Jahs from Sierra Leone?"

"Yes. Amina Jah is Kono, her husband is a Kissy man."

OPRAH IS LIKE A STORYTELLER. In the theatrical arena of her show, she conjures a vision of life as deeply troubled yet ultimately open to renewal and resolution. Our efforts pay off. Virtue is rewarded. Adversity is overcome through confession, contrition, and compassion. The official Oprah website posted a report on the show in which Fina appeared. It was titled "A mother's love." On the show, Oprah had told Damba, "You have an amazing mother. If all the mothers in the world were like your mother, this would be a different kind of world. We are honored to have you here." The implication was that a mother's moral duty was to sacrifice her own happiness for her daughter's well-being, and since well-being was synonymous with achieving the American dream, Fina had made the right decision in giving Damba a chance of a life in the United States.

Sometimes we forget that the passage to modernity through education, money, and mobility is, despite appearances, often accompanied by grief and guilt. This gap between the simplicity of our idealizations and the complexity of our lived situations is the subject of one of Guy de Maupassant's most troubling stories.

"The Adopted Son" begins like a folktale: two peasant families live in neighboring cottages near a seaside resort, the parents struggling to make ends meet, the children of each family nonetheless happy. One hot August afternoon a carriage stops in front of one of the cottages, and a well-born and wealthy young woman steps down to admire the peasant children playing in the road. Madame Henri d'Hubières, who is childless, becomes attached to the only son of the Tuvaches, and after several weeks of visiting the family she offers to adopt him. Monsieur d'Hubières draws up a contract to cover all eventualities. If the boy turns out well, he will in time inherit the d'Hubières estate. In any event, he will receive a handsome sum when he comes of age and his parents will be paid a pension of 100 francs a month until their death. However, the boy's parents are outraged by this suggestion and refuse to give up their son for adoption. Madame d'Hubières then asks after the other boy who she had observed playing with Charlot and assumed to be his brother. On being told that this boy belonged to the Vallins family who lived next door, the d'Hubières took their proposition to the Vallins, who, after some haggling, accepted it. The Vallins were now able to live comfortably on their pension, while the Tuvaches, though miserably poor, consoled themselves with the thought that they had done the right thing in not selling their child. Years passed, and one day a brilliant carriage stopped again outside the peasant cottages. The young man who stepped down from the carriage was Jean Vallin, now twenty-one. Entering the Vallins' house, he greeted his astonished parents who, later that day, proudly introduced their successful son to the local mayor, deputy, cure, and schoolmaster. Faced with the good fortune of his erstwhile friend, Charlot Tuvaches reproached his parents for stupidly refusing to give him the opportunity that the Vallins had given Jean. "See what I should have been by now," he said. And he declared that he would never forgive his parents for depriving him of his one chance of happiness. On the night he walked out on his parents, he heard the sounds of celebration from the neighboring cottage. The Vallins were celebrating the return of their son.

THIS CONFLICT BETWEEN the bonds and obligations of kinship, traditionally conceived, and the freedom to embrace a life beyond the world into which one is born entails several moral quandaries. How, for example, can one fulfill one's filial obligations without compromising one's own ambitions, if to remain in one's natal village may doom one to the same poverty that oppressed one's parents, and caring for them in their dotage may mean the abandonment of one's own dreams of improving one's lot? And how can a migrant reconcile the material gains he makes in his own life with the abandonment of his ancestral world and possible estrangement from kith and kin? Through remittances alone? And how can one decide the good, when local and global worlds seem so mutually antithetical, and the tug of tradition comes into conflict with the allure of modernity?

School fees for Fina's eldest son, Magba, were paid by the Nar-Sarah clinic. This clinic was established in Kabala in 2002 by a Kuranko expatriate, Dorcas Kamanda, and her husband Dan. Born into a family of twenty-six, Dorcas converted to Christianity in the late 1960s and moved to Colorado to study for a nursing degree under the auspices of the United Methodist Church. She recalls her Sierra Leonean childhood as a happy time. "We were hungry but we were happy. Everybody took care of you. Everybody was your mother or father. It was simply life as we knew it [and] any missing creature comfort that we have become accustomed to in modern America was more than replaced by the undying support of family members and fellow villagers, each of whom did their share to make life just that much more comfortable. We were really, really happy."

Dorcas speaks in equally glowing terms of her American life, her conversion to Christianity, and her commitment to a mini-medical and spiritual revolution in Sierra Leone. In the words of the NarSarah project, Dorcas is committed to "funding materials and personnel in areas such as prayer and worship, health, education, agriculture, transport and communications." But the irony is that utopia (*ou-topos*) is literally nowhere. And while the vision of a perfect world or a better place—whether in the distant past or the near future—helps us explain and escape our present reality, it remains a state of mind—a "heaven," in Dylan Thomas's words, "that never was nor will be ever" yet is "always true."[14] In reality, life must always be lived within limits, and the difference between traditional and modern societies is simply a difference between the kinds of limits that people struggle against. If poverty, disease, and limited educational or employment opportunities define the limits in Sierra Leone, spiritual impoverishment, loveless marriages, stress, loneliness, and the struggle to lose weight are the things we struggle with most in the United States, at least in Oprah's worldview. Still, there are some limits that hold true for all human beings, such as the difficulty of reconciling the ontological security that comes from the bond between mother and child with the inevitable separation from home that initiates the beginning of our own adulthood. This difficult transition from attachment to autonomy constitutes the Oedipal project—the eternal struggle of the young to come into their own, frequently against the criticisms, constraints, and dictates of the old. In my view, this is the same struggle that is entailed in the passage from tradition to modernity, which is why every migrant, leaving home to make his or her way in the wider world, is Everyman, and why the attainment of new life inevitably means the severing of primary bonds, a departure from a natal place, and the symbolic death of the old.

WHEN I FIRST MET FINA KAMARA, I saw only her tragedy—her autonomy lost because of the loss of a limb, her life overshadowed by the loss of her only daughter. But I now ask whether it is not the destiny of a parent to sacrifice her own well-being for the well-being of her child, even at the risk of her own welfare—as Fina did, attempting to rescue her mutilated daughter from the bloody machetes of the RUF boys. Is it not imperative that one give up one's own emotional claim on one's offspring in order that they flourish in the world, just as it is in the nature of every young life to break free from primary bonds and constrictive roots so that it may branch out, reach up, and find the sun? The choice between attachment and separation is never easy. Intimate bonds are as basic to our security as they are potentially inimical to our autonomy. And while separation is inevitable, it entails losses we may mourn forever. When Kaimah asked Fina Kamara to describe the hardest thing in her life, she replied, "It is the pain of losing my arm, of being unable to farm and provide for my children. It is the pain of struggling to improve their chances in life, to get them an education, so they can help me and their father who is old and almost blind." But like any good parent, Fina Kamara readily admits that her children's happiness matters more than her own. As for Damba, she describes the moment she left for America as "terrifying." "I was crying and my mom was crying. She had to let me go because she knew I'd get a better life." But will Damba ever lament the life she may never have in Sierra Leone, the extended family she may never know, the natal village to which she may never return? These are questions that an anthropologist cannot answer, because culture never completely determines such matters and each individual, at different times in his or her life, will construe such existential dilemmas differently. Thus, while I sometimes rue the partial eclipse of my ties with my natal New Zealand, I am aware that in escaping the confines of a provincial upbringing I truly came into my own.

Still, the movement from a local to a global world, or from tradition to modernity, is as fraught as the journey of life itself. There are always losses as well as gains, and it is never possible to decide in retrospect which of our decisions, or our parents' decisions, were for the best. Rather than strive to do the maximum good, I prefer the Hippocratic principle of doing the least harm, and hold to the existential tenet that every human being needs to have some hand in deciding his or her own destiny. This is why I remain troubled about the events that overwhelmed Fina Kamara's life, leaving her no option but to go along with the decisions of others. And why I find in her story uncanny echoes of a story that broke in late October

2007 when a group of seventeen European "charity workers" were arrested in Chad and charged with the attempted kidnapping of 103 local children.

According to parents and relatives of many of these children, the charity workers had visited villages in the Chad-Sudan border region, offering free schooling in the nearby town of Abeche. Marc Garmirian, a journalist traveling with the Zoe's Ark group at the time of their arrest, felt that the charity workers' judgment had been "clouded by idealistic zeal." "What struck me was their state of mind," he told a BBC reporter, "their conviction. They were sure they were doing good and had a mission to carry out." Indeed, one is struck, in remarks by one of the French detainees, by a total insensitivity to the wishes of the children (who believed their departure from home would only be temporary), not to mention the rights of the children's parents and relatives, many of whom traveled long distances to Abeche after hearing of the alleged abductions

Responding to a BBC journalist who asked Christine Peligat to explain the motives of Zoe's Ark, Peligat said that the team was "rescuing children from Sudan's Darfur region. And the only thing they wanted [was] to give these children a better life. That's it. This is the only aim of this operation."

"But what were they going to do with the children?" the journalist asked. "They were going to take them back to France?"

"Yes, and find some families so that they can have these children. It was not like some people have said, that we were like an organization for adoption. That's not true. All we wanted was to save the children. There was no trafficking. We are not child traffickers."

A few days after the story broke in Europe, the BBC news service initiated an Internet debate, asking, "Would you ever give up your child in hope of a better life?"

Some respondents, imagining a life-threatening situation, said they would do anything to keep their child from mortal danger, even if this meant losing their child. Others were critical of the assumption that Europe was necessarily a better place to bring up one's children than Africa. Others spoke of the need to help Africa look after its own, rather than assume that the continent was a place of ignorance and savagery from which children had to be rescued. Still others made a case against adoption, arguing that the bond with one's biological parents is more important than anything else in life—educational opportunities, medical care, physical comfort. As I read through these various responses, many of them from people who had themselves been stolen or adopted as children in order to receive "a better life," I was reminded of Kuranko dilemma tales that sharpen one's awareness of life's aporias and suggest that accepting them may be preferable to the illusions of moral closure and intellectual certainty to which so many of us cling.

The Shape of the
Inconstruable Question

A COUPLE OF DAYS AFTER getting back to Freetown, Sewa drove me to Hill Station to visit Rose Marah. When last I saw Rose, she and her husband S.B. were living in P. K. Lodge, a large ministerial residence overlooking the city. But since S.B.'s death in 2003, Rose had withdrawn from the world, resisting even her children's plans and pleas that she visit them in London and spend time with her grandchildren. I found it difficult to understand Rose's reclusion, and my brief long-distance phone conversations with her had given me little insight into why, four years after S.B.'s death, she was still so consumed by grief. For I had fully expected her to return to her dressmaking business, or enthusiastically embrace the activities that she had long insisted S.B. had forbidden — traveling, seeing her friends, visiting her family, earning her own income.

We found the house without too much difficulty, a newish bungalow on an eroded dirt road that descended steeply into a gully. The house was half-hidden by exotic plants with large mottled leaves, the porch shaded by flowering bougainvillea. At the wrought iron gate I told Joshua to look back across the valley. I wanted him to see the recently completed American embassy — an immense white concrete building, resembling a fortress, within a perimeter wall. The hillside around the compound had been bulldozed clear of vegetation, and behind the embassy, on a high peak, stood a phalanx of communications towers.

The elaborate surveillance and security that protected the embassy was a reminder that human well-being is always a compromise between enclosure and openness. As Kuranko see it, the protection of one's body, one's house, the space of the village and the chiefdom with magical medicines (*kandan li fannu*, lit. "enclosing things") is, ironically, counterpointed with a moral ideal of personhood (*morgoye*) that emphasizes openness, transparency, and generosity in one's relations to the others.

It took some time after I knocked on the door before the man of the house appeared. I explained that I was an old friend of Rose's and of her late husband, S. B. Marah. Was Rose in?

"She dae," he said, but with such a pained expression on his face that I wondered whether I was intruding.

"Would it be all right if I saw Rose?" I asked.

"Waittin na you name?"

After I had identified myself, he asked me to wait, then closed the door.

And so we waited, Joshua, Sewa, and I, sitting on the balustrade, speculating on why the American embassy should be so large, and what might justify such a massive presence in a small West African country.

Ten minutes passed before the man opened the door again and asked us in. In the parlor, he invited us to sit, then slumped in a chair well away from us with an open hand shielding his eyes.

Several minutes passed before Rose appeared. She floated out of the shadows, smiling and welcoming, and we embraced. Referring to Sewa as "Small S.B." and as "my husband," she explained to her "friend" that Sewa had worked for S.B. as a driver and general factotum. She greeted Joshua as though he were her long-lost son.

I was both moved and troubled. Her face was swollen as though she had been weeping. Her perfume did not disguise the alcohol on her breath. And her words were slurred, her manner overly effusive. It was painfully clear why she had kept us waiting so long.

THAT NIGHT, WHEN WE HAD RETURNED to our hotel, I tried to tell Joshua something of Rose's story. I wanted him to understand her unhappiness, even as I was struggling to understand it myself.

As long ago as 1985, Rose had confided to me some of the tribulations of her marriage. I was in Freetown at the time, staying with Rose after a few miserable weeks up-country, still in a state of shock after Pauline's death two years before. Perhaps this was the reason why Rose presumed such intimacy—that, and the fact that S.B. was in Zimbabwe at a parliamentary conference.

We were sitting in the parlor, the daylight fading.

"The children must miss S.B. when he goes away," I said.

"I think it is a relief," she said.

"For you or the kids?"

Rose laughed. "It's not so bad, Michael. When S.B. isn't here I get to see my own friends for a change."

"You mean you don't see them when he is here?"

"I haven't even been home since I married S.B."

I must have looked incredulous.

"I was born in Bonthe," Rose said. "In 1945. I married S.B. in 1966. I was actually in form two when we first met. My parents were both dead and I was living with my aunt and older sister, Pat. S.B. said he intended to make me his wife, and he began to give gifts to my aunt so that she would approve the match. When Pat found out what was going on she was furious. She removed all my things from the house, told my aunt not to take them back inside, and took me to Freetown, where I completed my secondary schooling. I met S.B. again in 1966, a year after I left school. I was twenty-one at the time, and wanted to go overseas and study to be a pediatrician. In the meantime I was working in the prime minister's office with Pat. Pat was still dead set against the marriage. She pointed out that S.B. had been married twice already and that one of his wives had left him, and, besides, we were from a Christian family and therefore had very different backgrounds."

"But that hasn't stood in the way . . ." I said.

"No, but it has added to the difficulties."

I was not altogether comfortable listening to Rose's grievances. In marriage, as in all things, there are always two sides to any story. But Rose was persistent. It wasn't that she wanted to undermine my friendship with S.B., she said. It was a matter of trust. And she launched into an exasperated account of Sierra Leonean men.

"My sister's husband is on trial for stealing money from his firm. Years ago he was an accountant for the Aureol Tobacco Company, but he was sacked with several other men for embezzlement. After fifteen years out of work he was given a second chance. But he spoiled it. Now he is out of work again. But he never lifts a finger to help my sister. Never shows any interest in the kids. And it is my sister [a teacher] who earns the money and keeps the family together."

Rose then mentioned another man, a lecturer at Fourah Bay College. Someone I knew.

"Do you know, he keeps all the family food, the palm oil, the tomato paste, everything, in the boot of his car! He doesn't give his wife any money to spend. But now she's finishing an MA in education and happy with her independence. If she had stayed with him, what would have happened? Waiting up every night for him to get home. Wondering what affairs he was having."

I was aware that Rose was not regaling me with these anecdotes because of their ethnographic value. This was her indirect if not altogether discrete way of letting me know how she felt about her own situation.

We sat in silence for a while. And then, as if we had passed a point of no return, Rose suddenly declared that S.B. had taken a second wife, and that they had two children.

I was taken aback. I wasn't sure I wanted to hear this. But Rose wanted me to know everything.

"A few years ago I had a call from a friend who nurses at the Jalloh Hospital. Something had confused her. S.B. had turned up with a Mrs. Marah who had gone into labor. My friend knew I wasn't pregnant, so she rang the house to find out what was wrong. She was surprised when I answered the phone. How could I be here and there at the same time? Then she told me about this second Mrs. Marah. The awful thing was, it wasn't even her first child with S.B. She had already borne him a daughter. He had built them a house somewhere up-country."

I muttered something about what a shock this must have been.

"At first he denied it. Pat wanted me to take him to court on a bigamy charge. Finally I confronted him! Do you know what he said? He said 'I am not a white man. I am a Kuranko man.' As if this explained and justified everything."

Suddenly, the shadow passed from her face, and she smiled. "It's all right, Michael. I've got used to the arrangement now. We African wives always do!"

In 2002, little had changed. Rose and S.B. were still at loggerheads, exchanging few words, going their separate ways, sleeping in separate rooms, and S.B.'s occasional show of affection or words of praise were meant to impress me, not Rose. Indeed, the tension in P. K. Lodge had been the reason S.B. had put me up in the Cape Sierra Hotel during the weeks we worked on his biography, not wanting me to observe his "tricks and bullying," as Rose put it. Their marriage was now "a marriage in name only." The love and trust that had once existed between them had been killed when S.B. began his affair with Lois, favoring her children over Rose's. And even though Rose had committed herself wholeheartedly to caring for Lois's children during the war when she and S.B. were exiled in Conakry, she was bitter and unforgiving. Loyal and faithful for so long, she felt betrayed. "I am afraid of him. I would like to start up my dressmaking business again but I cannot bring myself to ask him if the lease on my shop has expired or could be renewed. He does not want me to leave the house. He insists I stay home with the children. 'Who will cook and take care of the house if I am not there?'"

S.B. was not so much jealous of his wife's affairs but concerned for his political reputation should she be seen in public with other men. But what did I care? I was finding it impossible to accommodate Rose's and S.B.'s different versions of the story of their life, with S.B. telling me not to trust anything Rose told me, and Rose telling me not to set any store by S.B.'s accounts.

One morning we were in the kitchen. Rose was preparing a meal of dried fish, cassava leaf, and chili sauce for me and complaining about S.B.'s temper, which had driven the hired cook from the house only days before. "I have to work like this every day, now," she said. "Like a slave. Preparing food for the security guards, the houseboys, and for S.B. I look forward to the afternoon, when I can go to my room and do some sewing. To get away from the mess. The house is like a storeroom. Bags of rice everywhere. Sacks of onions. Tables covered with his papers and medicines which I am not allowed to clear away. But you know, Michael, the hardest thing to bear is his criticisms of our sons in London. He thinks they are useless."

Rose spoke of Abu, their eldest. At school he had displayed a talent for soccer. "He used to play with Mohamed Kallon," Rose said, "and Mohamed is now a professional player and a billionaire. If S.B. had taken seriously the word of a scout many years ago who saw Abu's talent and wanted to take him to Côte d'Ivoire for training, Abu would be now as successful as Mohamed Kallon. But S.B. didn't want to let his eldest son go, didn't want to lose him."

I thought, *Just as S.B.'s father, a generation ago, did not want his eldest son Kulifa to continue his education, wanting him to keep the home fires burning in Firawa.*

"You don't get another chance in life," Rose said. "That was Abu's chance. He missed it, and now he's too old. Even though he plays nonprofessional football for a team in London. As for getting a house in London, when S.B. was minister of energy and power, I asked Tony Yazbeck to help S.B. buy a house in London. Tony agreed to put up three quarters of the money. S.B. said he didn't have the remaining amount, so we lost this opportunity. Recently, Abu went all out to find a house in London we could buy, and sent details to S.B. S.B. finally agreed to send twenty thousand pounds for the deposit. But he sent it to his daughter Fatmata [from his first marriage] and the money never reached Abu or our other children. Fatmata could not be reached. Only an answering machine message. S.B. never broached with her the question of this money. Had Fatamata sent it to her mother in America as her benefit for the years she had spent married to S.B., working for him? So you see, Michael. Yet another item to add to the list of S.B.'s bad decisions that will one day have fatal consequences. Like the security guards at the gate. We should have four, but there is often only one because of the way S.B. abuses them all the time."

I suppose I was witnessing in Rose's unflagging critiques of S.B. not only a marriage that had succumbed to external pressure and internal decay, as many marriages do, but an unresolvable conflict between two very different worldviews. In this sense, it presaged the kind of conflict I had seen emerging among young women in Firawa, desiring love, education, and freedom of choice in a world that still adhered to traditional notions of hierarchy and duty. And where the young were impatient with waiting and with keeping faith with old ideas of deferred gratification and delayed rewards, the old adhered to the ancient virtues of stoicism, patience, and forbearance.

Quite early on in my first fieldwork, I had become familiar with two crucial Kuranko concepts—that of duty (*wale*) and that of blessings (*duwe*). One's duty is "that which you have to do"—the actions, obligations, and demeanor that come with one's role as a chief, a praise-singer, a wife, a farmer, or whatever. This is why *wale* is also work—the work one does in order to enact one's role, uphold custom, and play one's part in the order of things. A common phrase, used in greeting a person and in acknowledging a gift, approving words well spoken, or behavior that conforms to the ideal, is i n *wale* (lit. "you and work," meaning you are doing the right thing by your forebears, you are doing the right thing by your wife, husband, brothers, subjects, etc.). But while *wale* emphasizes a person's agency—his savoir-faire, his social *nous*, his personal conduct—

the notion of *duwe* denotes the *outcome* of working well, which is *baraka*, the state of being blessed. Thus, the exemplary conduct of a paternal ancestor bestows good fortune, or blessings, on his descendants. However, these blessings come to a person through his or her mother. If she is a hard-working, and a faithful and dutiful wife to her husband, then her children will receive the blessings of their patrilineal forebears, and become *duwe dannu* (blessed children). If she fails in her duty by being lazy, unfaithful, or disobedient, the path along which the patrilineal blessings flow will become blocked, and her children will be cursed. This is why Kuranko say, "A man has many children; a woman bears them; a man's children are in her hands" (*Ke l dan sia; musu don den; ke l den wo bolo*) and observe that you (i.e., your destiny) is in your mother's hands (*i i na le bolo*) or that the book your mother wrote is what you are reading now (*i na l kedi sebene, i wole karantine kedi*) — which is to say that one's actions and disposition are direct reflections of one's mother's actions and disposition. *Fe-é wa serine ne-é n'serine dan ti serine* (if the father brays and the mother also brays, their child will never bray) — meaning that if a wife is always challenging her husband's authority in public, the child of this marriage will never amount to very much.

Ideally, there is a complementarity between work and blessings. A person who is blessed is disposed to work hard and do his or her duty. A person who works hard and does his or her duty brings blessings to his or her family. But in practice people may give very different existential emphases to these cultural ideas. For instance, birth does not necessarily decide a person's worth, as Keti Ferenke Koroma explained to me many years ago by punning on the word *kina*, which, depending on a subtle inflection, can mean either beehive or elder. His argument was that someone who is nominally elder could forfeit the right to be considered superior if he behaved unjustly or stupidly. A person might be designated an elder, he said, but if he acted like a child he was a child. Superiority, he observed, derived not only from being born first, or from being big and powerful; it also stemmed from one's social *nous*, one's moral courage, or one's cleverness. Not surprisingly, Keti Ferenke was a brilliant storyteller and marvelous informant, but not the firstborn of the firstborn! A second example, again drawn from my earlier Kuranko ethnography, is equally telling. Kuranko traditional medicine is conventionally divided into three categories — curative, prophylactic and protective, and lethal. In the course of his apprenticeship, any medicine-master (*besetigi*) becomes adept in all three.[1] But what defines a practitioner's duty or work? Is it to draw on both his curative and lethal powers if public consensus gives him the right to do so? Or is his "duty" partly a question of his own individual judgment? Here, we need to have recourse to both ethnography and biography if we are to understand why a particular medicine-master should decide, as did my key informant Saran Salia Sano, to devote his energy and expertise to protecting the vulnerable and curing the sick rather than selling his services to the envious and aggrieved, or using his powers to prosecute private vendettas through sorcery.

NO ONE CAN HAVE WORKED harder or more dutifully than Rose Marah. And her children had been blessed, their well-being the fruit of her love and (to follow Kuranko reasoning) their patrilineal ancestors' benevolent recognition of her good work. Though she expressed deep misgivings about her marriage, her children and grandchildren "meant the world to her"; she had been blessed. But was this sufficient compensation for what she had given up, all that she had suffered? What of her dalliances? Partly from a desire to get even with her husband, partly to find consolation in physical intimacy for the love she lacked, she undoubtedly found pleasure in acting on her own initiative even if it was clandestine. And I thought of Sira, singing in Firawa of her desire to marry for love. Her desire to control her own destiny.

One can never know how life will turn out. But of one thing I am sure—that the final measure of a life does not consist in whether one has been blessed or cursed; it is a matter of *how* one responds to what befalls one in the course of one's life, the rough as well as the smooth. This is the enduring message of Viktor Frankl's notion of having an "inner hold" on life that enables one to bear one's burden well.[2] For Frankl, well-being has three sources—our work (which in Kuranko is also one's duty), our relations with others, and "the attitude we take toward unavoidable suffering"[3]—an observation that resonates with the Kuranko adage *dunia toge ma dunia; a toge le a dununia*, which, translated literally, means "the name of the world is not world; its name is load."[4]

This emphasis on the way we bear a load or on the attitude we adopt places in parenthesis the question of the moral *quality* of the relationship we are in. To put it another way, it recognizes that relationships are dynamic, not static, and inevitably move between the poles of affection and animosity, attraction and repulsion. Yet most of us adopt a Manichaean view of relationships; they are either good or bad; they work or they do not work. It may be that Rose's failure to get beyond a moral view of her marriage made it impossible for her to mourn its ending. That her ambivalence toward S.B. had not been resolved in life made it difficult to resolve it in death. Not only is it easier to mourn the loss of someone we love than someone we have ceased to love; it is easier to accept loss when we accept the messiness of life than when we expect it to conform to our ideas of order.

Surpassing the positive and negative values we tend to assign to our relationships with others is the sheer force of their existence over time—good times as well as bad, children brought into the world, a war survived, and the everyday routines, both loving and unloving, of living under the same roof. Well-being is, accordingly, more than mere happiness (*eudaimonia*), or even virtue. In the movie *McLintock* (1963), an Arizona rancher called G. W. McLintock (played by John Wayne) is talking to his daughter Becky, who has just returned home after two years at a boarding school in the East. During Becky's time away, G.W. and his wife Katie (Maureen O'Hara) have been living apart, and Becky expresses distress and mystification, believing that her parents have fallen out of love and no longer have any regard for each other. G.W. struggles to explain that his estrangement from Katie has nothing to do with loss of love or respect. He says, "All the gold in the U.S. Treasury and all the harp music in heaven can't equal what happens between a man and a woman with all that growin' together. I can't explain it any better than that."

I think the reason I have never forgotten this corny phrase "all that growin' together" is that, like G.W., I have always been of the opinion that what evolves and emerges in the course of any relationship is not reducible to any script or template—cultural or phylogenetic—and that, moreover, human bonds are not necessarily a function of their quality or even their quotidian viability. This was what Alfred Schutz had in mind when, alluding to the phenomenon of "growing old together," he spoke of the synergy of two time spans or life courses unfolding together, face-to-face, and of the profound effect of our being in and belonging to a single community in space and in time.[5]

Schutz's observation has as much bearing upon kinship as marriage.

In his monumental work on kinship, Lewis Henry Morgan observed that "in considering the elements of consanguinity the existence of marriage between single pairs must be assumed. Marriage forms the basis of relationships."[6] A comparable assertion prefaces Meyer Fortes's account of kinship among the Tallensi. "Every genealogical relationship goes back, eventually, to one pair of parents."[7] The abstract Tallensi verb *dog* means to bear or beget a child; hence the abstract noun *dogam* (kinship) that "describes the process, or the act, or the physiological capacity, of bringing a child into the world, as well as the ties thus created."[8] My own assumption, however, is that no human relationship is simply given—either as a fact of nature or as a cultural ascription; rather, every human relationship has its own history and undergoes many transformations in the course of different encounters, circumstances, and crises over time.

Like most human beings, Kuranko speak of kinship in absolute and abstract terms, as though context were irrelevant. Thus kinship is a matter of being born (*mui*, to give birth; hence *mui nyorgoye*, birth relationship or agnatic kinship), or of feeding at the same breast (*demba*, a nursing mother; hence *dembaiya*, breast-feeding relationship or close kinship), or an expression of the mother-child bond, as is suggested by the most common term for kinship: *nakelinyorgoye*, "mother-one-relationship." All of this echoes the Fulani term *enDam* (kinship or bond), which derives from the word for breast (*endu*) and whose basic meaning is "mother's milk."[9] But, as Paul Riesman observes, despite the fact that the "we-ness" or "oneness" of kinship implies for the Fulani that one's character is imbibed with the mother's milk, kinship amity does not naturally follow and "an enormous effort goes into maintaining those relations in a stable form."[10] Indeed, Riesman goes on to say that the Fulani "are well aware that being a relative is not in fact the automatic result of biological kinship, but *is a way of living with others that involves both hard work and frustration. 'Being together is not easy'* is a phrase that I heard many times during my stay with the Fulani."[11] The Kuranko have a similar phrase—*siginyorgoye ma di*, "neighborliness is not sweet"—and it also prompts us to ask how closely the words for kinship capture the realities of life.

Consider the Kuranko adage: *Dan soron ma gbele, koni a ma kole,* "Bearing a child is not hard; raising a child is." The irony here is that nothing would seem to be more difficult (*gbele* means hard, difficult, problematic) than bringing a child into the world, especially when infant mortality is so high (between 40 percent and 50 percent, birth to three years of age) and many women die in childbirth or suffer from pregnancy-related problems like vesico-vaginal fistula.[12] But the fact remains that the labor of nursing a child through its earliest years, caring for a child through times of famine and illness, protecting a child from the pitfalls of a politically unstable world, and working hard for a hard-hearted or indifferent husband so that one's child is blessed by its patrilineal ancestors amounts to greater hardship than the labor of giving birth. At the same time, the adage implies that while the bond between mother and child *begins* with birth, it is actually born of the intimate interactions and critical events that characterize primary intersubjectivity. In other words, it is the intense protolinguistic relationship between mother and infant, mediated by synchronous movement and affect attunement, including smell, touch, gaze, sympathetic laughter and tears, cradling, lulling embraces, interactive play, and the rhythmic interchanges of motherese that create the "enlarged" and "collaborative" field of consciousness that we construe as a primary bond.[13] To speak of kinship as a "natural" bond, or to invoke images of shared substances—blood (consanguinity), breast milk, semen, placenta, genes—or of common parentage, names, place, and ancestry *seems* to explain the strength of kinship ties. But such figurative language is a way of *retrospectively* and *selectively* acknowledging those experiences of a relationship that have confirmed a moral ideal. This is what William James means when he claims that "truth *happens* to an idea. It *becomes* true, is *made* true by events. Its verity *is* in fact an event, a process; the process of verifying itself."[14]

Does James's view of truth apply to well-being, and if so, how?

In early 2004, Alberto Corsín Jiménez invited me to a conference at the University of Manchester on the topic "Well-Being: Anthropological Perspectives."[15] I declined Alberto's kind invitation because I had never explored this question, never done fieldwork explicitly on this topic, and had, I felt, little to contribute to discussions. But Alberto's proposition that "the concept of well-being has emerged as a key category of social and political thought in recent times, especially in the fields of moral and political philosophy, development studies, and economics," intrigued me, and I found myself returning to it over the next two years.[16]

My starting point was the panoply of surveys that went under such names as "the meaning of life," "happy planet index," "gross national happiness," "subjective life satisfaction," and "world values survey."

The study I examined most closely was the "quality of life survey" published every few years under the direction of Richard Estes, president of the International Society of Quality of Life Studies. In surveys between 1970 and 2003, covering 98 percent of the world's population, Denmark topped the list, while at the bottom came countries like Afghanistan, Ethiopia, Guinea Bissau, and Sierra Leone. Any Sierra Leonean reading the forty-six factors that determined the quality of life rankings—factors that include school enrollments, literacy rates, GNP, civil rights, child immunization, life expectancy, and public debt—might agree that his or her country was relatively impoverished when it came to "social development and progress" but object to the conclusion that his or her life was thereby bereft of quality. He or she might want also to ask why the survey excluded such factors as family, friendship and community ties, or attachment to home.[17] This skepticism would be nothing new to Professor Estes, who has been criticized in one English newspaper (*Times*, 17 September 1986) for placing Denmark at the top of his list when Danes "consume more tranquilizers than any people on earth and have the worst psychiatric problems," and in another (*Daily Telegraph*, 20 September 1986) for ignoring such factors as "the weather, the food and the wine" which also make up "the good life." Clearly there is a problem here of using measurable factors such as "percent arable land mass" or "crude death rate of population over 60 years" to assess immeasurable factors such as happiness or well-being, and it is this that makes the term "quality of life" (QOL) a misnomer. Indeed, a World Economic Forum survey carried out by Gallup International in January 2006 found that people in Europe and the United States were the most pessimistic about the future, while Africa, the "hopeless continent," was home to some of the most optimistic people in the world. Given that so few people in Sierra Leone have paid work or enjoy long lives, why should they be so upbeat? What have they got to celebrate?

For me, the most compelling answer to these questions is given by

James Baldwin, meditating on the history of the Negro in America. For all its horrors, "this past, this endless struggle to achieve and reveal and confirm a human identity" contains "something very beautiful." Though not wanting to romanticize suffering, Baldwin asserts that "people who cannot suffer can never grow up, can never discover who they are," for it is by "continually surviving the worst that life can bring" that "one eventually ceases to be controlled by a fear of what life can bring; whatever it brings it must be borne."[18]

A sense of hope, a sense of a way out,[19] is crucial to this ability to endure. Equally critical is a sense that one is able to act on the situation that is acting on you—that one can give as much as one can get. For, in spite of being aware that eternity is infinite and human life finite, that the cosmos is great and the human world small, and that nothing anyone says or does can immunize him or her from the contingencies of history, the tyranny of circumstance, the finality of death, and the accidents of fate, *every human being struggles for some modicum of choice, craves some degree of understanding, demands some say, and expects some sense of control over the course of his or her life.*[20] But there is a third existential precondition for well-being, and that is a sense of being-with-others.

Consider, for instance, the quandary of Franz Kafka, who lived in dread of losing his freedom to write—either from long hours in his civil service job or in matrimonial bondage. When, in the late summer of 1917, Kafka discovered that he had pulmonary tuberculosis, he felt strangely liberated; "it was a release from all the responsibilities (office, marital obligations, parents) that for many years he had believed he must assume."[21] But for Kuranko individuals like Sewa, who also found their social obligations onerous, their hope was not to be released from all responsibility but to find a more bearable balance between personal needs and the equally imperative needs of others. By implication, well-being could not be found within oneself but only in relation to significant others.

The most disgruntled people I met in Sierra Leone were children like Sira, Ferenke, and Fasili whose parents were dead or not there for them, women like Rose and Saran Marah whose husbands were dead and whose children were living abroad, or men like Abdul and Kaimah Marah who were thwarted in completing the projects they had embarked upon. Yet none of these individuals lived in despair. This was not solely because a stoic spirit prevails in a country like

Sierra Leone, instilling the view that "endurance is fundamentally more important than happiness."[22] It was because these individuals *had* a place in their local communities, despite their dreams of widening their horizons, and because their utopian fantasies, projected in folktales or daydreams, were never so abstract as to encourage a cult of inwardness or eclipse practical reason.[23]

Despite economic hardship, ill health, and political powerlessness, what remained foundational and constant was one's relation to others. In Rugie's comments on her home as a place where she was "surrounded by people who love you, who care," in Sewa's distress over "the lack of love" in the village where he was raised, in Sira's determination to marry for "love," in Fina Kamara's hopes for her children or Kaimah's devotion to his son, happiness issued from one's affectional bonds and the social world of which one was a part.

That such relational virtues transcend culture and class is suggested by a longitudinal study, initiated in 1937, of the health and well-being of two hundred and sixty-eight Harvard sophomores.[24] Documenting these lives through war and peace, marriage and divorce, sickness and health, success and failure, the Harvard files provide no recipes or rules for happiness. But they do afford glimpses into what seems to matter most in surviving adversity and achieving contentment.

Dr. George Vaillant, who has directed the Harvard study for the past forty-two years, speaks of a man whose shipwrecked life led to emergency hospitalization. The loving care this man received in hospital was inspirational and turned his life around. He became, in his eighties, "beloved of a great many people." "Happiness isn't about me," Vaillant observes. Nor can it be achieved by trying; it arises unbidden from our relations with others. "My image of real happiness in the Grant Study," Vaillant concludes, "is a man whose laundry room was just filled with the laundry that came from his children, all loving him and being there and bringing their grandchildren who all helped him garden and helped him sail and produced dirty clothes that needed to be cleaned . . . The take home lesson is always to enjoy where you are now . . . The job is playing and working and loving, and loving is probably the most important. Happiness is love, full stop."

However, as James Baldwin trenchantly observes, love is as "desperately sought" as it is "cunningly avoided," for "love takes off the masks that we fear we cannot live without and know we cannot live within."[25] To fully love another implies, to some degree, the sacrifice or surrender of one's ego. This kenosis does not, however, imply abjection or servility. It is a matter of seeing oneself through the eyes of another, and of confronting the distorted perspective that is born of focusing solely on oneself. For Baldwin, therefore, love is not a personal state of being but a synonym for the "quest and daring and growth" that comes from ceasing to regard one's own received view of the world as the natural standard against which all other views are to be measured. By extension, this means ceasing to see the West as the sole source of Africa's salvation.

Not to Find One's Way in a City

I HAVE ALWAYS DRAWN STRANGE comfort from the fact that the author of the "earliest perfect specimen of the novel" pretends to be apologetic about the tale he has told and the character he has created, for in his prologue to Don Quixote, Miguel de Cervantes confesses that his book lacks "erudition and doctrine" and has "nothing to note in the margin or to annotate at the end."[1] In the same ironic vein, he goes on to say that, unlike other tomes, his book lacks those "citations from Aristotle, Plato, and the entire horde of philosophers" that readers so admire and is even devoid of references to Holy Scripture. This irony is compounded when Cervantes turns to a fictitious friend for advice. As his "friend" reels off a series of arcane references and classical allusions, we are left in no doubt as to Cervantes's mastery of the academic and literary canon and are made aware that what is "new" about the novel as a genre is that it engages directly with life, "sincere and uncomplicated," as Cervantes puts it. Life, for the novelist, is not something to be interpreted or a problem to be solved; it is a journey embarked upon, an adventure to be described, a mystery to be fathomed. Don Quixote is an eccentric figure not simply because he is a living parody of the chivalric tradition in which he has so ardently schooled himself but because his errant career subverts that tradition. The world of books *not only drives him mad but drives him out into the real world.*[2]

I sometimes think that I was drawn to ethnography because, of all the intellectual disciplines with which I became acquainted at university, this was the one that would draw me out of myself, obliging me, like Don Quixote, to periodically leave the sanctuary of libraries and seminar rooms and cast myself adrift in the world, subject to its unsettling, surprising, and sometimes dangerous twists and turns. If my writing retains a picaresque element, resisting closure, it is because I can never bring myself to organize as a lineal argument the improvisatory and open-ended experiences of fieldwork, where one is typically embroiled in events over which one has minimal control. Ethnography is an errant art.

I DID A LOT OF WALKING during my last few days in Freetown. Sometimes with Joshua, showing him around the city or strolling along the beach. Sometimes with Kaimah, making plans for his new life in London. Sometimes with Sewa, who had enlisted my help in securing a visa for his mother from the British High Commission. She wanted to visit her daughters in London and find a treatment for her diabetes. Since the gate-keepers at the High Commission demanded dashes from Sierra Leoneans, and otherwise hindered them, Sewa relied on my Anglo identity and Harvard affiliation as his laissez-passer. But even with my help, progress was frustratingly slow. Twice, Sewa was sent away to get more documentation, and it took me the best part of a morning at the Rokel Bank before I could get an advance on my Visa card to cover the costs of his application. All these obstacles, Sewa said, were intended to drive away would-be migrants and thwart the efforts of Sierra Leoneans in London to bring ailing or dependent relatives to the UK. The day before we were to fly out, Sewa's application had still not been processed, and he appealed to me for advice. His sister Aminatta had paid his college fees when he first went to London; now she expected Sewa to find ways and means of getting their mother to London. But though morally indebted to Aminatta, he was fast running out of money, and Ade, his wife, was impatient for him to return to London. Perhaps he could file the paperwork in London. Perhaps he should postpone his return flight and finalize matters in Freetown. What should he do?

I suggested we return to the city and see if it was possible for him to reschedule his flight at no extra charge. On discovering that this could be done, Sewa confessed that delaying his departure was in fact his only option. If he went back to London with Joshua and me, and his mother fell ill or died, he would never forgive himself. His hands were tied. Ade would be upset and his jobs in London might be jeopardized, but his family in Freetown would have to come first.

Despite these rationalizations, Sewa was distressed by the dilemma he faced. Moreover, his mother simply could not understand what was involved; she imagined that getting a visa was a straightforward matter and that she would have the same access to the National Health in London as her children.

When we left the airline office we set off for the waterfront, hoping to buy some small souvenirs that Joshua and I could take back to America. But our progress through the thronged streets was constantly interrupted. A policeman on point duty turned out to be S.B's former bodyguard, Lansana Marah, and a good friend of Sewa's. I remembered Lansana from a trip we made with S.B. to Koinadugu just before the end of the war. After exchanging recollections of what now seemed a very distant event, Sewa and Lansana fell to bantering, with Sewa referring to his friend as "monitor lizard" (*kane*), the slave of the crocodile (*bambe*)—since the Marah from Barawa and the Koroma from Diang were affinally related. Yet the joking relationship was based on more than the classificatory relationship between Lansana, the "sister's son," and Sewa, the "mother's brother." Though the relationship between the chiefdoms of Barawa and Diang was based on an old political alliance, cemented by intermarriage and expressed in the phrase *Diang n Barawa* (implying the closeness of the two polities), there had been, as in any arranged marriage, stresses and strains. In Sewa's grandfather's time, for example, Barawa gave a woman in marriage to the Diang chief Bala Koroma who turned out to be a witch. Not only was she sent back to whence she came but Diang warriors hassled Barawa farmers working near the border between the chiefdoms, and a piece of land alienated at that time has never been returned. "But," Sewa explained later, when I asked him about his friendship with Lansana Marah, "we would not just joke because I am his mother's brother and he is my sister's son; it's because we know each other so well, because we spent so much time together in S.B.'s service, both in the same inferior position under him, and always at his beck and call."

I was the next to call a halt, wanting to take photographs of the posters on the concrete walls advertising various evangelical ministries. But it wasn't long before Sewa had run into another acquaintance, this time one of the renegade soldiers (sobels) from the Sierra Leone army who joined the RUF and directed the sacking of Kabala in 1994 in which Sewa's cousin was killed and he and his father narrowly escaped with their lives. Much to my astonishment, Sewa started joking with the man, asking ironically if he had gone back home (to Kabala) for New Year. The ex-sobel saw nothing amusing in his situation. "I can't go back'" he said. "I have been discouraged from going there. Since the war ended, I have not been home."

"He fears retaliation," Sewa said as we walked on. "Even now, you can never be sure of the feeling against you if you were in the RUF."

THAT LAST DAY IN FREETOWN with Sewa reminded me of the days we had wandered through the streets of London together, and an army recruiting office, a particular tube station, department store, or street corner would remind Sewa of some encounter, epiphany, or episode during his first disoriented months in the city. And as he shared these experiences with me, I scribbled notes, gathering glimpses into what it meant to be a stranger in a world where so much was unfamiliar and forbidding. As in London, so in Freetown, I marveled that my fieldwork, so minimally planned and so improvisatory, should have proved so fruitful. It was as if I had entered a theater without much thought of what was playing, with little inkling of what I might see, and been afforded insights into a lifeworld where every event echoed others, contributing to a mosaic, a composite, whose emergent meaning could not have been guessed at the outset. It was a little like the "purposeless journey" of which David Haberman speaks in his account of the Ban-Yatra pilgrimage in North Central India, where the peregrinations of the pilgrim through the twelve forests of Krishna's childhood lead neither to the ascetic goal of enlightenment nor the philosophical goal of certain knowledge. Rather, the journey provides a mythical space for storytelling and opens up the possibility of seeing "that all life is *lila*, or purposeless play."[3] Faithful to this spirit of openness and play, Haberman elected to write his ethnography in a free narrative style, in which "episodic beads . . . are strung together on several strands of thought."[4] Accordingly, he abandoned "the search for the real or essential . . . replacing it with an effort to give voice to the multitude of agents involved in the production of culture."[5] But, he adds, "the culture of Braj, like any culture, resists final summation . . . could never be pinned down or fully known."[6]

Many ethnographers, myself included, have had very similar experiences and arrived at very similar conclusions. After thirteen years of living and "endless learning" among the Tz'utujil-speaking

Maya of Santiago Atitlán, Vincent James Stanzione reflects on the "pilgrimage of learning" he embarked upon — "a pilgrimage with no definitive point or termination in a conversation with the Tz'utujil that remains unfinished" yet finds its justification in "knowing one's own humanness in the reflection of the only-too-human 'other.'"[7]

But what kind of meaning is it that we find, but never fully fathom, that informed such everyday encounters as those of Sewa and Lansana, or Sewa and the ex-sobel, yet resist interpretation as simply instantiations of a cultural rule or as products of culture? What is it that fieldwork discloses that a preconceived view may prevent us seeing? And in what ways are mental maps transformed in the act of walking through the country that the maps abstractly represent?[8]

Philosophically, I like to draw an analogy between life and light — an analogy that echoes certain strains in Kuranko thought. Like light, life energy penetrates and permeates our human world, only to be subtly altered, refracted, filtered, impeded, and distorted by the particular milieus through which it must pass. Accordingly the light or life of our shared humanity (or divinity) becomes so changed by historical, cultural, physical, or biographical contexts that we may get the impression that our humanity is as diverse in its essence as it appears in our discursive reflections. Ethnography provides a method whereby the occluded, denigrated, or masked dimensions of our common humanity may be recovered, not through thought alone but through practical engagement with others in the world. Ethnography thus implements Jacques Derrida's call to rethink philosophy from the margins, from the nonphilosophical, from otherness, from outside the logos[9] — domains that Kuranko speak of as the bush or wild.

Methodologically, this movement is not away from the empirical but toward it, and entails a radicalization of the empirical as encompassing what is illuminated as well as what lies in shadow, the fluid as well as the fixed, the transitive as well as the intransitive, the verbal as well as the nonverbal, the personal as well as the transpersonal, the worldly as well as the extra-worldly.

Consider the curious relationship between the two great French writers, Gustave Flaubert and Guy de Maupassant. Contemporary accounts describe their relationship as affectionate — characterized by the exchange of good humor and obscene banter. In anthropological parlance, it was a joking relationship.

Although the following story may be apocryphal, I have carried it in my head for forty years. According to this story, the master, Flaubert, having decided that his young friend was worthy of tuition, sent Maupassant out onto the street to observe what was happening there. When Maupassant reported that nothing much had happened, that the day was much like any other day, Flaubert sent him back onto the street until he returned with a story to tell. "Reminding his pupil that 'talent is a long patience,' he told him again and again: 'There is a part of everything which is unexplored, because we are accustomed to using our eyes only in association with the memory of what people before us have thought of the thing we are looking at. Even the smallest thing has something in it which is unknown. We must find it.'"[10]

Would Flaubert's method of training his protégé work for anthropologists as well? For myself, I find the idea of "philosophical walking" to be an apt description of ethnographic practice.[11] "Walking" and "the street" are metaphors for direct engagement with others, involving oneself in what they are doing, attempting to put oneself in their shoes, as we say, and balancing one's tendency to have one's head in the clouds with the imperative of keeping one's feet firmly on the ground. This grounded view echoes the view of Jean-Jacques Rousseau, who confessed, "I can meditate when I am walking. When I stop, I cease to think; my mind only works with my legs."[12] But while walking teaches one to see thought as a "spatial practice,"[13] to recognize the interplay between the rhythms of walking and the rhythms of thought, and to realize that the form of all discourse—theoretical as well as poetical and narrative—echoes the forms of bodily movement within a social environment, the most elementary of which is walking,[14] such a direct involvement in the world of others has its dangers, which may be why many choose textual analysis and armchair anthropology as a safer bet. One may easily lose one's footing, lose one's way, and even lose one's reason.

Like Rousseau, Søren Kierkegaard was not only a keen walker; he thought when afoot and received his greatest insights when strolling through the streets of his beloved Copenhagen. But there is always something a little absurd about an intellectual on the street, as though bookishness were incompatible with the public square, and the scholar's proper place a library, a study, or retreat where silence reigns and one is free of worldly distractions. But Kierkegaard did not see himself this way, at least not at first, as his friend Hans Brochner recalls:

> I once walked through a whole street with him while he explained how one can make psychological studies by so putting oneself *en rapport* to passers-by. As he explained his theory he put it in practice with almost everybody we met. There was no one on whom his glance did not make an obvious impression . . .
>
> The occasion of these experiments was this. I was walking before him deep in thought, and had not heard him call me, nor noticed that he tapped me on the shoulder. When finally I did notice, he said that it was wrong to be so immersed in oneself, and not make the observations one might in so rich a field. To show me his method he dragged me up and down several streets, and surprised me by his talent for psychological experiment. He was always interesting to accompany, but there was one drawback. His movements were so irregular because of his crooked figure that you could never walk straight when he was with you. You were successively pushed in towards the houses and cellar-holes, and out towards the gutter. And when he gesticulated with his arm and his Spanish cane, walking became still more difficult. You had from time to time to get round the other side of him to keep your place![15]

There is, as Roger Poole points out, an uncanny relationship between Kierkegaard's irregular and surprising manner of comporting himself in public and his philosophical method of indirect communication—refusing to deliver clear univocal communication, disseminating doubt.[16] Poole also notes that the life of this largely unremarkable, if idiosyncratic, figure was transformed utterly when, in 1846, a cartoonist on the Copenhagen daily, *The Corsair,* published a series of vindictive caricatures, exaggerating the philosopher's spindly shanks, curved back, broad-brimmed hat, and uneven trouser legs. Kierkegaard became the laughingstock of the city. "An entire terrorism of the street was rapidly invented and deployed, and the daily walks turned into a nightmare," driving the ironist to despair and reclusion and radically transforming the style of his writing and the tenor of his thought.[17]

If the beginning of Kierkegaard's nightmare was a series of malicious cartoons, the *origin* of this peculiarly Danish form of vilification (familiar to many of us when the right-wing Danish newspaper

Jyllands-Posten published its anti-Islamic cartoons in early 2006) is a species of humor known as *det Kobenhavnske grin*—"the Copenhagen Laugh"—whose aim is to cut any outstanding figure down to size or force them out of the public square. Laughing them off stage, as we say.[18] But behind even this leveling mechanism we may glimpse a problem that is as old as humanity itself—how a group that is struggling to maintain itself as a secure and stable unity can accommodate a stranger in its midst.

Perhaps this is why I often felt incongruous in the streets of Freetown, with my notebook and pale skin, and why I felt a certain kinship with Clarence in Camara Laye's *The Radiance of the King*. Though I never experience myself as an outsider in Firawa, Freetown is different. Yet I was not alone in feeling out of place and ambivalent in this vast and overcrowded city. For the thousands that had flocked there during the war, or migrated to Freetown in search of a better life, the questions as to who you could trust or ask for favors, who was friend and who was foe, were as vexed and unavoidable as they had been for the rural poor who flocked to the new industrial cities of Europe in the early-eighteenth century. And this may explain the origin of the joking relationships, the strong sense of irony, that people spontaneously deploy in their urban encounters with others who are at once vaguely familiar yet disconcertingly strange.[19] This same irony informs many of our responses to situations that elude our grasp or overwhelm, as when Kuranko jokingly respond to the question "Are you well?" by saying "I am as healthy as hunger," since the pangs of hunger are stronger than any emotion and defy all one's efforts to bring them under control. Since there is no way of reducing the ambiguity inherent in these experiences, one laughs them off or, as Richard Sennett observes, one has recourse to *theatrical* means of coping with situations in which one's known *social* skills and personal capacities prove inadequate. But should some stranger become too conspicuous, either because of his or her unusual attire, different appearance, or peculiar habits, he or she is likely to be made the scapegoat that the fearful community drives out, ghettoizes or drives into reclusion in a magical attempt to confirm its sense of solidarity and security. I wonder if this is why one is never completely comfortable in a space of strangers—for in your own eyes, you may be the odd one out—an experience I recognize in Jean Rouch's intriguing comment that "when you make films with

Africans, you have a strange relationship — a 'joking relationship' — because the activity involves both collaboration and dissent, bringing identity and difference together in an unsettling and possibly unresolvable way."[20]

IT IS SOMETIMES ASSUMED that in traditional societies, difference is a matter of age, gender, status, and role, but that a collective ethos prevails in which individual identity is eclipsed. However, fieldwork among the Kuranko has brought home to me that the *social* values of coexistence and cooperation cannot be achieved unless everyone actively and mindfully works toward the common weal *and finds personal fulfillment in doing so.* Well-being is therefore dependent on an adjustment or balance between our sense of what we owe others and what we owe ourselves.

And everyone struggles to strike this balance in his or her own way. To speak of balance is to suggest that life is not a problem that can be solved but a situation with which we struggle, a mystery that cannot be fully fathomed.

Of these paradoxes of well-being, Amartya Sen observes, "You could be *well off*, without being *well*. You could be *well*, without being able to lead the life you *wanted*. You could have got the life you *wanted*, without being *happy*. You could be *happy*, without having much *freedom*. You could have a good deal of *freedom*, without *achieving* much."[21]

But what of my paradoxical relationship with Kuranko, who have contributed so much to my own well-being, a significant part of the *"upstream* region of myself?"[22] When I think of the grasslands around Firawa and their hold over my imagination, or the poems and prose for which I have Sierra Leone to thank, I have to admit that both my aesthetic and intellectual responses to my fieldwork experience have produced a little knowledge, to be sure, but more importantly, perhaps, they bear witness to a struggle to cope with relationships that were never easy, a language that was never mastered, food that was never entirely palatable, customs that often seemed cruel, and living conditions that were seldom comfortable. More like an arranged marriage than a love match, my bond with Kuranko was also a kind of bondage, a curious mix of obligation and affection. And yet, by seeing this relationship through, I have gained the satisfaction of survival—which is so much deeper than the satisfaction of success. I have been with Kuranko friends through sickness and health, thick and thin, constancy and inconstancy. It has been like walking together on a difficult journey, with no end in sight. What affinities there have been have come from this prolonged experience of moving through life together—and it is this that lies at the heart of human sociality, and even of love, which, for Kuranko, is a form of kindness. One can never fully close the gap between oneself and another. But identification and empathy are not what anthropology should aim for, any more than keeping one's distance and striving for a view from afar is a viable way of understanding the other. Ethnography is a way of thinking oneself through in the place of another, and this task is perhaps far more demanding when the other is a stranger rather than a kinsman. Yet it is overcoming one's resistance to engage, stretching oneself as far as one possibly can, and accepting the situation into which one has been thrown and making something of it that define not only the scope of anthropology but the essence of coexistence. And if, at the end of the day, we no longer see the other as an alien and a threat but as oneself under other circumstances, struggling with similar existential issues—such as the scarcity and inaccessibility of the goods that make our lives complete or worthwhile—then we will have gone some way toward redeeming ourselves, whose self-interests and perspectives often contribute to deepening the divide between haves and have-nots, making mutuality impossible and dismissing the notion of the common weal as an outmoded or unattainable ideal. In fact, it may be as impossible to meliorate the conditions under which we live as it is to arrive at a single formula for what makes life worth living or what might change it for the better.

And so I return to the question of existential dissatisfaction with which this book began—the quest for the unknown something or someone without which one's life feels incomplete. That our wishful thinking and passionate imaginings fasten, restively and transiently, on disparate objects—a better world, mobility, money, love, learning, recognition—suggests that human desire rarely originates in the thing or person that is held to be necessary for its consummation. We must be analytically careful, therefore, not to infer the true source of a person's longings and frustrations from the way that person identifies them, for though we act in the name of certain convictions, our actions often have their origin in situations we cannot name. Moreover, for those who fulfill their ambitions and achieve their goals, new dissatisfactions invariably arise, new objects of desire. This is not to pour scorn on human aspirations for a better life, or argue against helping others achieve their goals to the extent that one's own resources allow. Rather, it is to remind oneself that the imagination typically gets ahead of itself, producing a cognitive surplus to survival needs and fostering the illusion that we can transcend our circumstances, reborn into a world where losses are made good, injustices redressed, prayers answered, patience rewarded, and knowledge achieved. For most of the people I met in Firawa, Kondembaia, and Kamadugu Sukurela, such hopes were tempered by an awareness of the limits within which one's life unfolds, and an acceptance that happiness consists in knowing how to make the most of what one has rather than staking everything on the chance of something else.[23] That we might find merit in such an attitude, I leave to my readers to decide.

AT LUNGI AIRPORT WE TAXIED to the end of the runway and were preparing for takeoff when the captain announced that we would be returning to the terminal. A passenger, angered at having been assigned an aisle seat when he had expressly asked for a window, had abused a stewardess and could not be mollified. The palaver went on for ten minutes. The stewardess informed the man that the airline had a "zero tolerance policy" and that the abuse of airline staff would be met with instant action. When the man responded by using the "c" and "f" words, and another passenger supported him in vociferous protest, the captain was informed, our takeoff delayed, and airport security notified. When security came aboard, the man was asked to disembark. Suddenly as contrite as he had had been abusive, the man begged the crew to give him a second chance. But he and his supporter were both ushered off the plane. It took another forty-five minutes for their bags to be offloaded.

I experienced mixed feelings about the incident. While it was irksome to wait seventy minutes while the dispute was resolved, it was disconcerting to see that the "zero tolerance" policy extended to a way of life in which the pleasures of making palaver, of turning minor incidents into a theatrical performance, of creating social bonds through confrontation, were so familiar.

But then I slept, oblivious to everything, until a cabin attendant was shaking me by the shoulder, telling me to wake up and fasten my seatbelt; we were approaching Gatwick.

I looked blankly out the cabin window. A horizon of glowing embers, a fading strip of ultramarine. In the paler empyrean, the merest sliver of a moon with Venus, its beloved wife, below it.

At Gatwick, the bracing air of the January dawn swept me back into another time. The ringing silence of empty streets. Everything orderly and subdued. I pitied the Sierra Leoneans at the immigration counters, their solemn and disgruntled faces, their tawdry clothing. At Freetown airport, we had waited together in the hot, clammy departure lounge for three long hours. Hi-life jangled from the bar. Ceiling fans turned slowly in the cloying air. And malfunctioning fluorescent lights imparted a sickly pallor to our skins—the UN soldiers in battle fatigues, the Lebanese businessmen, the young Sierra Leoneans heading to Europe for the first time. Now they dutifully formed a queue, and in their bewilderment I saw myself descending into the turmoil of a long-ago African night.

Coda

A FEW MONTHS AFTER our return to the United States, Joshua began applying for admission to various colleges. He decided to make his experiences in Firawa the basis of his application essay.

Beyond Firawa

IT WAS THE HEAT OF THE DAY. Almost everyone was asleep, and the few that had chosen to brave the sun were quietly sitting, staring down the dirt road that led out of the village. My father and I had been in Sierra Leone for three weeks. He had been coming there for over forty years, doing anthropological research in the remote village of Firawa, but this was the first time he had ever brought me with him. I still felt as if I was in a dream, the heavy dust settling on me, lulling me into a deep sleep that I thought I would eventually wake from, but recall nothing.

Abdul, the Firawa chief, was leaning into his chair. His nickname, "heavy-foot," had been earned during his youth as a wrestler when no one could move him once he had taken his stance. Today, though, he was sitting with eyes half open, watching those around him with an air of philosophical speculation. The only sound in the village came from his old radio, which no one understood and therefore all ignored. However, at that moment, a BBC newscaster began talking about Sierra Leone.

The radio journalist seemed to pronounce every word with a melancholy air of pity; she wove her voice with the script so well that I almost believed she meant every word she said. She was talking about Sierra Leone being the poorest country in the world. As she spoke, the men, women and children did not move, as if frozen in a separate dimension, far from the facts and figures that I was obliged to live and breathe. Abdul lifted his head when he heard the name of his country, but I don't think anyone except my father and I understood what the BBC newscaster's words meant.

Then, as the climax of her broadcast drew near, the journalist held her breath for a fraction of a second, before diving headfirst into her final point.

"The average Sierra Leonean man," she triumphantly declared with her soft, but powerful voice, "makes less than a dollar a day."

Her voice reverberated in the stifling heat. It initially struck me as a powerful point. Like the journalist, I lived in a society that judged success by the amount of money one made every day, and assumed that money would cover all the problems one faced. Yet there seemed to be something wrong with her assumption. I looked around at the village men and women, some hanging up clothes on a line, some lying down in the shade of a porch, completely un-aware that they were being judged as the poorest individuals in the world. They would never see themselves this way, because their lives were focused on raising children, growing enough rice to see them through the long months of the rainy season, and celebrating their sense of close community. The mountain that stood so solidly over the countryside suggested to me that Firawa would abide, despite war and suffering, while the rest of the world, with its volatile mar-kets, energy crises and moral confusion, might not.

The hammock swayed below me and a soft wind explored the natural beauty of this unspoiled village. I briefly closed my eyes, and imagined my father, some thirty years ago; sitting in the house he had shared with an old medicine master in Firawa, writing up his research notes. His late wife was buying fruit from the local mar-ket while his nine-year old daughter was outside, playing with some kids she had met the day before; the very kids who would grow up to make less than a dollar a day. I saw the world through my father's eyes and understood why that BBC journalist was so mistaken. I understood that even though the people of Firawa did not pos-sess what Westerners consider essential to life or liberty, they had learned to accept hardship and found the infinite joy that is human companionship. I opened my eyes again, more awake than I had ever been in my life, and wondered where the red road that led further into the mountains might take me.

Acknowledgments

I AM GRATEFUL to Bill Graham, Dean of the Harvard Divinity School, for his timely help in making research money available for my travel and fieldwork in Sierra Leone. To Sierra Leonean friends, appreciatively named in the pages of this book, I owe a great debt— for their warm hospitality and unstinting help, as well as their acceptance of research that may bring none of the benefits they hope from the outside world. I am particularly indebted to my old friend, Abdul Marah, who gave up his own room to me and my son and saw that our daily needs were met. I also acknowledge, with pride and affection, my son Joshua Jackson, who undertook this journey with me, and my boon companion, Sewa Magba Koroma, on whom I so often relied for assistance and advice. Finally, warm thanks are due to Sverker Finnström, Kirin Narayan, Bhrigupati Singh, and an anonymous reviewer for their incisive readings of my manuscript, and to Ken Wissoker, Mandy Earley, Tim Elfenbein, Cherie Westmoreland, and the staff at Duke University Press for undertaking the publication of yet another of my books with such care.

Notes

Imagining Firawa

1. If GNP per capita based on global purchasing power parity (PPP) is taken into account, Sierra Leone is the poorest country in the world and, according to the UN, "the world's least liveable country" considering "its poverty and the poor quality of life that its citizens must endure." Daniel Workman, "World's Poorest Countries: Lowest GNP Nations Highlight African Poverty," posted 22 October, 2006, on Suite101.com, http://internationaltrade.suite101.com/ (accessed 1 June, 2010).

2. See Viktor Frankl, *Man's Search for Meaning* (Boston: Beacon Press, 2006), 104–5.

3. The questions are echoed in the opening lines of Ernst Bloch's masterpiece, *The Principle of Hope*, trans. Neville Plaice, Stephen Plaice, and Paul Knight (Cambridge, Mass.: MIT Press, 1986), 3. "Why are we? Where do we come from? Where are we going? What are we waiting for? Who awaits us?"

4. Coincidentally, the etymology of Firawa ("bush place," i.e., a cleared space in the bush) echoes the etymology of Inglewood, my hometown in New Zealand (from the Gaelic *aingeal*, "fire"—hence a fire-cleared space in a forest).

5. The idea of anteriority brings to mind the déjà vu effect, but, like Walter Benjamin, I prefer an acoustic metaphor for "events that reach us like an echo awakened by a call, a sound that seems to have been heard somewhere in the darkness of past life." Walter Benjamin, "A Berlin Chronicle," *Reflections: Walter Benjamin Essays, Aphorisms, Autobiographical Writings* (New York: Schocken, 1978), 59. Robert Desjarlais provides a compelling account of the Yolmo Buddhist conception of the soul's transmigration from one incarnation to another (*bhaja*) as a kind of "visual echo"—illusory, repeating, always moving, yet recalling "something of an original sound or phenomenon." Robert Desjarlais, *Sensory Biographies: Lives and Deaths among Nepal's Yolmo Buddhists* (Berkeley: University of California Press, 2003), 279, 281.

6. Gabriel Marcel, *Being and Having*, trans. Katharine Farrer (Boston: Beacon Press, 1951), 100.

7. Paul Ricoeur, *Critique and Conviction: Conversations with François*

Azouvi and Marc de Launay, trans. Kathleen Blamey (New York: Columbia University Press, 1998), 100.

8. Ibid., 98.

9. William James, *The Will to Believe* (London: Longmans, 1898), viii.

10. Gabriel Marcel, *Homo Viator: Introduction to a Metaphysic of Hope*, trans. Emma Craufurd (New York: Harper, 1962), 53.

11. Bourdieu, *Pascalian Meditations*, trans. Richard Nice (Cambridge: Polity Press, 2000), 216–18.

12. Hannah Arendt, *The Human Condition* (Chicago: University of Chicago Press), 178.

13. Marcel, *Homo Viator*, 43.

14. Pierre Bourdieu, "Social Being, Time and the Sense of Existence," *Pascalian Meditations*, 206–45. See also Michael Jackson, *Existential Anthropology: Events, Exigencies and Effects* (New York: Berghahn, 2005).

15. "Something's Missing: A Discussion between Ernst Bloch and Theodor W. Adorno on the Contradictions of Utopian Longing," *The Utopian Function of Art and Literature: Selected Essays*, trans. Jack Zipes and Frank Mecklenburg (Cambridge, Mass.: MIT Press, 1988), 1–17.

Fathers and Sons

1. Michael Jackson, *In Sierra Leone* (Durham, N.C.: Duke University Press, 2004).

2. The distinctions are those of Ernst Bloch, for whom wishful thinking is "immature" and "unworldly" and leads a person to become lost in fantasy and memory rather than engaged in the achievement of what is actually attainable. *The Principle of Hope*, trans. Neville Plaice, Stephen Plaice, and Paul Knight, 3 vols. (Oxford: Basil Blackwell, 1986), 1:144–45.

Forty Days

1. Orhan Pamuk, "My Father's Suitcase: The Nobel Lecture, 2006," *New Yorker*, 25 December 2006, and 1 January 2007, 82–96, 90.

2. Literally "lying down/forty," *labinane* is the period of sequestration imposed on women after their husband's death and bears comparison with the Italian *quarantina* (forty) which was traditionally the number of days of confinement expected of a widow. C. M. Parkes, *Bereavement: Studies of Grief in Adult Life* (Harmondsworth: Penguin, 1975), 188.

3. *Purity and Danger: An Analysis of Concepts of Pollution and Taboo* (Harmondsworth: Penguin, 1966).

4. Heavy stones or logs of *turé* wood are placed over the lower trench of a grave, and the topsoil shoveled back before the clay, to prevent the spirit

finding its way back to its body. The logic here is similar to the logic that prevents any contact between the bereaved and the spirit of the deceased.

5. It was actually burned to the ground in a bush fire that spread into the village some years before the war.

Scenes from a Marriage

1. Divorce was also difficult on account of the bridewealth that had been transferred from the husband's lineage to the wife's lineage (and used to fund the marriage of one of her brothers). This bridewealth was simply not available to be refunded.

2. It is customary and not uncommon for the maternal uncles to intervene if their sisters' children are being neglected or mistreated in their father's household.

3. Fina's generalizations echo Chris Coulter's recent and more systematic research on changing marriage patterns in the neighboring chiefdom of Kamadugu. *Bush Wives and Girl Soldiers: Women's Lives through War and Peace in Sierra Leone* (Ithaca, N.Y.: Cornell University Press, 2009), 80–89.

4. In effect, cross-cousin marriages (in which a man marries his mother's brother's daughter) effectively unite the children of a brother and sister in marriage, which is why Kuranko speak of such unions metaphorically as echoing or repeating a previous bond. *Wore koro, woro feran* (lit. "small kola under a large kola tree") or *sogei bora ka minto meeye n'yo* (lit. "meat comes to a place where there is a hearty appetite for meat").

5. Accordingly, many older men would tolerate their wives living with their lovers, rather than make a public issue out of it, though the arrangement required that any children of such a union be legally recognized as belonging to the husband and not the lover.

6. Lit. "Father Bori from Mande."

7. The Kuranko harp-lute is much smaller than the twenty-one stringed Mande *kora*, but its construction is similar: a half calabash resonator, a hide tympanum, a notched bridge, metal objects attached to the neck, and the strings plucked with thumbs and forefingers while the remaining fingers clasp two posts atop the gourd. The harp-lute is called *seraima* or *serama*; the praise-singer of the hunters is known as the *serawayili*.

8. Daniel Biebuyck and Kamombo C. Matene, eds., *The Mwindo Epic: From the Banyanga (Congo Republic)* (Berkeley: University of California Press, 1971); Jack Goody, *The Myth of the Bagre* (Oxford: Clarendon, 1972).

9. Shaving is here a metaphor for taming, domesticating, initiating, i.e., transforming Bori from an unruly or wild state into being a fully socialized member of the community.

10. In the Mande epic of Sundiata, Bori is a half-brother and close friend

of the powerful ruler, and their relationship compared to that of a man and his shadow. D. T. Niane, *Sundiata: An Epic of Old Mali*, trans. G. D. Pickett (London: Longman, 1965), 25.

11. Kuranko hunters say that a wounded buffalo (*segei*) will often retrace its steps along a trail in order to ambush hunters following its spoor.

12. The bush cow (*Syncerus caffer nanus*), or dwarf forest buffalo, is smaller than the buffalo.

13. Hunters allegedly have "second sight" (lit. "four-eyes"); the second pair enables them to see in the dark, and sometimes to see djinn or witches.

Smoke and Mirrors

1. The Kuranko term for a diviner is *bolomafelne* (lit. "hand-on-looker") and covers anyone who manipulates or 'lays down" various objects — pebbles, cowries, kola nuts — in order to "see" what kind of sacrifice a client should make to avert misfortune or ensure an improvement in his or her lot. Muslim diviners (called moris or alphas in Krio) use techniques from consulting the Qu'ran to mirror-gazing, water-gazing, astrology, and oneiromancy.

2. During my fieldwork in 1970, older men recalled a particularly bad year, known as *porobonkonke* (lit. "palmtree heart take out hunger"), when even secondary foodstuffs were in short supply and people were forced to live on bush food. During this time, women were barren, allegedly because rice — the staff of life — was not available.

3. This process of perpetually recalibrating our notions of what we need in order to be happy or satisfied is known as the adaptation-level principle. Adaptation is never a state that can be attained, for every gain we make simply redefines the nature of what we lack. Harry Helson, *Adaptation-Level Theory: An Experimental and Systematic Approach to Behavior* (New York: Harper and Row, 1964).

4. Amartya Sen, *Development as Freedom* (New York: Anchor Books, 1999), 74, 87.

5. Amartya Sen, "Capability and Well-Being," *The Quality of Life*, ed. Martha Nussbaum and Amartya Sen (Oxford: Clarendon, 1993), 30.

6. Anthropologists have made a similar "communitarian critique" of Rawls's theory of distributive justice and Sen's notions of capability and freedom, arguing that in many non-Western societies, moral reasoning does not proceed from the standpoint of the individual (and his or her self-sufficiency, rights, or capabilities) but rather from the "obligations, debts, and ties of solidarity that weave us into a community" and find expression in "a *minima moralia* represented by roundedness or completeness." Alberto Corsin Jiménez, "Introduction: Well-Being's Re-Proportioning of Social Thought," *Culture and Well-Being: Anthropological Approaches to*

Freedom and Political Ethics, ed. Alberto Corsin Jiménez (London: Pluto Press, 2008), 6, 10.

7. It is notoriously difficult to be medically objective about the effects of female genital cutting, when moral panic, cultural prejudice, and descriptive inexactness abound, but in a recent Swedish OB-GYN study, only 10 percent of sexual dysfunctionality and medical complications among circumcised African women could be attributed to female genital cutting, and there is no evidence that FGC impairs or destroys sexual sensitivity, since the "female penis" is so deeply embedded and the sexually sensitive parts of the body so extensive that clitoridectomy alone cannot reduce sexual pleasure. See Ylva Hernlud and Bettina Shell-Duncan, eds., *Transcultural Bodies: Female Genital Cutting in Global Context* (New Brunswick, N.J.: Rutgers University Press, 2007).

8. See James Vernon, *Hunger: A Modern History* (Cambridge, Mass.: Belknap Press of Harvard University Press, 2007). Vernon shows how the hungry became objects of compassion in mid-nineteenth-century Europe, challenging Malthusian assumptions that death by hunger was a natural form of population control.

9. Recent research suggests that the greater one's sense of uncertainty and *not* being in control of one's life, the greater the likelihood that one will have recourse to the "futile pursuit" of "illusory patterns." "For example, children of lower economic status overestimate the size of coins as compared with the wealthy, and hungry individuals are more likely to see food in ambiguous images." Jennifer A. Whitson and Adam D. Galinsky, "Lacking Control Increases Illusory Pattern Perception," *Science* 322, no. 5898 (3 October 2008), 115–17.

10. On the distinction between supplement and substitute, see Michael Jackson, *Existential Anthropology: Events, Exigencies and Effects* (New York: Berghahn, 2005), 95.

11. Ernst Bloch, *The Spirit of Utopia*, trans. Anthony A. Nassar (Stanford, Calif.: Stanford University Press, 2000), 167–71.

12. I am indebted to Bhrigupati Singh for pointing out to me the echoes of Gilles Deleuze's concepts of pure immanence, transcendental empiricism, and "a life" in my allusion to the Greek Stoics. Gilles Deleuze, *Pure Immanence: Essays on a Life*, trans. Anne Boyman (New York: Zone Books, 2001), 25–33.

13. *Suma* is a rare generic term for a grain; by extension, it connotes the germ of anything (e.g., *sumafan*, secret thing, i.e., a secret society). More commonly, grains and seeds are *kuli* (e.g., *kor' kuli* = rice seed). *Kuli* also means "bone" or "pith" and figures in such phrases as *i la kume wo kuli sa ro*, "your words are boneless" (i.e., hollow and without substance).

14. *Kore* is uncooked rice (cooked rice is *kine*). The word is cognate with *koro* (elder sibling; elder). Rice is thus the senior and most respected of all foodstuffs.

My appropriation of René Girard's compelling phrase for the title of this chapter does not imply an endorsement of his thesis that the origin of violence lies in mimetic desire, but it does echo it. René Girard, *Things Hidden Since the Foundation of the World*, trans. Stephen Bann and Michael Metteer (Stanford, Calif.: Stanford University Press, 1987).

1. Alhaji Hassan Sanoh's grandfather came to Barawa from Guinea, accompanied by his brother. Both were Koranic scholars, and the Marah rulers in Barawa allowed them to settle and to proselytize.

2. For an extended, cross-cultural account of such stories, see Michael Jackson, *Minima Ethnographica: Intersubjectivity and the Anthropological Project* (Chicago: University of Chicago Press, 1998), 108–24.

3. According to a Limba narrative from northern Sierra Leone, Africans and Europeans were once brothers. That one became less advantaged than the other was a result of their father's favoritism. He wrote a book, containing instructions on how to make money, ships, and airplanes, intending to give it to his dark-skinned son. But his wife smuggled the book to her favorite son — the one with white skin. The dispossessed son ended up with a hoe and a basket of millet, rice, and groundnuts.

> "You see us, the black people, we are left in suffering. The unfairness of our birth makes us remain in suffering. That is why they want to send us to learn the writing of the Europeans. But our mother did not agree, she did not love us. She loved the white people. She gave them the book . . . Yesterday we were full brothers with them. We come from one descent, the same mother, the same father, but the unfairness of our birth, that is why we are different. We will not know what you know unless we learn from you." (Ruth Finnegan, *Limba Stories and Story-Telling* [Oxford: Clarendon, 1967], 263).

4. Paul Ricoeur, *Critique and Conviction: Conversations with François Azouvi and Marc de Launay* (New York: Columbia University Press, 1998), 98.

5. Ibid., 94.

6. I follow Sartre's and Merleau-Ponty's situated ethics, on the grounds that Kant's ethics was "too well-ordered to be true; to be, alas, too removed from human life — and death —; and probably even culpably remote, morally speaking, given the shattering realities of postwar Europe." Forrest Williams, preface to Gail Evelyn Linsenbard, *An Investigation of Jean-Paul Sartre's Posthumously Published "Notebooks for an Ethics"* (Lampeter, Wales: Edwin Mellen Press, 2000), viii.

7. Jean-Paul Sartre and Benny Levi, *Hope Now: The 1980 Interviews*, trans. Adrian van der Hoven (Chicago: University of Chicago Press, 2007), 71. I am following Sartre's precept that ontology precedes and produces ethics, in the same way that existence precedes essence.

8. Maurice Merleau-Ponty, *Phenomenology of Perception*, trans. Colin

Smith (London: Routledge and Kegan Paul, 1962), 347, 353–54. Merleau-Ponty's comments find recent confirmation in the work of Ed Tronick on primary intersubjectivity. It is never enough to declare simply that sociality is the measure of well-being, since everything depends on the consummation of what Tronick calls "dyadic consciousness"—the collaborative incorporation of complex information, experience, and mutual mappings into a relatively coherent whole that functions as a self-regulating system that effectively expands the consciousness of one person into the consciousness of another. Dyadic consciousness begins in the stage of primary intersubjectivity, and should an infant be "deprived of the experience of expanding his or her states of consciousness in collaboration with the other . . . this limits the infant's experience and forces the infant into self-regulatory patterns that eventually compromise the child's development." Ed Tronick, *The Neurobehavioral and Social-Emotional Development of Infants and Children* (New York: W.W. Norton, 2007), 292.

9. The etymology of the term *namuge* or *namui* (custom) is relevant here, for it literally means "mother-birth"; by extension, what is given, what is found, where you start from, as in the Kuranko adage "Never forget the one who first filled your belly."

10. Sartre also begins his comments on ethics by saying that ethics is a reciprocal mode of consciousness, and therefore a consciousness of obligation. *Hope Now*, 69–70.

11. Marcel Mauss, *The Gift*, trans. Ian Cunnison (London: Cohen and West, 1954), 5.

12. I share the view of T. M. S. Evens that sacrifice must be grasped as a dimension of human sociality before it is subject to analysis as a religious rite. See his *Anthropology as Ethics: Nondualism and the Conduct of Sacrifice* (New York: Berghahn, 2008), 77.

13. This idea finds expression in the Christian assertion that it is more blessed to give than receive (Acts 20:35), and in the logic of forgiveness, in which a person forfeits or gives up all thought of revenge.

14. The impossibility of deciding how an ethical *disposition* (altruism) can be compared with a social *position* (chieftaincy) creates an ambiguous situation, thereafter managed through a formalized joking relationship between the clans—which is a *ritual* way of making light of a contradiction that does not admit of any other resolution.

15. Although Mauss invoked the Maori conceptions of reciprocity (*utu*), he failed to elaborate on the ambiguity of the Maori term, which covers both the giving of life and the taking of life.

16. On the connection between paying damages or discharging a debt through inflicting pain and degradation on the body of a culprit or debtor, see Friedrich Nietzsche, *On the Genealogy of Morals* (Oxford: Oxford University Press, 1996), 46. On the relationship between accounting, counting, sacrifice, and social order, see Derek Hughes, *Culture and Sacrifice:*

Ritual Death in Literature and Opera (Cambridge: Cambridge University Press, 2007).

17. I know of only one instance of this sacrifice, known as *baramawulan saraké*. In 1979, chief Kulio of Sambaia told me that his ancestor, Mali Yan (tall) Jallo—a Fula—had migrated to present-day Sierra Leone some eleven generations ago. Mali Yan's three sons, Samba, Bubu, and Kalo settled in different areas (Sambaia, Buiyan, and Kalian). The country that Fula Manse (Fula chief) Bubu entered was already inhabited by the Kargbo. But the Kargbo were living in caves to escape the depredations of Tegere (Temne) warriors. The Kargbo asked Fula Manse Bubu to help them drive the Temne away. With the help of his younger brother, Kalo, and a renowned warrior, Morogbe Kundu Togele, Bubu succeeded in repulsing the Temne. As a reward, the Kargbos offered Bubu land to settle, though they would first have to consult with their allies and "brothers," the Sisé of Sambadugu. After much deliberation, the Kargbo and Sisé decided to make Fula Manse Bubu protector and lord of the land, but only on condition that he make a sacrifice to the land. Fula Manse Bubu asked his wife, Ma Hawa, to give their daughter as a human sacrifice. The girl stood in a pit (*baramawulan*), her head inside a copper receptacle, gold in her mouth, then buried alive. In addition, "one hundred of everything" had to be distributed among the populace. The Kargbo now declared, *m'bol fa ma kin fa*, meaning "my hands and my feet are yours." Fula Manse Bubu then released an arrow into the air that fell to earth in a straight line, signifying that the sacrifice had been accepted by the ancestors and a covenant made. Bubu then built his courthouse on the spot where the arrow landed and gave part of his chiefdom to Morogbe Kundu.

18. Davíd Carrasco, *City of Sacrifice: The Aztec Empire and the Role of Violence in Civilization* (Boston: Beacon Press, 1999), 179, 148. In "The Other Mexico," Octavio Paz writes that the real rivals of the Aztecs are not to be found in the East (he first suggests the Assyrians) but in the West, "for only among ourselves has the alliance between politics and metaphysics been so intimate, so exacerbated, and so deadly: the inquisitions, the religious wars, and above all, the totalitarian societies of the twentieth century." *The Labyrinth of Solitude and Other Writings*, trans. Lysander Kemp (New York: Grove Press, 1985), 307–8.

19. It should be emphasized, moreover, that what applies in any dyadic relationship also applies in relations between groups, and in relations between persons and nonpersons (animals, gods, objects, and ideologies). A concrete example is the parallelism between state sacrifice and autosacrifice among the Aztecs, where ritualized bloodletting for the well-being of the state was analogous to individual acts of bloodletting as a way of achieving an amelioration of one's personal circumstances. Carrasco, *City of Sacrifice*, 85.

20. Even a small child's sense of fairness carries this dual connotation—

that fairness means both getting what is one's due but also getting even when someone else has received more than his or her fair share.

21. Alfred Schutz borrows this concept from Husserl to explore "the interchangeability of standpoints" and "the congruence of relevances" that produce a sense that despite our human diversity we share a common ground. Alfred Schutz, *Collected Papers*, ed. Maurice Natanson (The Hague: Martinus Nijhoff, 1973), 1:10–13, 1:312–16.

22. Jean-Jacques Rousseau, *Discours sur l'origine de d'inégalité parmi les hommes* (Paris: Editions Garnier, 1962), 37.

23. Leslie Marmon Silko, "Notes on the Deer Dance," *The Delicacy and Strength of Lace: Letters between Leslie Marmon Silko and James Wright*, ed. Anne Wright (Saint Paul, Minn.: Graywolf Press, 1986), 9–10.

24. Patricia Vinnecombe, *People of the Eland: Rock Paintings of the Drakensberg Bushmen as a Reflection of their Life and Thought* (Pietermaritzburg: University of Natal Press, 1976), 180, emphasis in original. Vinnecombe's insights are reminiscent of Walter Buckert's argument that hunting rituals involve expiation for the guilt of killing of an animal. A classical example is the annual Athenian slaying of the ox (Bouphonia) that was followed by a trial for the murder of the animal, with the axe and knife found guilty and cast into the sea. *Homo Necans: The Anthropology of Ancient Greek Sacrificial Ritual and Myth*, trans. Peter Bing (Berkeley: University of California Press, 1983), 20.

25. Which is why murder or genocide are never straightforward and require extraordinary imaginative, discursive, and ritual preparation— transforming a person or persons who are manifestly human, like oneself, into radical others, alien objects, or mere beasts.

26. Michael Serres, *The Natural Contract*, trans. Elizabeth MacArthur and William Paulson (Ann Arbor: University of Michigan Press, 1995), 38.

Reopening the Gate of Effort

The chapter title (from the Arabic *fatah al ijtjihad*) is borrowed from Jean Duvignaud's *Change at Shebika: Report from a North African Village* (New York: Vintage, 1970), chapter 5. It is intended as a reminder to the reader that the issues that emerged in the course of my conversations with young Kuranko men and women are almost identical to those that preoccupied the thoughts of young Tunisian villagers in 1960–66, and a further reminder that the existential issues that underlie a desire for education, to travel abroad, to become rich, and to resist the imposition of state decrees or foreign protocols on local polities are longstanding and universal. But where Duvignaud calls his work of "the sociological imagination" utopian, I would call it allegorical since, like my ethnography of Firawa, it tries to go beyond a purely local narrative and speak to the human condition.

1. Claude Lévi-Strauss, *The Savage Mind* (London: Weidenfeld and Nicolson, 1966), 166. Among the Akan of Ghana, the notion of "sympathetic impartiality" expresses a similar vision of human rights. See Kwasi Wiredu, *Cultural Universals and Particulars: An African Perspective* (Bloomington: Indiana University Press, 1996), 29–31.

2. Kenelm Burridge, *Mambu: A Melanesian Millennium* (Princeton, N.J.: Princeton University Press, 1960), 6.

3. Alan Badiou, *Saint Paul: The Foundation of Universalism*, trans. Ray Brassier (Stanford, Calif.: Stanford University Press, 2003), 93.

4. Even though many Kuranko have embraced Islam, villagers tend to use Altala rather than Allah in referring to god.

5. *Fa San* (lit. "Father Hare") may be translated "Mr. Hare," though in Kuranko stories, hare — who is the younger brother — is the trickster, while hyena — the elder brother — is the dupe.

6. Charles Long, *Significations: Signs, Symbols, and Images in the Interpretation of Religion* (Aurora, Colo.: Davies Group, 1986), 196, emphasis added.

7. In a compelling account of the ethical gray zone of the *favelas* of northeast Brazil, Nancy Scheper-Hughes describes the *jeitoso* "personality type" as "attractive, smooth, handy, sharp and a real operator" who can con people, beat the system, and even "get away with murder." Like the tactical ingenuity of the "rascals" of Papua New Guinea, the Brazilian trickster is amoral and opportunistic, with shallow loyalties and a thick skin. Nancy Scheper-Hughes, "A Talent for Life: Reflections on Human Vulnerability and Resilience," *Ethnos* 73, no.1 (2008): 47.

8. Norman O. Brown, *Hermes the Thief: The Evolution of a Myth* (Great Barrington, Mass.: Lindisfarne Press, 1990), 32–45.

Something's Missing

The chapter title is taken from a line from Bertolt Brecht and calls to mind a story about Brecht, whose early plays were staged by the Berliner Ensemble, including the world premiere of Brecht and Weill's *The Threepenny Opera* in 1928. The theater was severely damaged in a bombing raid but rebuilt after the war. In 1954 Brecht and Weigel were appointed its directors, and after Brecht's death Helene Weigel carried on the Brechtian tradition at the "Schiff" for another fifteen years. She only gave up acting when she found she no longer had the strength to pull the wagon in *Mother Courage*, though she retained an iron grip on the company until her death. Today, the Berliner Ensemble no longer receives a state subsidy and has to generate its own income. Though Brecht's plays are still included in the repertoire, older theater-goers who remember the Brecht-Weigel productions of the fifties and sixties "claim that something is missing" from contemporary performances of Brecht's plays. Perhaps the Brecht-Weigel partnership did produce something special. In the same way there are veteran theater-goers in England who look back with nostalgia on the Old Vic's productions of 1944–48 when Laurence Olivier, Ralph Richardson, and Sybil Thorndike trod the boards at the grand old theater in the Waterloo Road.

1. Plato, *Symposium*, trans. Robin Waterfield (Oxford: Oxford University Press, 1994), 25–28.

2. Called *fafei*—from *fafa*, meaning "hot," with its symbolic overtones of emotionality, ordeal, and consternation—this tentlike temporary house is thatched with palm fronds and has a long pole (the *lumbon*) rising from its center and topped with leaves.

3. Ernst Bloch, *The Spirit Of Utopia*, trans. Anthony A. Nassar (Stanford, Calif.: Stanford University Press, 2000),165, 3; Clifford Geertz, *The Interpretation of Cultures: Selected Essays* (New York: Basic Books, 1973), 49.

4. Ernst Bloch, *Traces*, trans. Anthony A. Nassar (Stanford, Calif.: Stanford University Press, 2006), 1.

5. George Lakoff and Mark Johnson refer to these as "experiential" or "ontological" metaphors since they reflect universal structures of our being-in-the-world. *Metaphors We Live By* (Chicago: University of Chicago Press, 1980).

6. On this waxing and waning of being, see my account of the dialectic of "town" and "bush" in Kuranko discourse and my account of the dialectic of *tupu* (coming into existence) and *mate* (fading away, dying) in Maori thought. Michael Jackson, *Existential Anthropology: Events, Exigencies and Effects* (New York: Berghahn, 2005), 62, 186. Also relevant are my comments on the dialectic of *palka* (presently embodied) and *lawa* (presently absent) in Warlpiri thought and ritual. Michael Jackson, *Minima Ethnographica: Intersubjectivity and the Anthropological Project* (Chicago: University of Chicago Press, 1998), 132–33, 139.

7. Baruch Spinoza, *Ethics*, trans. Samuel Shirley (Indianapolis: Hackett, 1982), 109–12, especially propositions 6, 12, and 13.

8. Psychoanalytical thought claims, I think correctly, that the universality of such ontological images is grounded in the experience of primary intersubjectivity, particularly images of being up or down, contained or containing, large or small, attached or detached, entire or broken. See also Lakoff and Johnson, *Metaphors We Live By*, 30–31. It is also worth remarking that Lakoff's account of the "fundamental" economic metaphor of well-being as wealth, "which brings quantitative reasoning into the qualitative realm of morality," works less well in traditional Africa than in the modern West. George Lakoff, *Moral Politics: What Conservatives Know That Liberals Don't* (Chicago: University of Chicago Press, 1996), 62–63.

9. See Pierre Bourdieu, *Pascalian Meditations*, trans. Richard Nice (Cambridge: Polity Press, 2000), 207–9.

10. Like the latent power of the coiled snake or kundalini in tantric yoga, num is said, by Kung healers, to "work its way up" the backbone from the base of the spine with a tingling sensation. "Then num makes your thoughts nothing in your head." Richard Katz, *Boiling Energy: Community Healing among the Kalahari Kung* (Cambridge, Mass.: Harvard University Press, 1982), 42.

11. Sigmund Freud, *Beyond the Pleasure Principle*, trans. James Strachey (New York: W. W. Norton, 1989), 30–35.

12. Katz, *Boiling Energy*, 46.

13. Michael Jackson, "Migrant Imaginaries: With Sewa Koroma in Southeast London," *Excursions* (Durham, N.C.: Duke University Press, 2007), 102–34.

14. One is expected to respond to the riddle by "pointing out" an appropriate answer. *Sosogoma* is from the verb *ka sogo*, "to point out, to indicate."

15. There were mobile phone networks in Freetown from as early as 1999, but it wasn't until the war ended in January 2001 that the first nationwide networks were put in place. Kabala was only "connected to the world" in May 2006 and, as Chris Coulter reported, "young women had already started to 'love' to get money to buy mobile phones." "Being a Bush Wife: Women's Lives through War and Peace in Northern Sierra Leone" (PhD diss., Uppsala University, 2006), 394.

16. I am referring to a Kuranko man with whom I worked in 1979 and 1985, who could transform himself into an elephant—the totem of his clan—as a way of augmenting his flagging powers. See Michael Jackson, *Paths toward a Clearing: Radical Empiricism and Ethnographic Inquiry* (Bloomington: Indiana University Press, 1989), 102–18.

17. Monica Ali, writing about Nazreen, a young woman from a Bangladeshi village, now living in London and suddenly alone, surrounded by the "muffled sounds of private lives sealed away above, below, and around" but isolated from people, as though she were in a box. *Brick Lane* (New York: Scribner's, 2003), 12.

18. Lyndall Gordon, *A Private Life of Henry James: Two Women and His Art* (London: Chatto and Windus, 1998), 329.

19. Henry James to Grace Norton (1880). Cited by Colm Tóibín, "A Man with My Trouble," *London Review of Books*, 3 January 2008, 15–18.

20. Jean Duvignaud, *Change at Shebika: Report from a North African Village*, trans. Frances Frenaye (New York: Vintage, 1972), 300.

Politics of Storytelling

1. Alexander Gordon Laing, *Travels in the Timannee, Kooranko, and Soolima Countries in Western Africa* (London: John Murray, 1825), 428–33.

2. The story told in Nieni is that Yelimusu Keli Koroma had come under attack from the Limba in the West. When the Nieni capital, Yifin, fell to the Limba, a corridor was opened up through which the Kono could invade Barawa.

3. Abdul recalls taking his father's petition to the district commissioner in Kabala.

4. Meyer Fortes, "The First Born," *Religion, Morality and the Person: Essays on Tallensi Religion*, ed. Jack Goody (Cambridge: Cambridge University Press, 1987), 218–46, 234, emphasis added.

5. The principle is beautifully captured in the Tibetan Buddhist notion that "dying does not mean dying; dying means moving" (i.e., a shift or transfer into a new life that is, however, never an exact repetition or recapitulation of a previous incarnation). Robert Desjarlais, *Sensuous Biographies: Lives and Deaths among Nepal's Yolmo Buddhists* (Berkeley: University of California Press, 2003), 275.

6. Children who die before weaning are buried in the rubbish heap area (*sundu kunye ma*) behind the house. Often slivers of stick are inserted under a fingernail so that the child will be recognized if it is reincarnated. And of course names are recycled, so that, for example, Tina Kome's firstborn son Kulifa inherited his paternal grandfather's name, which means, literally, "leopard-slayer."

Road to Kabala

1. Blaise Pascal, *Pensées* (Paris: Éditions du Seuil, 1962), 89.

2. Cf. the Maori myth from Aotearoa–New Zealand of the culture hero Maui attempting to enter the vagina of the goddess of the underworld, Hine-nui-te-Po, and steal from her the gift of life/birth, but being squeezed to death in her thighs when some fantails break into laughter at the absurd sight of this mortal human being trying to reenter the womb of the earth mother. Also see Wendy Doniger, "The Land East of the Asterisk," *London Review of Books* 30, no.7 (2008): 27–29.

3. In the late 1930s J. Fashole Luke reported that Lake Sonfon was "regarded as sacred and as alligators abound in it these also are considered sacred, and to kill any of them is considered a very grave offence tantamount to a spiritual sin." Luke also reported on the sacrifices made at the head of the lake, and a belief that "a ship used to appear and submerge now and again near the islet, but because of violation of certain laws this ceased." J. Fashole Luke, "Some Impressions of the Korankos and their Country," *Sierra Leone Studies* o.s. 17 (1939): 90–94.

4. Golden Prospects, a UK corporation, in conjunction with Mano River Resources (managing diamond exploration in the area), owns the mining leases at Lake Sonfon.

5. I first recorded the legend of Lake Sonfon from Keti Ferenke Koroma of Kondembaia in January 1970. Details were corroborated by Sewa Magba Koroma in January 2008.

Their Eyes Were Watching God

My chapter title mimics the title of Zora Neale Hurston's great novel.

1. Verbatim reports by eyewitnesses.

2. A pale-complexioned virgin girl signifies an uncorrupted mind and transparency in human relations. Accordingly, diviners will sometimes advise a chief to be seen in the company of such a young girl, for she will bring good fortune upon the ruling house.

3. It is significant that the well that neither received nor gave water was in Yogomaia, the Kuranko quarter of the town of Kabala, where an impersonal market economy based on money had supplanted traditional reciprocities.

Albitaiya

1. As a known individual with a long association with the village, I was regarded as an honorary member of the community; by contrast, Joshua and Sewa were, in local parlance, newcomers, guests, or "strangers" (*sundannu*). Nevertheless, a strong alliance or "friendship" had always existed between Diang (Sewa's natal chiefdom) and the neighboring chiefdoms of Kamadugu and Barawa.

2. The *Dimusukuntigi* (head of the women) was one of Morowa's wives, and her daughter Mantene was attending high school in Kabala, her fees and expenses paid by Chris Coulter.

3. One evening, strolling around the village and greeting people, I found this young man lying on a mat in a fetid house, feverish, moaning, flailing about, eyes dilated and terror-stricken. Outside the house, his kin had gathered, grim-faced. The following day, I gathered details of the sick man's story. He had eloped with another man's wife and brought her to Sukurela to live with him. The husband and the girl's father-in-law brought their case before the district court in Kabala, asking that the girl be ordered to end her affair and return home. The lover, who was the Kometigi in Sukurela, considered himself above the law and rejected the court order. The girl's father now traveled to Sambaia Bendugu chiefdom and in the village of Kunya sought the services of the town chief, a powerful medicine-master who, for a fee, laid a curse on the errant lover. Earlier, the cursed man's family had begged the girl's father to allow her to divorce her husband. Now they implored the town-chief of Kunya, whose

name was Kona, to lift the curse. Kona's response was that, despite being warned, the man had ignored the court order and defied everyone who attempted to advise him. I tried to pressure the town chief and elders to allow me to take the young man to Kabala hospital, but I was rebuffed; the curse would first have to be lifted. The young man died a few days later (probably of insect-borne encephalitis). There was no public mourning. The burial was unceremonious, and no sympathy was expressed. Finally, the deceased man's wives, children, and property (including the rice in the granary) were taken to Kunya where the curse—which had contaminated them all—was lifted for a fee of £7.

4. This Panglossian view of human resilience is discussed in Daniel Gilbert's *Stumbling on Happiness* (New York: Vintage, 2007), chap. 8. "The world is *this* way, we wish the world were *that* way, and our experience of the world—how we see it, remember it, and imagine it—is a mixture of stark reality and comforting illusion. We can't spare either. If we were to experience the world exactly as it is, we'd be too depressed to get out of bed in the morning, but if we were to experience the world exactly as we want it to be, we'd be too deluded to find our slippers" (176–77).

5. E. F. Sayers, "Notes on the Clan or Family Names Common in the Area Inhabited by Temne-Speaking People," *Sierra Leone Studies* o.s. 12 (1927): 14–108, 91–92.

6. Michael Jackson, *Paths toward a Clearing: Radical Empiricism and Ethnographic Inquiry* (Bloomington: Indiana University Press, 1989), 8.

7. I have elaborated the view elsewhere. Michael Jackson, *Minima Ethnographica: Intersubjectivity and the Anthropological Project* (Chicago: University of Chicago Press, 1998), 28–32; Michael Jackson, *Existential Anthropology: Events, Exigencies and Effects* (New York: Berghahn, 2005), chap. 6.

8. Joyce Johnson, *Minor Characters: A Beat Memoir* (London: Virago, 1983), 83.

Year of Supernatural Abundance

1. See J. S. Trimingham, *Islam in West Africa* (Oxford: Clarendon Press, 1959), 40–42. More recently, Stephen Ellis has remarked the ease with which initiates into the Poro cult association in Liberia identify Poro with the Christian God. "This combination of Poro and Christian belief, obviously a fairly recent development, illustrates clearly the way in which even the most revered tradition may accommodate novelty and change." *The Mask of Anarchy: The Destruction of Liberia and the Religious Dimension of an African Civil War* (London: Hurst, 1999), 225–26.

2. I should add that Bockarie did manage to send me a message from Firawa that Sira's supplies had been safely delivered.

3. *Conversations with Woody Allen: His Films, the Movies, and Movie-making*, Eric Lax (New York: Knopf, 2009), 123.

4. *Four Films by Woody Allen* (London: Faber and Faber, 1983), 105.

5. Ernst Bloch, *The Principle of Hope*, trans. Neville Plaice, Stephen Plaice, and Paul Knight (Cambridge, Mass.: MIT Press, 1986), vol. 2, 454.

6. Orhun Pamuk notes, "If we give what we treasure most to a Being we love with all our hearts, if we can do that without expecting anything in return, then the world becomes a beautiful place." *The Museum of Innocence* (New York: Knopf, 2009), 41.

7. Robin Law, "Human Sacrifice in Pre-Colonial West Africa," *African Affairs* 84, no. 334 (1985): 53–87.

8. Derek Hughes, *Culture and Sacrifice: Ritual Death in Literature and Opera* (Cambridge: Cambridge University Press, 2007), cited by Frank Kermode in "Offered to the Gods," *London Review of Books* 30, no. 1 (2008): 11.

9. What is foregrounded in one culture will be backgrounded in another, but psychological analogues of a cultural trait will be found universally. In a compelling study of "concretized metaphors" in the discourse of anorexics, Finn Skårderud shows that images of voiding, emptying, vomiting, and purging convey a desire to escape an oppressive external circumstance that allows no freedom of direct negotiation, shifting a weight, lightening a burden, restoring a sense of firmness, security, stability, and control that had not been experienced before. "Eating One's Words, Part 1: 'Concretised Metaphors' and Reflective Function in Anorexia Nervosa—An Interview Study," *European Eating Disorders Review* 15 (2007):163–74.

Strings Attached

1. Kuranko refer to the umbilical cord as *bara yile* (the maternal cord). Only when the umbilical stump had dried is the child said to have passed from the spirit to the earthly world.

2. René Devisch and Claude Brodeur, *The Law of the Lifegivers: The Domestication of Desire* (Amsterdam: Harwood, 1999), 51.

3. Ibid., 54.

4. R. B. Onians, *The Origins of European Thought* (Cambridge: Cambridge University Press, 1951), 331.

5. Ibid., 336.

6. Ibid., 381.

7. Ibid., 356.

8. The Latin term *necesse* is related to *necto* and *nexus* and refers originally to binding or being bound. While there is no obvious relation between necessity and kinship, "both have a natural point of contact in binding which implies not only constraint but also union and proximity." Onians cites, in this regard, the Sanscrit *bándhu-h*, "kinsman," and the

widespread idea that kinship ties are given in nature and cannot be changed. Ibid., 333.

9. Aristotle, *The Basic Works of Aristotle*, ed. Richard McKeon (New York: Random House, 1941), 1059 (1155b).

10. "The Prose of Suffering and the Practice of Silence," *Spiritus* 4, no. 1 (2004): 44–59.

11. I am indebted to Martha Carey for her help in this research.

12. Rather than the Eurocentric term "fostering," Esther Goody favors the more neutral term "pro-parenthood." *Parenthood and Social Reproduction: Fostering and Occupational Roles in West Africa* (Cambridge: Cambridge University Press, 1982).

13. The NarSarah health clinic in Kabala is funded by CITA (Commission on International Trans-Regional Accreditation)—a United Methodist Church organization based in Golden, Colorado.

14. Dylan Thomas, "Poem on His Birthday," *Collected Poems, 1934–1952* (London: J. M. Dent, 1952), 171.

Shape of the Inconstruable Question

The chapter title is from Ernst Bloch's *The Spirit of Utopia*, trans. Anthony A. Nassar (Stanford, Calif.: Stanford University Press, 2000), 165.

1. Michael Jackson, *Paths toward a Clearing: Radical Empiricism and Ethnographic Inquiry* (Bloomington: Indiana University Press, 1989), 24.

2. Viktor Frankl, *Man's Search for Meaning*, trans. Ilsa Lasch (Boston: Beacon Press, 2006), 69, 78.

3. Ibid., 111.

4. The adage exploits oxymoron and pun (*dunia*, "world," and *dununia*, "load," are near homonyms) and implies that the world is like a head-load, the weight of which depends on the way one chooses to carry it.

5. Alfred Schutz, *The Phenomenology of the Social World*, trans. George Walsh and Frederick Lehnert (London: Heinemann, 1972), 163.

6. Lewis Henry Morgan, *Systems of Consanguinity and Affinity of the Human Family* (Lincoln: University of Nebraska Press, 1995 [1870]), 10.

7. Meyer Fortes, *The Web of Kinship among the Tallensi* (Oxford: Oxford University Press, 1949), 16.

8. Ibid.

9. Paul Riesman, *First Find Your Child a Good Mother: The Construction of Self in Two African Communities* (New Brunswick, N.J.: Rutgers University Press, 1992), 89.

10. Ibid., 181–82.

11. Ibid.,182–83, emphasis added. Cf. Paul Riesman, *Freedom in Fulani Social Life: An Introspective Ethnography* (Chicago: University of Chicago Press, 1977), 175.

12. Vesico-vaginal fistula may occur when a girl becomes pregnant before her body is fully developed. The fetus is often too large to enter the birth canal. It compresses the bladder against the sidewall of the pelvis. To make matters worse, midwives sometimes try to expel the baby by pushing down hard on the girl's belly. The baby dies. Tissue dies in the girl's bladder, creating a hole through which urine leaks continually. The girl is condemned to lifelong incontinence and is often stigmatized and shunned.

13. Ed Tronick, *The Neurobehavioral and Social-Emotional Development of Infants and Children* (New York: W. W. Norton, 2007), 292. The most recent and exemplary ethnographic account of mother-infant interactions in a West African society is Alma Gottlieb's monograph on the Beng of Côte d'Ivoire: *The Afterlife Is Where We Come From: The Culture of Infancy in West Africa* (Chicago: University of Chicago Press, 2004).

14. William James, *Pragmatism* (Cambridge: Mass.: Harvard University Press, 1978), 97.

15. The conference papers were subsequently published as *Culture and Well-Being: Anthropological Approaches to Freedom and Political Ethics*, ed. Alberto Corsín Jiménez (Ann Arbor: University of Michigan Press, 2008). Another collection of conference papers on well-being appeared the following year, calling for an anthropology of well-being, and a comparative approach to understanding what constitutes, in different cultures, "the optimal state for an individual, a community, and a society." *Pursuits of Happiness: Well-Being in Anthropological Perspective*, eds. Gordon Matthews and Caroline Izquierdo (New York: Berghahn, 2009).

16. Ibid., 2.

17. And then there is the question as to the relative weight one gives to one's inner feelings over one's external circumstances, a problem that has bedeviled the cross-cultural evaluation of well-being. As shown by a recent study by Han, Leichtman, and Wang, four-to-six-year-old Korean and Chinese children are far less inclined to schematize experience in terms of self-referents and internal emotional words than American children at the same age. "Autobiographical Memory in Korean, Chinese and American Children," *Developmental Psychology* 34, no. 4 (1998): 701–13. Moreover, while normative concerns with roles and social obligations figure prominently in Asian and African discourse on life satisfaction, individual emotions are foregrounded among middle-class Europeans and Americans. *Culture and Subjective Well-Being*, ed. Ed Diener and Eunkook M. Suh (Cambridge, Mass.: MIT Press, 2000), 70–71.

18. James Baldwin, *The Fire Next Time* (New York: Vintage International, 1993), 98–99. Baldwin's comment echoes the Nietzschean and Kuranko view that while suffering is hard (*gbele* connotes both hardness and strength), hardship (*gbeleye*) makes one strong.

19. See Anne-Line Dalsgaard's compelling study of fertility control in

an impoverished favela in Northeast Brazil where everyday life is interrupted by unpredictable violence, misery, and defeat yet always offers "a jeithinho—a way out." *Matters of Life and Longing: Female Sterilisation in Northeast Brazil* (Copenhagen: Museum Tusculanum Press, 2004), 14.

20. Michael Jackson, *The Politics of Storytelling: Violence, Transgression and Intersubjectivity* (Copenhagen: Museum Tusculanum Press, 2002), 14.

21. Klaus Wagenbach, *Kafka*, trans. Ewald Osers (Cambridge, Mass.: Harvard University Press, 2003), 116.

22. John Berger, *A Fortunate Man: The Story of a Country Doctor* (London: Writers and Readers Publishing Coop., 1976), 134.

23. On the distinction between "abstract" and "concrete" utopias, see Ernst Bloch, *The Spirit of Utopia*, 167–71.

24. Joshua Wolf Shenk, "What Makes Us Happy," *Atlantic Monthly*, June 2008.

25. *The Fire Next Time*, 95.

Not to Find One's Way in a City

The chapter title is taken from a line in Walter Benjamin's "A Berlin Chronicle," *Reflections: Walter Benjamin Essays, Aphorisms, Autobiographical Writings*, trans. Edmund Jephcott (New York: Schocken Books, 1978), 8.

1. The phrase "earliest perfect specimen of the novel" is Walter Benjamin's, in "The Storyteller," *Illuminations*, trans. Harry Zohn (New York: Schocken Books, 1968), 99.

2. "*The reason for the unreason to which my reason turns so weakens my reason that with reason I complain of thy beauty* . . . With [such] words and phrases the poor gentleman lost his mind, and he spent sleepless nights trying to understand them and extract their meaning, which Aristotle himself, if he came back to life for only that purpose, would not have been able to decipher or understand." Miguel de Cervantes, *Don Quixote*, trans. Edith Grossman (New York: HarperCollins, 2005), 20.

3. David Haberman, *Journey through the Twelve Forests: An Encounter with Krishna* (New York: Oxford University Press, 1994), viii.

4. Ibid., xvii.

5. Ibid., x.

6. Ibid., xvii.

7. Vincent James Stanzione, *Rituals of Sacrifice: Walking the Face of the Earth on the Sacred Path of the Sun: A Journey through the Tz'utujil Maya World of Santiago Atitlán* (Albuquerque: University of New Mexico Press, 2000), xx.

8. I am thinking here of Warlpiri (Central Australia) initiation, in which elders take neophytes on arduous journeys through ancestral lands, stopping at places where the ancestors stopped and performed groundbreak-

ing ceremony or earth-transforming acts, so ensuring that the novices embody their understanding as though the ancestral world were continuous with their own. For a compelling ethnographic example of the initiatory journey from a very different region of the world, see Vincent James Stanzione, "Walking Is Knowing: Pilgrimage through the Pictorial History of the Cuauhtinchantlacan," *Cave, City, and Eagle's Nest: An Interpretative Journey through the Mapa de Cuauhtinchan No. 2*, ed. David Carrasco and Scott Sessions (Albuquerque: University of New Mexico Press, 2007), 333–55.

9. Jacques Derrida, *Margins of Philosophy*, trans. Alan Bass (Chicago: University of Chicago Press, 1982).

10. Roger Colet, introduction to Guy de Maupassant, *Selected Short Stories*, trans. R. Colet, (Harmondsworth: Penguin, 1971), 10.

11. The phrase is Rebecca Solnit's, from *Wanderlust: A History of Walking* (New York: Viking Penguin, 200), 22.

12. Jean-Jacques Rousseau, *The Confessions*, trans. J. M. Cohen (Harmondsworth: Penguin, 1953), 182.

13. Michel de Certeau, *The Practice of Everyday Life*, trans. Steven Rendall (Berkeley: University of California Press, 1988), 91.

14. In *The Crowning Privilege* (London: Cassell, 1955), Robert Graves explores in great detail the origin of poetic meter in human activity—how Nordic poetry is steeped in the rhythmic slap of oars, the rattle of rowlocks, the ring of hammers on an anvil in a forge, the beat of feet around altar or tomb, or the ploughman turning at the end of each furrow (from *versus* to verse). It is not surprising that Graves's own early poems frequently allude to walking, the relaxed momentum of which is often made a metaphor for a balanced mind, and what Paul Valéry called "the quickened flow of ideas" (cited in A. Welsh, *Roots of Lyric* [Princeton, N.J.: Princeton University Press, 1978], 12).

15. T. H. Croxall, ed., *Glimpses and Impressions of Kierkegaard* (London: James Nisbet, 1959), 12–13.

16. Roger Poole, *Kierkegaard: The Indirect Communication* (Charlottesville: University of Virginia Press, 1993), 9.

17. Ibid., 15–22. I find it fascinating how, faced with a situation he could do nothing about, Kierkegaard decided to choose it himself, much as Genet, in Sartre's account, chose to be a thief when faced with the impossibility of being anything else. In his *Journal*, Kierkegaard writes of "The *Corsair* affair" as signaling a loss of freedom to gad about on the streets and be "a nobody in this way while thoughts and ideas were working within me." "Now," he goes on, "this is all upset; the rabble, the apprentices, the butcher boys, the schoolboys, and all such are egged on. *But I will not play to such a public.*" He then concludes in a characteristically ironic vein, "And now that I have remodeled my external life, am more withdrawn, keep to myself more, have a more momentous look about me, then in certain quarters it will be said that I have changed for the better." Cited in ibid., 217–18.

18. As Roger Poole observes (195), the cartoonist's focus on Kierke-gaard's legs implies an attempt to symbolically immobilize him, to pre-vent him perambulating in public, to drive him indoors — out of sight, out of mind.

19. Of the "gathering of strangers" in the burgeoning cities of eighteenth-century Europe, Richard Sennett observes that the stranger can be seen as an unknown, rather than as an alien. "A stranger can be experienced on these terms by someone who does have rules for his own identity, such as an Italian meeting someone he cannot 'place'; the stranger as an unknown can dominate, however, the perceptions of people who are unclear about their own identities, losing traditional images of themselves, or belonging to a new social group that as yet has no clear label." Richard Sennett, *The Fall of Public Man* (Cambridge: Cambridge University Press, 1977), 48.

20. Jean Rouch with Lucien Taylor, "A Life on the Edge of Film and An-thropology," in Rouch, *Ciné-Ethnography*, ed. and trans. Steven Feld (Min-neapolis: University of Minnesota Press, 2003), 128–46, 137.

21. Amartya Sen, *The Standard of Living*, ed. Geoffrey Hawthorn (Cam-bridge: Cambridge University Press, 1988), 1. Emphases in original.

22. Gabriel Marcel, *Homo Viator: Introduction to a Metaphysics of Hope*, trans. Emma Crauford (London: Gollancz, 1951), 71.

23. The English adage "Better the devil you know than the devil you don't" has an exact equivalent in Kuranko: "Better to be in the hands of an ordinary djinn than in the hands of Kome [the most powerful and un-predictable djinn of all]."

Index

death (*continued*)
157; tales of, 25–27, 74; witchcraft and, 137–40, 153
Derrida, Jacques, 191
Desjarlais, Robert, 203n5
destruction by rebels, 16, 20, 23, 82–83, 85, 127, 164
detachment, 19
development, 9, 156; socioeconomic, ix, 24, 61, 91, 134, 155, 183
Diang (chiefdom), 5–6, 16, 120–21, 125–26, 132, 189, 216n1
divination, 53, 60–61, 70, 206n1
divorce, 35, 205n1
djinn (*nyenne*), 39–45, 53–57, 96, 128–29, 142, 151
Douglas, Mary, 17
dreams, 11–12, 57, 105, 133, 166–67
drug trade, 116, 150, 153
duty (*wale*), 2, 60, 67, 177–79, 189; moral, 166; social, 25, 47, 159–60
Duvignaud, Jean, 99, 211

Economic Community of West African States Monitoring Group (ECOMOG), 149
education, 2, 8–12, 60–61, 104–5, 129–32, 166–68
Ellis, Stephen, 217n1
Estes, Richard, 183
ethics: distributive morality, 77; existential situation and, 68; of natural justice, 77–78; particularistic vs. universalistic, 77; proto-ethical sensibility, 68, 73; sociality and, 68–69
ethnicity and difference, 68
ethnography, x, 178–79, 187–88, 190–91, 196
Evans-Pritchard, E. E., 147
existentialism: dissatisfaction

and, ix, 38, 196, 197; satisfaction and, 60–61, 73

farming cooperatives, 37, 80, 124
Fa San story, 82–83, 85, 212n5
female genital cutting (FGC). *See* clitoridectomy
Firawa (village) 15, 23, 77, 148
Flaubert, Gustave, 191–92
Fortes, Meyer, 110, 181
fostering, 161
4th West India Regiment, 101
Frankl, Viktor, 179
Freud, Sigmund, 95
Fulani (ethnic group), 66, 101, 124, 153, 181

Gauguin, Paul, x
Gbangbe (witch-finding association), 136
gender relations, 89; between brother and sister, 113; between husband and wife, 30–35; in *Mande Fa Bori* epic, 42–44. *See also* marriage; trust and transparency
Gilbert, Daniel, 217n4
gold, 72–73, 121, 126
Gottlieb, Alma, 220n13
governmental corruption, 143

Haberman, David, 190
hardship, 23–25, 81, 92–93, 160, 169, 200, 220n18
Hippocratic principle, 169
Homer, 159
hope, xi–xiii, 9–12, 93, 147–48, 184
hopelessness, 115
human anxiety, 93–94, 99, 196
hunger, 36, 59, 61–62
Hurston, Zora Neale, 216

imagination, migrant, 96, 116
inheritance, 21–22, 68, 80, 109, 156, 166

initiation (*biriye*), 24, 33, 53, 88–91, 105–7, 221n8

intelligence (*hankilimaiye*), 28, 85

intersubjectivity, xiii; childbearing/rearing and, 182; vs. intrapsychic, 24; meaningful life and, 69, 73, 159–60

intrapsychic, 19, 24, 28, 139

Islam: anti-Islamic cartoons, 194; conversion to, 66–67, 129, 136–37, 141; jujus and, 63–64, 96; ummah and, 78; witchcraft and, 155

Jackson, Heidi Aisetta, 63, 80, 100, 134, 142

Jackson, Joshua, 1, 86–87, 135

Jackson, Pauline, 17, 20, 63, 80, 173

James, Henry, 99

James, William, xi, 182

Janneh, Imam, 135

Janneh, Musa, 80, 103–4

Jiménez, Alberto Corsín, 182

Johnson, Mark, 213n5

joking relationships, 22, 62, 71, 74, 189, 191, 209n14; irony and, 194–95

Jung, Carl Gustav, 133

Kabala (town), 13–14, 104, 140–41, 143, 162–63, 189–90

Kabbah, Tejan, 103

Kafka, Franz, 184

Kakoia (village), 141

Kallon, Mohamed, 154, 176

Kamadugu Sukurela (village), 134–35, 137, 139, 141, 197

Kamanda, Dorcas, 167–68

Kamara, Damba, 128, 161–66, 169

Kamara, Fina, 127–28, 161–62, 164, 168–69, 185

Katz, Richard, 95

Kierkegaard, Søren, 192–93, 222n17–18

kinship: animals, 74; marriages (*nakelinyorgoye fure*), 34, 137; nature of, 180–82; obligations of, 167; rope analogy of, 158–59

Koinadugu (*district*), 103, 106, 113, 118, 131, 141, 189

kola, in gift exchange, 30, 55, 59, 60, 135

Kome (men's cult association), 64, 66, 136

Kondembaia (town), 37–38, 125, 127–28, 131, 164

Kono (ethnic group), 104, 165, 215n2; region, 10, 48, 136–37, 141

Koroma (clan), 120, 126, 189

Koroma, Keti Ferenke, 126, 128, 178

Koroma, Kuna, 128–29

Koroma, Sewa Magba: ambition and, 117–19; anger and, 117–18; beliefs of, 119–20; city girls and, 45; as expatriate, 156; family pressures, 188–89; Fa San and, 85–86; father's grave and, 127; friendship and, 13–14; hometown of, 125; kinship obligations and, 4–9, 12–14; lineage, 16; in London, 1–3; marriage and, 36; respect for, 135; Rose Marah and, 172–73; self-confidence of, 93–94; Sewa Balansama and, 14; Sheku (brother) and, 125–26; Sira Marah and, 52–55; stress and, 118; as successful, 140; as travel companion, 1–8

Koroma (Paramount Chief Sheku Magba II), 6, 125, 127

Koroma (Paramount Chief Sheku Magba III), 6, 125–26

Kung (healing dance), 95, 214n10
Kuranko. *See specific topic*

labinane, 15, 18, 21, 27, 204n2
Laing, Alexander Gordon, 101–2, 105, 113
Lakoff, George, 213n5, 213n8
Laye, Camara, 194
Lévi-Strauss, Claude, 42, 133
life: afterlife, 65; in America, 80; analogy of, with light, 191; comparisons of, 58; as Euro-centric ideal, 116; everlasting, 73, 110; existential discontent and, xi, 196; fulfillment and, 61–62; as God-given, 132; life-energy, 93–96, 109, 155; masks of, 36–37; as meaningful, 69; moral, 147–48; opportunity and, 152; paradox of, 95, 40, 45, 58–65; predestination and, 159; promise of advertising and, 98, 122; quality of, sur-veys, 183; sacrifice and, 70–72, 75; unpredictability of, 115, 180
limits, 89, 105, 139, 150, 168, 197
Long, Charles, 84–86
Lumley beach, 148, 152, 156
Lungi (airport), 3, 197

magical thinking, 61, 109, 122, 194
magical medicine. See *bese koli* (sorcery medicines)
Mamiwata, 53, 112
Mande (region), 71–72, 84, 88, 104
Mande Fa Bori (ancestral hunter), 38–44
Marah, Abdul: chieftaincy struggles and, 101–10; family of, 67, 86, 88–90, 100; forgive-ness and, 23; funerary rites and, 20–21; hospitality and, 112–13, 215n3; as information

source, 29–33; introduction to, 15–16
Marah, Bockarie, 29, 50, 52–54, 97, 113, 118–19, 142, 147
Marah, Fasili, 80–86, 92, 99–100, 113, 116–17, 184
Marah, Fina: initiation and, 30–37, life story of, 30–37, 48, 50; on marriage, 33–36, 48, 50, 127–28
Marah, Kaimah B., 7; educa-tion and, 8–12, 148–56, 159, 162–65, 169, 184–85, 188; son Michael, 11–12
Marah, Kulifa, 23, 105–6, 109–10, 176, 215n6
Marah, Morowa, 101–2, 134, 136–40, 216n2
Marah, Noah, 9–12, 63, 67, 109, 113, 120, 138, 154
Marah, Rose, 106, 154, 172–77, 179–80, 184
Marah, Rugie (Rugiatu), 3–4, 6–9, 118, 185
Marah, S. B., 1, 4, 16, 103–6, 154, 160, 172–77
Marah, Sayon, 46–48, 58
Marah, Sira: divination and, 52–61; first encounter with, 49–52; poverty and, 70; resourcefulness of, 115–16
Marah, Tala Sewa, 9, 101–2
Marah, Tina Kome, 11–12, 104–5, 107, 109–10, 215n6
Marcel, Gabriel, xi
marriage, 35; arranged, 34, 36, 46, 137; betrothal and, 33; chil-dren and, 10, 34, 137; conjugal relations and, 34; divorce and, 35, 205n1; elopement and, 33, 216n3; kinship (*nakelinyorgoye fure*), 34, 137; love and, 24–25, 50–51, 58–59, 185–86; sororal polygyny, 34

Maupassant, Guy de, 166, 191–92
Mauss, Marcel, 69, 209n15
medicine-master. See *besetigi* (medicine-master)
medicines, sorcery. See *bese koli* (sorcery medicines)
memory, xi, 28, 38, 65, 192; among Kuranko, 27–28, 38, 65, 107, 132, 192
metaphors: acoustic, 203n5; for anorexia, 218n9; of bonds, 93, 158–60, 167, 185; of eating, 155, 218n9; hunger as, 59, 61–62; Kuranko, 94, 205n4; love as, 58–59; ontological, 94, 213n5; pregnancy as, xii; of sacrifice, 154–55; shaving as, 205n9; walking as, 192, 222n14; of weaving, 158; of well-being, 94, 213n8
Merleau-Ponty, Maurice, 69
mobile phones, 56, 97–98, 145, 214n15
mobility, 2, 96, 166, 196
mourning. *See under* death
Morgan, Lewis Henry, 181
Murraytown (amputee camp), 161

narrative, 42, 132, 144, 190, 192; Kuranko, 211; Limba, 208n3
NarSarah clinic, 163, 168, 219n13
natural standpoint, 73
Nieni (chiefdom), 103–5, 107–8, 110
Nietzsche, Friedrich, 72
Nigerian ministries, 149–50
Norse mythology, 159

Obama, Barack, 148
occult economy, 152, 157
Oedipal rivalries, 110
Onians, R. B., 218–19n8
Oprah Winfrey Show, 163

Pamuk, Orhan, 14, 218n6
Pascal, Blaise, 116

Paz, Octavio, 210n18
Pentecostalism, 96, 145, 151
Plato, 88, 187
play, 25, 42, 143–44, 177, 182, 185, 190
Poole, Roger, 193, 222n18
poverty, 52, 58, 61, 92–93, 115, 148, 165, 167–68, 203n1
pragmatism, 66
prosperity gospel, 155
Provost-Smith, Patrick, xiii
public/private space, 24

Qu'ran, 68, 129, 162

radical empiricism, xi
reciprocity, 69, 209n15
religion, 8, 96, 116, 141, 145–46
renunciation, 151
Revolutionary United Front (RUF), 10, 83, 126–28, 143, 169, 189–90
rice: flour and sacrifice, 21; as staff of life, 2, 59, 207n14
Ricoeur, Paul, xi, xiii, 68, 132
Riesman, Paul, 195
Rouch, Jean, 194
Rousseau, Jean-Jacques, 73–74, 192
Royal Africa Corps, 101
RUF. *See* Revolutionary United Front (RUF)

sacrifice (*sarake*): altruism and, 70–71; Aztec, 72; human, 150, 153–55, 210n17; life and, 70–72, 75; logic of, 70–72, 151; meat distribution and, 21; personal, 64–65, 70–72, 110, 146, 166, 168, 186; retaliation (*talsare*) and, 70–72; of rice flour (*dege*), 21, rituals, 20, 22–23, 64, 102, 120–21, 130; sibling rivalry (*fadenye*) and, 102, 109–10, 126–27, 144, 154
Sanoh, Alhaji Hassan, 64, 66–67, 76, 78, 80, 92, 208n1

MICHAEL JACKSON is Distinguished Visiting Professor in World Religions at Harvard Divinity School. He is the author of many books including *Palm at the End of the Mind: Relatedness, Religiosity, and the Real* (2009); *Excursions* (2007); *In Sierra Leone* (2004); *Existential Anthropology: Events, Exigencies, and Effects* (2004); *Minima Ethnographica: Intersubjectivity and the Anthropological Project* (1998); *At Home in the World* (1995); *Paths Toward a Clearing: Radical Empiricism and Ethnographic Inquiry* (1989); *Allegories of the Wilderness: Ethics and Ambiguity in Kuranko Narratives* (1982); and editor of *Things As They Are: New Directions in Phenomenological Anthropology* (1996).

Library of Congress
Cataloging-in-Publication Data

Jackson, Michael, 1940–
Life within limits : well-being in
a world of want / Michael Jackson.
p. cm.
Includes bibliographical references and index.
ISBN 978-0-8223-4892-4 (cloth : alk. paper)
ISBN 978-0-8223-4915-0 (pbk. : alk. paper)
1. Sierra Leone — Civilization.
2. Sierra Leone — Economic conditions.
3. Happiness — Sierra Leone.
4. Well-being — Sierra Leone.
5. Poverty — Sierra Leone. I. Title.
DT516.4.J33 2011
966.404 — dc22   2010035866